Elements of Literature®

Introductory Course

The Holt Reader

- ■ **Respond to and Analyze Texts**
- ■ **Apply Reading Skills**
- ■ **Develop Vocabulary and Practice Fluency**

HOLT, RINEHART AND WINSTON

A Harcourt Education Company

Orlando • **Austin** • New York • San Diego • Toronto • London

Contents

• PART ONE •

To the Student

A Book for You

....

A book is like a garden carried in the pocket.
—Chinese Proverb

....

The more you put into reading, the more you get out of it. This book is designed to do just that—help you interact with the selections you read by marking them up, asking your own questions, taking notes, recording your own ideas, and responding to the questions of others.

A Book Designed for Your Success

The Holt Reader goes hand in hand with *Elements of Literature.* It is designed to help you interact with the selections and master the language arts skills.

The book has two parts, each of which follows a simple format:

Part 1   Reading Literature

To help you master how to respond to, analyze, evaluate, and interpret literature, *The Holt Reader* provides—

For each collection:
- The academic vocabulary you need to know to master the literary skills for the collection, defined for ready reference and use.
- Two selections from the corresponding collection in *Elements of Literature,* reprinted in an interactive format to support and guide your reading.
- A new selection for you to read and respond to, enabling you to apply and extend your skills and build toward independence.

For each selection:
- A Before You Read page that preteaches the literary focus and provides a reading skill to help you understand the selection.
- A Vocabulary Development page that preteaches selection vocabulary and provides a vocabulary skill to use while reading the prose selections.
- Literature printed in an interactive format to guide your reading and help you respond to the text.
- A Skills Practice graphic organizer that helps you understand the literary focus of the selection.
- A Skills Review page that helps you practice vocabulary and assess your understanding of the selection you've just read.

Part 2   Reading Informational Texts

To help you master how to read informational texts, this book contains—

- The academic vocabulary you need to know to understand informational reading skills, defined for ready reference and use.
- New informational selections in interactive format to guide your reading and help you respond to the text.
- A Before You Read page that preteaches a reading skill to help you comprehend the selection. Selection vocabulary is also pretaught on this page.
- A Skills Practice graphic organizer that helps you understand the reading focus of the selection.
- A Skills Review page that helps you practice vocabulary and assess your understanding of the selection you've just read.

A Book for Your Own Thoughts and Feelings

Reading is about *you.* It is about connecting your thoughts and feelings to the thoughts and feelings of the writer. Make this book your own. The more you give of yourself to your reading, the more you will get out of it. We encourage you to write in it. Jot down how you feel about the selection. Question the text. Note details you think need to be cleared up or topics you would like to learn more about.

A Walk Through the Book

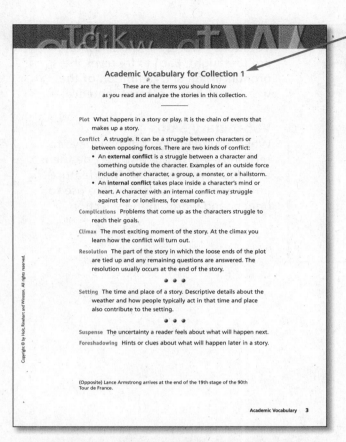

Academic Vocabulary for Collection 1

These are the terms you should know
as you read and analyze the stories in this collection.

Plot What happens in a story or play. It is the chain of events that makes up a story.

Conflict A struggle. It can be a struggle between characters or between opposing forces. There are two kinds of conflict:

- An **external conflict** is a struggle between a character and something outside the character. Examples of an outside force include another character, a group, a monster, or a hailstorm.
- An **internal conflict** takes place inside a character's mind or heart. A character with an internal conflict may struggle against fear or loneliness, for example.

Complications Problems that come up as the characters struggle to reach their goals.

Climax The most exciting moment of the story. At the climax you learn how the conflict will turn out.

Resolution The part of the story in which the loose ends of the plot are tied up and any remaining questions are answered. The resolution usually occurs at the end of the story.

• • •

Setting The time and place of a story. Descriptive details about the weather and how people typically act in that time and place also contribute to the setting.

• • •

Suspense The uncertainty a reader feels about what will happen next.

Foreshadowing Hints or clues about what will happen later in a story.

(Opposite) Lance Armstrong arrives at the end of the 19th stage of the 90th Tour de France.

Academic Vocabulary **3**

Academic Vocabulary

Academic vocabulary refers to the language of books, tests, and formal writing. Each collection begins with the terms, or academic language, you need to know to master the skills for that collection.

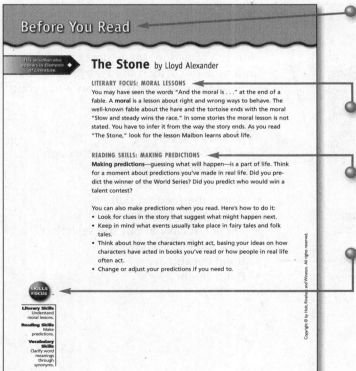

Before You Read

This selection also appears in *Elements of Literature.* ◆

The Stone by Lloyd Alexander

LITERARY FOCUS: MORAL LESSONS

You may have seen the words "And the moral is . . ." at the end of a fable. A **moral** is a lesson about right and wrong ways to behave. The well-known fable about the hare and the tortoise ends with the moral "Slow and steady wins the race." In some stories the moral lesson is not stated. You have to infer it from the way the story ends. As you read "The Stone," look for the lesson Maibon learns about life.

READING SKILLS: MAKING PREDICTIONS

Making predictions—guessing what will happen—is a part of life. Think for a moment about predictions you've made in real life. Did you predict the winner of the World Series? Did you predict who would win a talent contest?

You can also make predictions when you read. Here's how to do it:

- Look for clues in the story that suggest what might happen next.
- Keep in mind what events usually take place in fairy tales and folk tales.
- Think about how the characters might act, basing your ideas on how characters have acted in books you've read or how people in real life often act.
- Change or adjust your predictions if you need to.

SKILLS FOCUS

Literary Skills Understand moral lessons.

Reading Skills Make predictions.

Vocabulary Skills Clarify word meanings through synonyms.

18 Part 1 Collection 1/Plot: Moments of Truth

Before You Read

Previewing what you will learn builds success. This page tells you what the selection is about and prepares you to read it.

Literary Focus

This feature introduces the literary focus for the selection.

Reading Skills

This feature provides a reading skill for you to apply to the selection. It ties into and supports the literary focus.

Language Arts Skills

The skills covered with the selection are listed here.

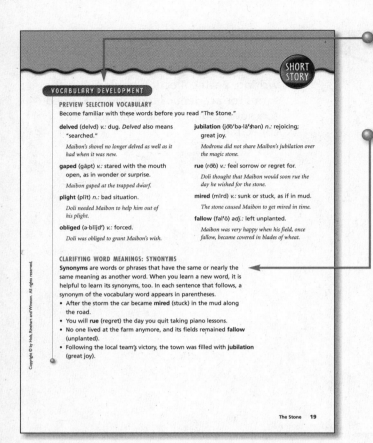

SHORT STORY

VOCABULARY DEVELOPMENT

PREVIEW SELECTION VOCABULARY

Become familiar with these words before you read "The Stone."

delved (delvd) *v.:* dug. *Delved* also means "searched."

Maibon's shovel no longer delved as well as it had when it was new.

gaped (gāpt) *v.:* stared with the mouth open, as in wonder or surprise.

Maibon gaped at the trapped dwarf.

plight (plīt) *n.:* bad situation.

Doli needed Maibon to help him out of his plight.

obliged (ə-blījd') *v.:* forced.

Doli was obliged to grant Maibon's wish.

jubilation (jōō'bə-lā'shən) *n.:* rejoicing; great joy.

Modrona did not share Maibon's jubilation over the magic stone.

rue (rōō) *v.:* feel sorrow or regret for.

Doli thought that Maibon would soon rue the day he wished for the stone.

mired (mīrd) *v.:* sunk or stuck, as if in mud.

The stone caused Maibon to get mired in time.

fallow (fal'ō) *adj.:* left unplanted.

Maibon was very happy when his field, once fallow, became covered in blades of wheat.

CLARIFYING WORD MEANINGS: SYNONYMS

Synonyms are words or phrases that have the same or nearly the same meaning as another word. When you learn a new word, it is helpful to learn its synonyms, too. In each sentence that follows, a synonym of the vocabulary word appears in parentheses.

- After the storm the car became **mired** (stuck) in the mud along the road.
- You will **rue** (regret) the day you quit taking piano lessons.
- No one lived at the farm anymore, and its fields remained **fallow** (unplanted).
- Following the local team's victory, the town was filled with **jubilation** (great joy).

The Stone **19**

Vocabulary Development

Vocabulary words for the selection are pretaught. Each entry gives the pronunciation and definition of the word as well as a context sentence.

Vocabulary Skills

When you read, you not only have to recognize words but also decode them and determine meaning. This feature introduces a vocabulary skill to use to understand words in the selection.

The Stone

Lloyd Alexander

There was a cottager named Maibon, and one day he was driving down the road in his horse and cart when he saw an old man hobbling along, so frail and feeble he doubted the poor soul could go many more steps. Though Maibon offered to take him in the cart, the old man refused; and Maibon went his way home, shaking his head over such a pitiful sight, and said to his wife, Modrona:

"Ah, ah, what a sorry thing it is to have your bones creaking and cracking, and dim eyes, and dull wits. When
10 I think this might come to me, too! A fine, strong-armed, sturdy-legged fellow like me? One day to go tottering and have his teeth rattling in his head and live on porridge like a baby? There's no fate worse in all the world."

"There is," answered Modrona, "and that would be to have neither teeth nor porridge. Get on with you, Maibon,

"The Stone" from *The Foundling and Other Tales of Prydain* by Lloyd Alexander. Copyright © 1973 by Lloyd Alexander. Reproduced by permission of **Henry Holt and Company LLC.**

The Stone **21**

IDENTIFY

Pause at line 7. Circle the names of the characters you meet.

INFER

Re-read lines 8–13. In what sort of shape is Maibon now? How does Maibon feel about getting old?

Side-Column Notes

Each selection is accompanied by notes in the side column that guide your interaction with the selection. Many notes ask you to underline or circle in the text itself. Others provide lines on which you can write your responses to questions.

Types of Notes

The different types of notes throughout the selection help you—

- Focus on literary elements
- Apply the reading skill
- Apply the vocabulary skill
- Think critically about the selection
- Develop word knowledge
- Build vocabulary
- Build fluency

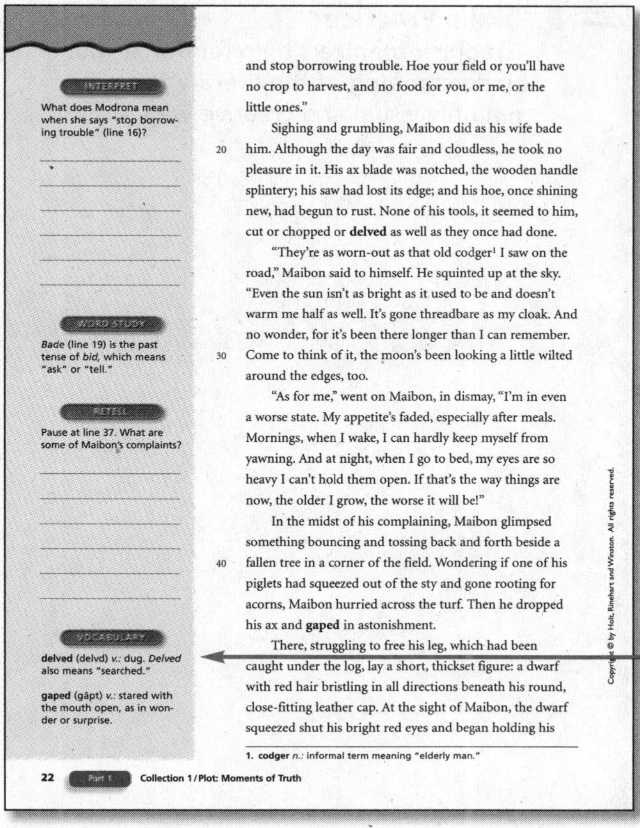

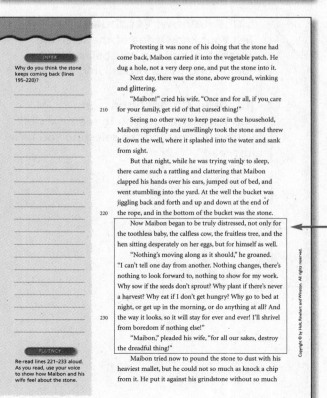

First reproduced page (page 22):

INTERPRET

What does Modrona mean when she says "stop borrowing trouble" (line 16)?

WORD STUDY

Bade (line 19) is the past tense of *bid,* which means "ask" or "tell."

RETELL

Pause at line 37. What are some of Maibon's complaints?

VOCABULARY

delved (delvd) *v.:* dug. *Delved* also means "searched."

gaped (gāpt) *v.:* stared with the mouth open, as in wonder or surprise.

and stop borrowing trouble. Hoe your field or you'll have no crop to harvest, and no food for you, or me, or the little ones."

20   Sighing and grumbling, Maibon did as his wife bade him. Although the day was fair and cloudless, he took no pleasure in it. His ax blade was notched, the wooden handle splintery; his saw had lost its edge; and his hoe, once shining new, had begun to rust. None of his tools, it seemed to him, cut or chopped or **delved** as well as they once had done.

   "They're as worn-out as that old codger[1] I saw on the road," Maibon said to himself. He squinted up at the sky. "Even the sun isn't as bright as it used to be and doesn't warm me half as well. It's gone threadbare as my cloak. And no wonder, for it's been there longer than I can remember. 30 Come to think of it, the moon's been looking a little wilted around the edges, too.

   "As for me," went on Maibon, in dismay, "I'm in even a worse state. My appetite's faded, especially after meals. Mornings, when I wake, I can hardly keep myself from yawning. And at night, when I go to bed, my eyes are so heavy I can't hold them open. If that's the way things are now, the older I grow, the worse it will be!"

   In the midst of his complaining, Maibon glimpsed something bouncing and tossing back and forth beside a 40 fallen tree in a corner of the field. Wondering if one of his piglets had squeezed out of the sty and gone rooting for acorns, Maibon hurried across the turf. Then he dropped his ax and **gaped** in astonishment.

   There, struggling to free his leg, which had been caught under the log, lay a short, thickset figure: a dwarf with red hair bristling in all directions beneath his round, close-fitting leather cap. At the sight of Maibon, the dwarf squeezed shut his bright red eyes and began holding his

1. **codger** *n.:* informal term meaning "elderly man."

Vocabulary

The vocabulary words that were pretaught are defined in the side column and set in boldface in the selection, allowing you to see them in context.

Second reproduced page (page 28):

INFER

Why do you think the stone keeps coming back (lines 195–220)?

FLUENCY

Re-read lines 221–233 aloud. As you read, use your voice to show how Maibon and his wife feel about the stone.

   Protesting it was none of his doing that the stone had come back, Maibon carried it into the vegetable patch. He dug a hole, not a very deep one, and put the stone into it.

   Next day, there was the stone, above ground, winking and glittering.

   "Maibon!" cried his wife. "Once and for all, if you care 210 for your family, get rid of that cursed thing!"

   Seeing no other way to keep peace in the household, Maibon regretfully and unwillingly took the stone and threw it down the well, where it splashed into the water and sank from sight.

   But that night, while he was trying vainly to sleep, there came such a rattling and clattering that Maibon clapped his hands over his ears, jumped out of bed, and went stumbling into the yard. At the well the bucket was jiggling back and forth and up and down at the end of 220 the rope, and in the bottom of the bucket was the stone.

   Now Maibon began to be truly distressed, not only for the toothless baby, the calfless cow, the fruitless tree, and the hen sitting desperately on her eggs, but for himself as well.

   "Nothing's moving along as it should," he groaned. "I can't tell one day from another. Nothing changes, there's nothing to look forward to, nothing to show for my work. Why sow if the seeds don't sprout? Why plant if there's never a harvest? Why eat if I don't get hungry? Why go to bed at 230 night, or get up in the morning, or do anything at all? And the way it looks, so it will stay for ever and ever! I'll shrivel from boredom if nothing else!"

   "Maibon," pleaded his wife, "for all our sakes, destroy the dreadful thing!"

   Maibon tried now to pound the stone to dust with his heaviest mallet, but he could not so much as knock a chip from it. He put it against his grindstone without so much

Fluency

Successful readers are able to read fluently—clearly, easily, quickly, and without word identification problems. In most selections, you'll be given an opportunity to practice and improve your fluency.

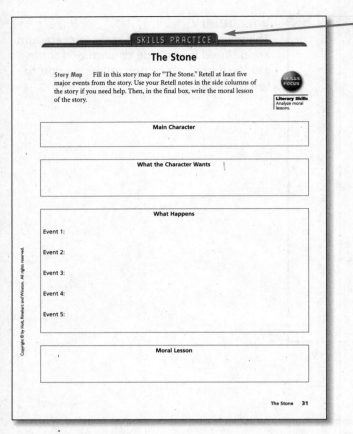

The Stone

Story Map   Fill in this story map for "The Stone." Retell at least five major events from the story. Use your Retell notes in the side columns of the story if you need help. Then, in the final box, write the moral lesson of the story.

SKILLS FOCUS
Literary Skills
Analyze moral lessons.

Main Character

What the Character Wants

What Happens

Event 1:

Event 2:

Event 3:

Event 4:

Event 5:

Moral Lesson

The Stone   **31**

Skills Practice
Graphic organizers help reinforce your understanding of the literary focus in a highly visual and creative way.

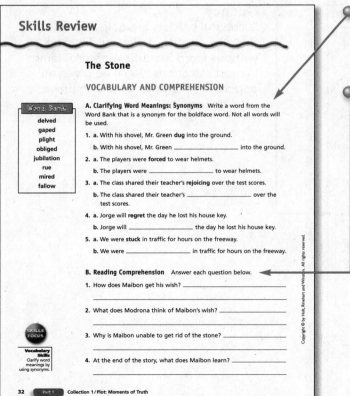

Skills Review

The Stone

VOCABULARY AND COMPREHENSION

Word Bank

delved
gaped
plight
obliged
jubilation
rue
mired
fallow

A. Clarifying Word Meanings: Synonyms   Write a word from the Word Bank that is a synonym for the boldface word. Not all words will be used.

1. a. With his shovel, Mr. Green **dug** into the ground.

   b. With his shovel, Mr. Green _____ into the ground.

2. a. The players were **forced** to wear helmets.

   b. The players were _____ to wear helmets.

3. a. The class shared their teacher's **rejoicing** over the test scores.

   b. The class shared their teacher's _____ over the test scores.

4. a. Jorge will **regret** the day he lost his house key.

   b. Jorge will _____ the day he lost his house key.

5. a. We were **stuck** in traffic for hours on the freeway.

   b. We were _____ in traffic for hours on the freeway.

B. Reading Comprehension   Answer each question below.

1. How does Maibon get his wish? _____

_____

2. What does Modrona think of Maibon's wish? _____

_____

3. Why is Maibon unable to get rid of the stone? _____

_____

4. At the end of the story, what does Maibon learn? _____

_____

SKILLS FOCUS
Vocabulary Skills
Clarify word meanings by using synonyms.

Skills Review: Vocabulary
Test your knowledge of the selection vocabulary and the vocabulary skill by completing this short activity.

Reading Comprehension
This feature allows you to see how well you've understood the selection you have just read.

Part One

Reading Literature

Plot:
Moments of Truth

Academic Vocabulary for Collection 1

These are the terms you should know
as you read and analyze the stories in this collection.

Plot What happens in a story or play. It is the chain of events that makes up a story.

Conflict A struggle. It can be a struggle between characters or between opposing forces. There are two kinds of conflict:

- An **external conflict** is a struggle between a character and something outside the character. Examples of an outside force include another character, a group, a monster, or a hailstorm.
- An **internal conflict** takes place inside a character's mind or heart. A character with an internal conflict may struggle against fear or loneliness, for example.

Complications Problems that come up as the characters struggle to reach their goals.

Climax The most exciting moment of the story. At the climax you learn how the conflict will turn out.

Resolution The part of the story in which the loose ends of the plot are tied up and any remaining questions are answered. The resolution usually occurs at the end of the story.

● ● ●

Setting The time and place of a story. Descriptive details about the weather and how people typically act in that time and place also contribute to the setting.

● ● ●

Suspense The uncertainty a reader feels about what will happen next.

Foreshadowing Hints or clues about what will happen later in a story.

(Opposite) Lance Armstrong arrives at the end of the 19th stage of the 90th Tour de France.

Before You Read

This selection also appears in *Elements of Literature.* ◆

Just Once by Thomas J. Dygard

LITERARY FOCUS: CONFLICT

Conflict happens when a character struggles to get what he or she wants. A character who struggles with something outside himself or herself is facing an **external conflict**. A character who struggles with something within his or her own mind or heart is dealing with an **internal conflict**. Here are some examples:

External Conflict	Internal Conflict
A dangerous animal escapes its pen and tries to attack its handlers.	A student wants to play basketball but has to study for a math test.
Two best friends compete in a track event.	A new student wants to make friends but is afraid to take the first step.
Astronauts trapped in a space station are running out of air.	A singer keeps forgetting the words to a song because of her incredible stage fright.

READING SKILLS: RETELLING

Sometimes you use the skill of retelling just for fun. For example, you may describe to a friend what happened in a great movie you saw last week. Sometimes, however, you retell to clarify something. For example, you may retell or rephrase a series of directions in order to make sure you got them right.

When you retell a story, it can be both fun and useful. As you read "Just Once," pause at the retell notes to explain what's been happening.

SKILLS FOCUS

Literary Skills
Understand conflict.

Reading Skills
Retell story events.

Vocabulary Skills
Clarify word meanings through context.

VOCABULARY DEVELOPMENT

PREVIEW SELECTION VOCABULARY

Before you read "Just Once," get to know these words from the story.

devastating (dev′ə·stāt′iŋ) *v.* used as *adj.*: causing great damage.

The Moose's devastating attack punched a hole through the opposing team's line.

nurturing (nʉr′chər·iŋ) *v.*: promoting the growth of; nursing.

The Moose's teammates suspected that he had been nurturing his dream for a while.

anonymous (ə·nän′ə·məs) *adj.*: unknown; unidentified.

The Moose was tired of being anonymous.

tolerant (täl′ər·ənt) *adj.*: patient; accepting of others.

A less tolerant coach might have become angry.

ponder (pän′dər) *v.*: think over carefully.

Coach Williams walked off to ponder the Moose's request.

CLARIFYING WORD MEANINGS: USING CONTEXT

Do you know how to figure out the meaning of an unfamiliar word? Here's a tip—use **context clues.** These are the words and phrases around the unfamiliar word. In the paragraph below, the context clue for each boldface word is in italics.

The coach read aloud the **anonymous** note, *wondering who had written it.* "Please take some time to **ponder** our request *carefully.* You may *think* that it would have a **devastating** effect, *but we're sure it won't ruin* the sports program. It's time to be **tolerant** and *fair to all people.* After all, we've been **nurturing** our dream, *practicing and working toward this opportunity* all our lives. Please let girls try out for the team."

JUST ONCE

Thomas J. Dygard

IDENTIFY

In lines 1–15, underline the words that tell about the Moose's special talents in football. Circle the position he plays.

INFER

Pause at line 21. Based on what you've read so far, what inferences, guesses based on clues in the text, can you make about the Moose's **character**?

_____

_____

_____

_____

_____

_____

_____

VOCABULARY

devastating (dev′ə·stāt′iŋ) v. used as *adj.*: causing great damage.

nurturing (nur′chər·iŋ) v.: promoting the growth of; nursing.

Everybody liked the Moose. To his father and mother he was Bryan—as in Bryan Jefferson Crawford—but to everyone at Bedford City High he was the Moose. He was large and strong, as you might imagine from his nickname, and he was pretty fast on his feet—sort of nimble, you might say—considering his size. He didn't have a pretty face but he had a quick and easy smile—"sweet," some of the teachers called it; "nice," others said.

But on the football field, the Moose was neither
10 sweet nor nice. He was just strong and fast and a little bit **devastating** as the left tackle of the Bedford City Bears. When the Moose blocked somebody, he stayed blocked. When the Moose was called on to open a hole in the line for one of the Bears' runners, the hole more often than not resembled an open garage door.

Now in his senior season, the Moose had twice been named to the all-conference team and was considered a cinch for all-state. He spent a lot of his spare time, when he wasn't in a classroom or on the football field, reading
20 letters from colleges eager to have the Moose pursue higher education—and football—at their institution.

But the Moose had a hang-up.

He didn't go public with his hang-up until the sixth game of the season. But, looking back, most of his teammates agreed that probably the Moose had been **nurturing** the hang-up secretly for two years or more.

The Moose wanted to carry the ball.

For sure, the Moose was not the first interior lineman in the history of football, or even the history of Bedford

30   City High, who banged heads up front and wore bruises like badges of honor—and dreamed of racing down the field with the ball to the end zone[1] while everybody in the bleachers screamed his name.

But most linemen, it seems, are able to stifle the urge. The idea may pop into their minds from time to time, but in their hearts they know they can't run fast enough, they know they can't do that fancy dancing to elude tacklers, they know they aren't trained to read blocks. They know that their strengths and talents are best utilized in the line.

40   Football is, after all, a team sport, and everyone plays the position where he most helps the team. And so these linemen, or most of them, go back to banging heads without saying the first word about the dream that flickered through their minds.

---

1. **end zone** *n.:* area between the goal line and the end line (the line marking the boundary of the playing area) at each end of a football field.

IDENTIFY

Pause at line 33. What does the Moose want to do?

IDENTIFY

Underline, and then number, three reasons linemen usually don't carry the ball (lines 34–44).

_____

_____

_____

_____

_____

_____

_____

_____

_____

_____

_____

_____

_____

_____

_____

_____

_____

_____

VOCABULARY

anonymous (ə·nän′ə·məs)
adj.: unknown; unidentified.

Not so with the Moose.

That sixth game, when the Moose's hang-up first came into public view, had ended with the Moose truly in all his glory as the Bears' left tackle. Yes, glory—but uncheered and sort of **anonymous.** The Bears were trailing 21–17 and had the ball on Mitchell High's five-yard line, fourth down,[2] with time running out. The rule in such a situation is simple— the best back carries the ball behind the best blocker—and it is a rule seldom violated by those in control of their faculties.[3] The Bears, of course, followed the rule. That meant Jerry Dixon running behind the Moose's blocking. With the snap of the ball, the Moose knocked down one lineman, bumped another one aside, and charged forward to flatten an approaching linebacker. Jerry did a little jig behind the Moose and then ran into the end zone, virtually untouched, to win the game.

After circling in the end zone a moment while the cheers echoed through the night, Jerry did run across and hug the Moose, that's true. Jerry knew who had made the touchdown possible.

But it wasn't the Moose's name that everybody was shouting. The fans in the bleachers were cheering Jerry Dixon.

It was probably at that precise moment that the Moose decided to go public.

In the dressing room, Coach Buford Williams was making his rounds among the cheering players and came to a halt in front of the Moose. "It was your great blocking that did it," he said.

"I want to carry the ball," the Moose said.

---

2. **fourth down:** In football the team holding the ball is allowed four downs, or attempts to carry the ball forward at least ten yards.
3. **faculties** *n.:* mental powers.

Coach Williams was already turning away and taking a step toward the next player due an accolade[4] when his brain registered the fact that the Moose had said something strange. He was expecting the Moose to say, "Aw, gee, thanks, Coach." That was what the Moose always said when the coach issued

80 a compliment. But the Moose had said something else. The coach turned back to the Moose, a look of disbelief on his face. "What did you say?"

"I want to carry the ball."

Coach Williams was good at quick recoveries, as any high school football coach had better be. He gave a **tolerant** smile and a little nod and said, "You keep right on blocking, son."

This time Coach Williams made good on his turn and moved away from the Moose.

90 The following week's practice and the next Friday's game passed without further incident. After all, the game was a road game over at Cartwright High, thirty-five miles away. The Moose wanted to carry the ball in front of the Bedford City fans.

Then the Moose went to work.

He caught up with the coach on the way to the practice field on Wednesday. "Remember," he said, leaning forward and down a little to get his face in the coach's face, "I said I want to carry the ball."

100 Coach Williams must have been thinking about something else because it took him a minute to look up into the Moose's face, and even then he didn't say anything.

"I meant it," the Moose said.

"Meant what?"

"I want to run the ball."

---

4. **accolade** (ak'ə·lād') n.: something said or done to express praise.

PREDICT

Pause at line 83. How do you think Coach Williams will answer the Moose? Explain.

_____

_____

_____

_____

_____

_____

_____

VOCABULARY

tolerant (tӓl'ər·ənt) adj.: patient; accepting of others.

INFER

Pause at line 99, and think about what you've read so far about Moose. What kind of person do you think he is? Explain.

_____

_____

_____

_____

_____

_____

_____

_____

INTERPRET

Pause at line 108. **Conflict** is a clash between opposing characters or forces. The Moose is on one side of the main conflict in this story. Who or what opposes him?

_____

_____

_____

_____

_____

_____

_____

_____

_____

_____

_____

_____

_____

_____

_____

_____

_____

IDENTIFY

The Moose tries to get support for what he wants (lines 109–126). Circle the names of the players he goes to. Underline how they respond.

"Oh," Coach Williams said. Yes, he remembered. "Son, you're a great left tackle, a great blocker. Let's leave it that way."

The Moose let the remaining days of the practice week
110 and then the game on Friday night against Edgewood High pass while he reviewed strategies. The review led him to Dan Blevins, the Bears' quarterback. If the signal caller would join in, maybe Coach Williams would listen.

"Yeah, I heard," Dan said. "But, look, what about Joe Wright at guard, Bill Slocum at right tackle, even Herbie Watson at center. They might all want to carry the ball. What are we going to do—take turns? It doesn't work that way."

So much for Dan Blevins.

The Moose found that most of the players in the back-
120 field agreed with Dan. They couldn't see any reason why the Moose should carry the ball, especially in place of themselves. Even Jerry Dixon, who owed a lot of his glory to the Moose's blocking, gaped in disbelief at the Moose's idea. The Moose, however, got some support from his fellow linemen. Maybe they had dreams of their own, and saw value in a precedent.[5]

© PhotoDisc, Inc.

---

5. **precedent** (pres′ə·dənt) _n.:_ action or statement that can serve as an example.

As the days went by, the word spread—not just on the practice field and in the corridors of Bedford City High, but all around town. The players by now were openly tak-
130 ing sides. Some thought it a jolly good idea that the Moose carry the ball. Others, like Dan Blevins, held to the purist[6] line—a left tackle plays left tackle, a ball carrier carries the ball, and that's it.

Around town, the vote wasn't even close. Everyone wanted the Moose to carry the ball.

"Look, son," Coach Williams said to the Moose on the practice field the Thursday before the Benton Heights game, "this has gone far enough. Fun is fun. A joke is a joke. But let's drop it."

140 "Just once," the Moose pleaded.

Coach Williams looked at the Moose and didn't answer. The Moose didn't know what that meant.

The Benton Heights Tigers were duck soup for the Bears, as everyone knew they would be. The Bears scored in their first three possessions and led 28–0 at the half. The hapless[7] Tigers had yet to cross the fifty-yard line under their own steam.

All the Bears, of course, were enjoying the way the game was going, as were the Bedford City fans jamming
150 the bleachers.

Coach Williams looked irritated when the crowd on a couple of occasions broke into a chant: "Give the Moose the ball! Give the Moose the ball!"

On the field, the Moose did not know whether to grin at hearing his name shouted by the crowd or to frown because the sound of his name was irritating the coach. Was the crowd going to talk Coach Williams into putting

---

6. **purist** (pyoor′ist) *n.* used as *adj.*: someone who insists that rules be followed strictly.
7. **hapless** *adj.*: unlucky.

MAKE A JUDGMENT

Pause at line 135. The people in town want the Moose to carry the ball. The coach and some players don't. How would you vote? Give reasons for your answer.

_____
_____
_____
_____
_____
_____
_____
_____

INTERPRET

What do you think Coach Williams's "look" means (line 141)?

_____
_____
_____
_____
_____
_____
_____
_____
_____

PREDICT

Pause at line 162. Is Coach Williams going to let the Moose carry the ball? Tell what you think will happen.

_____

_____

_____

_____

RETELL

Stop at line 172. Retell what's happened on the field and in the bleachers since the game started.

_____

_____

_____

_____

_____

_____

_____

_____

_____

IDENTIFY

Pause at line 188. Who has won the main **conflict** in this story? Underline the sentence that gives you this information.

the Moose in the backfield? Probably not; Coach Williams didn't bow to that kind of pressure. Was the coach going
160 to refuse to give the ball to the Moose just to show the crowd—and the Moose and the rest of the players—who was boss? The Moose feared so.

In his time on the sideline, when the defensive unit was on the field, the Moose, of course, said nothing to Coach Williams. He knew better than to break the coach's concentration during a game—even a runaway victory— with a comment on any subject at all, much less his desire to carry the ball. As a matter of fact, the Moose was careful to stay out of the coach's line of vision, especially when the
170 crowd was chanting "Give the Moose the ball!"

By the end of the third quarter the Bears were leading 42–0.

Coach Williams had been feeding substitutes into the game since half time, but the Bears kept marching on. And now, in the opening minutes of the fourth quarter, the Moose and his teammates were standing on the Tigers' five-yard line, about to pile on another touchdown.

The Moose saw his substitute, Larry Hinden, getting a slap on the behind and then running onto the field. The
180 Moose turned to leave.

Then he heard Larry tell the referee, "Hinden for Holbrook."

Holbrook? Chad Holbrook, the fullback?

Chad gave the coach a funny look and jogged off the field.

Larry joined the huddle and said, "Coach says the Moose at fullback and give him the ball."

Dan Blevins said, "Really?"

"Really."

190   The Moose was giving his grin—"sweet," some of the teachers called it; "nice," others said.

    "I want to do an end run," the Moose said.

    Dan looked at the sky a moment, then said, "What does it matter?"

    The quarterback took the snap from center, moved back and to his right while turning, and extended the ball to the Moose.

    The Moose took the ball and cradled it in his right hand. So far, so good. He hadn't fumbled. Probably both
200 Coach Williams and Dan were surprised.

    He ran a couple of steps and looked out in front and said aloud, "Whoa!"

    Where had all those tacklers come from?

    The whole world seemed to be peopled with players in red jerseys—the red of the Benton Heights Tigers. They all were looking straight at the Moose and advancing toward him. They looked very determined, and not friendly at all. And there were so many of them. The Moose had faced tough guys in the line, but usually one at a time, or maybe
210 two. But this—five or six. And all of them heading for him.

    The Moose screeched to a halt, whirled, and ran the other way.

    Dan Blevins blocked somebody in a red jersey breaking through the middle of the line, and the Moose wanted to stop running and thank him. But he kept going.

    His reverse had caught the Tigers' defenders going the wrong way, and the field in front of the Moose looked open. But his blockers were going the wrong way, too. Maybe that was why the field looked so open. What did it matter, though,
220 with the field clear in front of him? This was going to be a cakewalk;[8] the Moose was going to score a touchdown.

---

8. **cakewalk** *n.:* easy jŏb.

FLUENCY

Re-read the boxed passage aloud until you can read it smoothly. Pay attention to the punctuation marks as you read. Notice especially the questions and exclamations that make this dialogue between characters sound like real conversation.

INFER

Pause at line 210. What inference can you draw about how Moose feels at this point? Underline the details that lead to your inference.

VOCABULARY

ponder (pän′dər) *v.:* think over carefully.

VISUALIZE

Re-read lines 231–238. Circle the details that help you picture what's happening. Which of your senses do most of these details appeal to?

Then, again—"Whoa!"

Players with red jerseys were beginning to fill the empty space—a lot of them. And they were all running toward the Moose. They were kind of low, with their arms spread, as if they wanted to hit him hard and then grab him.

A picture of Jerry Dixon dancing his little jig and wriggling between tacklers flashed through the Moose's mind. How did Jerry do that? Well, no time to **ponder** that one 230 right now.

The Moose lowered his shoulder and thundered ahead, into the cloud of red jerseys. Something hit his left thigh. It hurt. Then something pounded his hip, then his shoulder. They both hurt. Somebody was hanging on to him and was a terrible drag. How could he run with somebody hanging on to him? He knew he was going down, but maybe he was across the goal. He hit the ground hard, with somebody coming down on top of him, right on the small of his back.

The Moose couldn't move. They had him pinned. 240 Wasn't the referee supposed to get these guys off?

Finally the load was gone and the Moose, still holding the ball, got to his knees and one hand, then stood.

He heard the screaming of the crowd, and he saw the scoreboard blinking.

He had scored.

His teammates were slapping him on the shoulder pads and laughing and shouting.

The Moose grinned, but he had a strange and distant look in his eyes.

250 He jogged to the sideline, the roars of the crowd still ringing in his ears.

"OK, son?" Coach Williams asked.

The Moose was puffing. He took a couple of deep breaths. He relived for a moment the first sight of a half dozen players in red jerseys, all with one target—him. He saw again the menacing horde of red jerseys that had risen up just when he'd thought he had clear sailing to the goal. They all zeroed in on him, the Moose, alone.

The Moose glanced at the coach, took another deep 260 breath, and said, "Never again."

INTERPRET

By line 255 you've found out who wins the main **conflict**. Read on to learn of an **internal conflict** the Moose faces. What does Moose decide?

_____

_____

_____

_____

_____

_____

EVALUATE

This story could have been called "Never Again." Write a sentence evaluating the story's title. Tell which title you prefer: "Just Once" or "Never Again." Give a reason for your answer.

_____

_____

_____

_____

_____

_____

_____

_____

Just Once

Literary Skills
Analyze conflict.

Conflict Scoreboard   A **conflict** is a struggle between characters or a difference of ideas. The scoreboard below lists some of the conflicts the Moose faces while trying to get what he wants: a chance to carry the ball. In the second column, fill in how each of those conflicts is **resolved,** that is, what happens to the conflict. (Are they all resolved?)

The Moose's conflict	How the conflict is resolved
With Coach in the dressing room	
With Dan Blevins	
With Coach on the practice field	
With Coach during the game	

Skills Review

Just Once

VOCABULARY AND COMPREHENSION

A. Clarifying Word Meanings: Using Context   Write the word from the Word Bank that fits in the context. Then, underline the context clues that helped you.

1. The team was _____ of the new player and treated her fairly and with kindness.

2. For weeks the girl had been _____ the idea of trying out for the boys' team.

3. The team's captain would have to _____, or think carefully about, his next move.

4. The team got an _____ donation. They never found out who gave them the money.

5. Because a loss would be _____ to their team, they worked especially hard to avoid such a terrible event.

B. Reading Comprehension   Answer each question below.

1. What does Moose want? _____

_____

2. Why doesn't Moose say what he wants right away? _____

_____

3. What happens when Moose goes "public"? _____

_____

4. How does Moose change at the end of the story? _____

_____

_____

SKILLS FOCUS

Vocabulary Skills
Use context clues.

The Stone by Lloyd Alexander

LITERARY FOCUS: MORAL LESSONS

You may have seen the words "And the moral is . . ." at the end of a fable. A **moral** is a lesson about right and wrong ways to behave. The well-known fable about the hare and the tortoise ends with the moral "Slow and steady wins the race." In some stories the moral lesson is not stated. You have to infer it from the way the story ends. As you read "The Stone," look for the lesson Maibon learns about life.

READING SKILLS: MAKING PREDICTIONS

Making predictions—guessing what will happen—is a part of life. Think for a moment about predictions you've made in real life. Did you predict the winner of the World Series? Did you predict who would win a talent contest?

You can also make predictions when you read. Here's how to do it:
- Look for clues in the story that suggest what might happen next.
- Keep in mind what events usually take place in fairy tales and folk tales.
- Think about how the characters might act, basing your ideas on how characters have acted in books you've read or how people in real life often act.
- Change or adjust your predictions if you need to.

SKILLS FOCUS

Literary Skills
Understand moral lessons.

Reading Skills
Make predictions.

Vocabulary Skills
Clarify word meanings through synonyms.

VOCABULARY DEVELOPMENT

PREVIEW SELECTION VOCABULARY

Become familiar with these words before you read "The Stone."

delved (delvd) *v.:* dug. *Delved* also means "searched."

Maibon's shovel no longer delved as well as it had when it was new.

gaped (gāpt) *v.:* stared with the mouth open, as in wonder or surprise.

Maibon gaped at the trapped dwarf.

plight (plīt) *n.:* bad situation.

Doli needed Maibon to help him out of his plight.

obliged (ə·blījd′) *v.:* forced.

Doli was obliged to grant Maibon's wish.

jubilation (jo͞o′bə·lā′shən) *n.:* rejoicing; great joy.

Modrona did not share Maibon's jubilation over the magic stone.

rue (ro͞o) *v.:* feel sorrow or regret for.

Doli thought that Maibon would soon rue the day he wished for the stone.

mired (mīrd) *v.:* sunk or stuck, as if in mud.

The stone caused Maibon to get mired in time.

fallow (fal′ō) *adj.:* left unplanted.

Maibon was very happy when his field, once fallow, became covered in blades of wheat.

CLARIFYING WORD MEANINGS: SYNONYMS

Synonyms are words or phrases that have the same or nearly the same meaning as another word. When you learn a new word, it is helpful to learn its synonyms, too. In each sentence that follows, a synonym of the vocabulary word appears in parentheses.

- After the storm the car became **mired** (stuck) in the mud along the road.
- You will **rue** (regret) the day you quit taking piano lessons.
- No one lived at the farm anymore, and its fields remained **fallow** (unplanted).
- Following the local team's victory, the town was filled with **jubilation** (great joy).

The Stone

Lloyd Alexander

There was a cottager named Maibon, and one day he was
driving down the road in his horse and cart when he saw
an old man hobbling along, so frail and feeble he doubted
the poor soul could go many more steps. Though Maibon
offered to take him in the cart, the old man refused; and
Maibon went his way home, shaking his head over such a
pitiful sight, and said to his wife, Modrona:

"Ah, ah, what a sorry thing it is to have your bones
creaking and cracking, and dim eyes, and dull wits. When
10   I think this might come to me, too! A fine, strong-armed,
sturdy-legged fellow like me? One day to go tottering and
have his teeth rattling in his head and live on porridge like
a baby? There's no fate worse in all the world."

"There is," answered Modrona, "and that would be to
have neither teeth nor porridge. Get on with you, Maibon,

IDENTIFY

Pause at line 7. Circle the
names of the characters you
meet.

INFER

Re-read lines 8–13. In what
sort of shape is Maibon now?
How does Maibon feel about
getting old?

_____

_____

_____

_____

_____

_____

INTERPRET

What does Modrona mean when she says "stop borrowing trouble" (line 16)?

_____

_____

_____

_____

_____

WORD STUDY

Bade (line 19) is the past tense of *bid*, which means "ask" or "tell."

RETELL

Pause at line 37. What are some of Maibon's complaints?

_____

_____

_____

_____

_____

VOCABULARY

delved (delvd) *v.*: dug. *Delved* also means "searched."

gaped (gāpt) *v.*: stared with the mouth open, as in wonder or surprise.

and stop borrowing trouble. Hoe your field or you'll have no crop to harvest, and no food for you, or me, or the little ones."

Sighing and grumbling, Maibon did as his wife bade him. Although the day was fair and cloudless, he took no pleasure in it. His ax blade was notched, the wooden handle splintery; his saw had lost its edge; and his hoe, once shining new, had begun to rust. None of his tools, it seemed to him, cut or chopped or **delved** as well as they once had done.

"They're as worn-out as that old codger[1] I saw on the road," Maibon said to himself. He squinted up at the sky. "Even the sun isn't as bright as it used to be and doesn't warm me half as well. It's gone threadbare as my cloak. And no wonder, for it's been there longer than I can remember. Come to think of it, the moon's been looking a little wilted around the edges, too.

"As for me," went on Maibon, in dismay, "I'm in even a worse state. My appetite's faded, especially after meals. Mornings, when I wake, I can hardly keep myself from yawning. And at night, when I go to bed, my eyes are so heavy I can't hold them open. If that's the way things are now, the older I grow, the worse it will be!"

In the midst of his complaining, Maibon glimpsed something bouncing and tossing back and forth beside a fallen tree in a corner of the field. Wondering if one of his piglets had squeezed out of the sty and gone rooting for acorns, Maibon hurried across the turf. Then he dropped his ax and **gaped** in astonishment.

There, struggling to free his leg, which had been caught under the log, lay a short, thickset figure: a dwarf with red hair bristling in all directions beneath his round, close-fitting leather cap. At the sight of Maibon, the dwarf squeezed shut his bright red eyes and began holding his

---

1. **codger** *n.:* informal term meaning "elderly man."

breath. After a moment the dwarf's face went redder than
50 his hair; his cheeks puffed out and soon turned purple.
Then he opened one eye and blinked rapidly at Maibon,
who was staring at him, speechless.

"What," snapped the dwarf, "you can still see me?"

"That I can," replied Maibon, more than ever puzzled,
"and I can see very well you've got yourself tight as a wedge
under that log, and all your kicking only makes it worse."

At this the dwarf blew out his breath and shook his fists.
"I can't do it!" he shouted. "No matter how I try! I can't make
myself invisible! Everyone in my family can disappear—
60 poof! Gone! Vanished! But not me! Not Doli! Believe me, if
I could have done, you never would have found me in such
a **plight.** Worse luck! Well, come on. Don't stand there
goggling like an idiot. Help me get loose!"

At this sharp command Maibon began tugging and
heaving at the log. Then he stopped, wrinkled his brow,
and scratched his head, saying:

"Well, now, just a moment, friend. The way you look,
and all your talk about turning yourself invisible—I'm
thinking you might be one of the Fair Folk."

70 "Oh, clever!" Doli retorted. "Oh, brilliant! Great
clodhopper! Giant beanpole! Of course I am! What else!
Enough gabbling. Get a move on. My leg's going to sleep."

"If a man does the Fair Folk a good turn," cried Maibon,
his excitement growing, "it's told they must do one for him."

"I knew sooner or later you'd come round to that,"
grumbled the dwarf. "That's the way of it with you ham-
handed, heavy-footed oafs. Time was, you humans got
along well with us. But nowadays you no sooner see a Fair
Folk than it's grab, grab, grab! Gobble, gobble, gobble!
80 Grant my wish! Give me this, give me that! As if we had
nothing better to do!"

Re-read lines 44–52. A new
character appears in the
story. What kind of story do
you predict this will be?

_____

_____

_____

_____

IDENTIFY

Circle the dwarf's name in
line 60. What is Doli unable
to do?

_____

_____

_____

VOCABULARY

plight (plīt) n.: bad situation.

CLARIFY

Re-read lines 67–74. What
does Maibon want from the
dwarf?

_____

_____

_____

_____

_____

"Yes, I'll give you a favor," Doli went on. "That's the rule; I'm **obliged** to. Now, get on with it."

Hearing this, Maibon pulled and pried and chopped away at the log as fast as he could and soon freed the dwarf.

Doli heaved a sigh of relief, rubbed his shin, and cocked a red eye at Maibon, saying:

"All right. You've done your work; you'll have your reward. What do you want? Gold, I suppose. That's the 90 usual. Jewels? Fine clothes? Take my advice, go for something practical. A hazelwood twig to help you find water if your well ever goes dry? An ax that never needs sharpening? A cook pot always brimming with food?"

"None of those!" cried Maibon. He bent down to the dwarf and whispered eagerly, "But I've heard tell that you Fair Folk have magic stones that can keep a man young forever. That's what I want. I claim one for my reward."

Doli snorted. "I might have known you'd pick something like that. As to be expected, you humans have it all 100 muddled. There's nothing can make a man young again. That's even beyond the best of our skills. Those stones you're babbling about? Well, yes, there are such things. But greatly overrated. All they'll do is keep you from growing any older."

"Just as good!" Maibon exclaimed. "I want no more than that!"

Doli hesitated and frowned. "Ah—between the two of us, take the cook pot. Better all around. Those stones—we'd sooner not give them away. There's a difficulty—"

"Because you'd rather keep them for yourselves," Maibon 110 broke in. "No, no, you shan't cheat me of my due. Don't put me off with excuses. I told you what I want, and that's what I'll have. Come, hand it over and not another word."

Doli shrugged and opened a leather pouch that hung from his belt. He spilled a number of brightly colored pebbles into his palm, picked out one of the larger stones, and handed it to Maibon. The dwarf then jumped up, took to his heels, raced across the field, and disappeared into a thicket.

Laughing and crowing over his good fortune and his cleverness, Maibon hurried back to the cottage. There he
120 told his wife what had happened and showed her the stone he had claimed from the Fair Folk.

"As I am now, so I'll always be!" Maibon declared, flexing his arms and thumping his chest. "A fine figure of a man! Oho, no gray beard and wrinkled brow for me!"

Instead of sharing her husband's **jubilation,** Modrona flung up her hands and burst out:

"Maibon, you're a greater fool than ever I supposed! And selfish into the bargain! You've turned down treasures! You didn't even ask that dwarf for so much as new jackets
130 for the children! Nor a new apron for me! You could have had the roof mended. Or the walls plastered. No, a stone is what you ask for! A bit of rock no better than you'll dig up in the cow pasture!"

Crestfallen[2] and sheepish, Maibon began thinking his wife was right and the dwarf had indeed given him no more than a common field stone.

2. **crestfallen** *adj.:* discouraged.

VOCABULARY

jubilation (jōō′bə·lā′shən) *n.:* rejoicing; great joy.

IDENTIFY

Pause at line 133. Underline what Modrona wants instead of the stone.

INFER

Do you think Maibon has learned a lesson yet (lines 134–136)? Tell why or why not.

_____

_____

_____

_____

_____

_____

_____

_____

_____

_____

_____

_____

In lines 147–149, what change does Maibon notice?

_____

_____

_____

_____

Brooding, in line 154, means "sitting on and hatching eggs." What other meaning does the verb brooding have?

_____

_____

_____

_____

What problem does Modrona notice in lines 150–154? What do you think might be the cause of this problem?

_____

_____

_____

_____

_____

_____

"Eh, well, it's true," he stammered; "I feel no different than I did this morning, no better or worse, but every way the same. That redheaded little wretch! He'll **rue** the day if 140 I ever find him again!"

So saying, Maibon threw the stone into the fireplace. That night he grumbled his way to bed, dreaming revenge on the dishonest dwarf.

Next morning, after a restless night, he yawned, rubbed his eyes, and scratched his chin. Then he sat bolt upright in bed, patting his cheeks in amazement.

"My beard!" he cried, tumbling out and hurrying to tell his wife. "It hasn't grown! Not by a hair! Can it be the dwarf didn't cheat me after all?"

150 "Don't talk to me about beards," declared his wife as Maibon went to the fireplace, picked out the stone, and clutched it safely in both hands. "There's trouble enough in the chicken roost. Those eggs should have hatched by now, but the hen is still brooding on her nest."

"Let the chickens worry about that," answered Maibon. "Wife, don't you see what a grand thing's happened to me? I'm not a minute older than I was yesterday. Bless that generous-hearted dwarf!"

"Let me lay hands on him and I'll bless him," retorted 160 Modrona. "That's all well and good for you. But what of me? You'll stay as you are, but I'll turn old and gray, and worn and wrinkled, and go doddering into my grave! And what of our little ones? They'll grow up and have children of their own. And grandchildren, and great-grandchildren. And you, younger than any of them. What a foolish sight you'll be!"

But Maibon, gleeful over his good luck, paid his wife no heed and only tucked the stone deeper into his pocket. Next day, however, the eggs had still not hatched.

170 "And the cow!" Modrona cried. "She's long past due to calve, and no sign of a young one ready to be born!"

"Don't bother me with cows and chickens," replied Maibon. "They'll all come right, in time. As for time, I've got all the time in the world!"

Having no appetite for breakfast, Maibon went out into his field. Of all the seeds he had sown there, however, he was surprised to see not one had sprouted. The field, which by now should have been covered with green shoots, lay bare and empty.

180 "Eh, things do seem a little late these days," Maibon said to himself. "Well, no hurry. It's that much less for me to do. The wheat isn't growing, but neither are the weeds."

Some days went by and still the eggs had not hatched, the cow had not calved, the wheat had not sprouted. And now Maibon saw that his apple tree showed no sign of even the smallest, greenest fruit.

"Maibon, it's the fault of that stone!" wailed his wife. "Get rid of the thing!"

"Nonsense," replied Maibon. "The season's slow,
190 that's all."

Nevertheless, his wife kept at him and kept at him so much that Maibon at last, and very reluctantly, threw the stone out the cottage window. Not too far, though, for he had it in the back of his mind to go later and find it again.

Next morning he had no need to go looking for it, for there was the stone, sitting on the window ledge.

"You see?" said Maibon to his wife. "Here it is, back again. So it's a gift meant for me to keep."

"Maibon!" cried his wife. "Will you get rid of it! We've
200 had nothing but trouble since you brought it into the house. Now the baby's fretting and fuming. Teething, poor little thing. But not a tooth to be seen! Maibon, that stone's bad luck and I want no part of it!"

RETELL

Pause at line 171. What trouble has the stone brought so far?

_____

_____

_____

_____

_____

_____

_____

_____

COMPARE & CONTRAST

Re-read lines 187–203. How are Maibon's ideas about the stone different from Modrona's?

_____

_____

_____

_____

_____

_____

_____

_____

_____

INFER

Why do you think the stone keeps coming back (lines 195–220)?

_____
_____
_____
_____
_____
_____
_____
_____
_____
_____
_____
_____
_____
_____
_____
_____

FLUENCY

Re-read lines 221–233 aloud. As you read, use your voice to show how Maibon and his wife feel about the stone.

Protesting it was none of his doing that the stone had come back, Maibon carried it into the vegetable patch. He dug a hole, not a very deep one, and put the stone into it.

Next day, there was the stone, above ground, winking and glittering.

"Maibon!" cried his wife. "Once and for all, if you care
210 for your family, get rid of that cursed thing!"

Seeing no other way to keep peace in the household, Maibon regretfully and unwillingly took the stone and threw it down the well, where it splashed into the water and sank from sight.

But that night, while he was trying vainly to sleep, there came such a rattling and clattering that Maibon clapped his hands over his ears, jumped out of bed, and went stumbling into the yard. At the well the bucket was jiggling back and forth and up and down at the end of
220 the rope, and in the bottom of the bucket was the stone.

Now Maibon began to be truly distressed, not only for the toothless baby, the calfless cow, the fruitless tree, and the hen sitting desperately on her eggs, but for himself as well.

"Nothing's moving along as it should," he groaned. "I can't tell one day from another. Nothing changes, there's nothing to look forward to, nothing to show for my work. Why sow if the seeds don't sprout? Why plant if there's never a harvest? Why eat if I don't get hungry? Why go to bed at night, or get up in the morning, or do anything at all? And
230 the way it looks, so it will stay for ever and ever! I'll shrivel from boredom if nothing else!"

"Maibon," pleaded his wife, "for all our sakes, destroy the dreadful thing!"

Maibon tried now to pound the stone to dust with his heaviest mallet, but he could not so much as knock a chip from it. He put it against his grindstone without so much as scratching it. He set it on his anvil and belabored it with hammer and tongs, all to no avail.

At last he decided to bury the stone again, this time
240 deeper than before. Picking up his shovel, he hurried to the field. But he suddenly halted and the shovel dropped from his hands. There, sitting cross-legged on a stump, was the dwarf.

"You!" shouted Maibon, shaking his fist. "Cheat! Villain! Trickster! I did you a good turn, and see how you've repaid it!"

The dwarf blinked at the furious Maibon. "You mortals are an ungrateful crew. I gave you what you wanted."

"You should have warned me!" burst out Maibon.
250 "I did," Doli snapped back. "You wouldn't listen. No, you yapped and yammered, bound to have your way. I told you we didn't like to give away those stones. When you mortals get hold of one, you stay just as you are— but so does everything around you. Before you know it, you're **mired** in time like a rock in the mud. You take my advice. Get rid of that stone as fast as you can."

"What do you think I've been trying to do?" blurted Maibon. "I've buried it, thrown it down the well, pounded it with a hammer—it keeps coming back to me!"
260 "That's because you really didn't want to give it up," Doli said. "In the back of your mind and the bottom of your heart, you didn't want to change along with the rest of the world. So long as you feel that way, the stone is yours."

"No, no!" cried Maibon. "I want no more of it. Whatever may happen, let it happen. That's better than nothing happening at all. I've had my share of being young; I'll take my share of being old. And when I come to the end of my days, at least I can say I've lived each one of them."

IDENTIFY

Pause at line 246. How does Maibon feel about the stone now?

_____

_____

_____

_____

VOCABULARY

mired (mīrd) v.: sunk or stuck, as if in mud.

IDENTIFY

Re-read lines 260–263. Underline the passage that explains why Maibon couldn't get rid of the stone.

_____

_____

_____

_____

IDENTIFY

How does Maibon feel now about growing old (lines 264–268)?

_____

_____

_____

_____

PREDICT

Pause at line 275. Will the stone come back again? Explain.

_____

_____

_____

_____

VOCABULARY

fallow (fal′ō) *adj.:* left unplanted; yielding no crops.

INTERPRET

Re-read lines 289–290. What is the **moral** of this story? Begin your answer with these words: "Maibon learns _____."

_____

_____

_____

_____

_____

_____

_____

270 "If you mean that," answered Doli, "toss the stone onto the ground right there at the stump. Then get home and be about your business."

Maibon flung down the stone, spun around, and set off as fast as he could. When he dared at last to glance back over his shoulder, fearful the stone might be bouncing along at his heels, he saw no sign of it, or of the redheaded dwarf.

Maibon gave a joyful cry, for at that same instant the **fallow** field was covered with green blades of wheat, the branches of the apple tree bent to the ground, so laden they were with fruit. He ran to the cottage, threw his arms around 280 his wife and children, and told them the good news. The hen hatched her chicks; the cow bore her calf. And Maibon laughed with glee when he saw the first tooth in the baby's mouth.

Never again did Maibon meet any of the Fair Folk, and he was just as glad of it. He and his wife and children and grandchildren lived many years, and Maibon was proud of his white hair and long beard as he had been of his sturdy arms and legs.

"Stones are all right in their way," said Maibon. "But 290 the trouble with them is, they don't grow."

The Stone

Story Map   Fill in this story map for "The Stone." Retell at least five major events from the story. Use your Retell notes in the side columns of the story if you need help. Then, in the final box, write the moral lesson of the story.

SKILLS FOCUS

Literary Skills
Analyze moral lessons.

Main Character

What the Character Wants

What Happens

Event 1:

Event 2:

Event 3:

Event 4:

Event 5:

Moral Lesson

Skills Review

The Stone

VOCABULARY AND COMPREHENSION

A. Clarifying Word Meanings: Synonyms   Write a word from the Word Bank that is a synonym for the boldface word. Not all words will be used.

1. **a.** With his shovel, Mr. Green **dug** into the ground.

   b. With his shovel, Mr. Green _____ into the ground.

2. **a.** The players were **forced** to wear helmets.

   b. The players were _____ to wear helmets.

3. **a.** The class shared their teacher's **rejoicing** over the test scores.

   b. The class shared their teacher's _____ over the test scores.

4. **a.** Jorge will **regret** the day he lost his house key.

   b. Jorge will _____ the day he lost his house key.

5. **a.** We were **stuck** in traffic for hours on the freeway.

   b. We were _____ in traffic for hours on the freeway.

B. Reading Comprehension   Answer each question below.

1. How does Maibon get his wish? _____

   _____

2. What does Modrona think of Maibon's wish? _____

   _____

3. Why is Maibon unable to get rid of the stone? _____

   _____

4. At the end of the story, what does Maibon learn? _____

   _____

SKILLS FOCUS

Vocabulary Skills
Clarify word meanings by using synonyms.

from The Martian Chronicles

by Ray Bradbury

LITERARY FOCUS: SETTING

Think of a time and place in the past, present, or future. Imagine a story taking place in that **setting.** Writers do this kind of imagining all the time. They think of or imagine a special time and place in which characters live. Setting is one of the most important parts of a story. In some stories, setting is as important as the characters.

The setting of the next story, "The Martian Chronicles," is—you guessed it—Mars. But what are *chronicles*? Chronicles are written records of the facts and events of a time and place. They are arranged in **chronological** order—the order in which they happened. The events described in this selection are dated November 2005. When "The Martian Chronicles" was first published in 1950, the year 2005 seemed far in the future. As you read, try to figure out what people in 1950 were worried about.

READING SKILLS: RETELLING

Retelling is a basic skill that proves useful time and time again. When you retell, you use your own words to explain what happened. When you're retelling a story, you should focus on retelling the main events. As you read, pause from time to time and review what has just happened. Think about the most important events, and retell them in your own words.

SKILLS FOCUS

Literary Skills
Understand setting.

Reading Skills
Retell events.

Vocabulary Skills
Use context clues.

VOCABULARY DEVELOPMENT

PREVIEW SELECTION VOCABULARY

Before you read the excerpts from "The Martian Chronicles," learn these words.

conscious (kän'shəs) *adj.:* having feeling; aware.

Because of the great shock, many people were not conscious of their moves that night.

anesthetic (an'es·thet'ik) *n.:* drug causing numbness.

Interplanetary space travel was like an anesthetic. It numbed the mind.

depopulated (dē·päp'yə·lāt·id) *v.:* reduced the number of people.

Earth was depopulated when its people moved to Mars.

extinguished (ek·stiŋ'gwisht) *v.:* put out; smothered.

The fire they had seen on Earth was extinguished by midnight.

atomized (at'əm·īzd) *v.:* destroyed by nuclear weapons.

The explosion had atomized the continent of Australia.

CLARIFYING WORD MEANINGS: CONTEXT CLUES

A good way to understand the meaning of new words is to look for context clues. **Context clues** are words and phrases near the word you want to learn. One type of context clue provides a restatement of the word, giving you its definition. Here are some examples. The words in italics define the words in boldface.

- The musician's humming was not **conscious.** He was not *aware of* what he was doing.
- The soft music was an **anesthetic** to Kyle's nerves. It was like *a drug that made him numb* and sleepy.
- The hurricane warning **depopulated** the town—*reducing the number of people* to just three.

from The Martian Chronicles

Ray Bradbury

November 2005
The Luggage Store

It was a very remote thing, when the luggage-store proprietor[1] heard the news on the night radio, received all the way from Earth on a light-sound beam. The proprietor felt how remote it was.

There was going to be a war on Earth.

He went out to peer into the sky.

Yes, there it was. Earth, in the evening heavens, following the sun into the hills. The words on the radio and that green star were one and the same.

10 "I don't believe it," said the proprietor.

"It's because you're not there," said Father Peregrine, who had stopped by to pass the time of evening.

"What do you mean, Father?"

"It's like when I was a boy," said Father Peregrine. "We heard about wars in China. But we never believed them. It was too far away. And there were too many people dying. It was impossible. Even when we saw the motion pictures we didn't believe it. Well, that's how it is now. Earth is China. It's so far away it's unbelievable. It's not here. You

20 can't touch it. You can't even see it. All you see is a green light. Two billion people living on that light? Unbelievable! War? We don't hear the explosions."

---

1. **proprietor** (prə·prī′ə·tər) *n.:* owner.

IDENTIFY

Circle words in the opening paragraph that give you clues about when and where this story takes place. What do they tell you about the **setting**?

_____

_____

_____

_____

_____

WORD STUDY

Peregrine (per′ə·grin) comes from a word that means "wander." Why do you think the author might have named this character Father Peregrine (line 11)?

_____

_____

_____

_____

_____

_____

"We will," said the proprietor. "I keep thinking about all those people that were going to come to Mars this week. What was it? A hundred thousand or so coming up in the next month or so. What about *them* if the war starts?"

"I imagine they'll turn back. They'll be needed on Earth."

"Well," said the proprietor, "I'd better get my luggage
30 dusted off. I got a feeling there'll be a rush sale here any time."

"Do you think everyone now on Mars will go back to Earth if this *is* the Big War we've all been expecting for years?"

"It's a funny thing, Father, but yes, I think we'll *all* go back. I know, we came up here to get away from things—politics, the atom bomb, war, pressure groups, prejudice, laws—I know. But it's still home there. You wait and see. When the first bomb drops on America the people up
40 here'll start thinking. They haven't been here long enough. A couple years is all. If they'd been here forty years, it'd be different, but they got relatives down there, and their home towns. Me, I can't believe in Earth any more; I can't imagine it much. But I'm old. I don't count. I might stay on here."

"I doubt it."

"Yes, I guess you're right."

They stood on the porch watching the stars. Finally Father Peregrine pulled some money from his pocket and
50 handed it to the proprietor. "Come to think of it, you'd better give me a new valise.[2] My old one's in pretty bad condition. . . ."

---

2. **valise** (və·lēs′) *n.*: suitcase.

November 2005
The Watchers

They all came out and looked at the sky that night. They left their suppers or their washing up or their dressing for the show and they came out upon their now-not-quite-as-new porches and watched the green star of Earth there. It was a move without **conscious** effort; they all did it, to help them understand the news they had heard on the radio a moment before. There was Earth and there the coming war, and there hundreds of thousands of mothers or grandmothers or fathers or brothers or aunts or uncles or cousins. They stood on the porches and tried to believe in the existence of Earth, much as they had once tried to believe in the existence of Mars; it was a problem reversed. To all intents and purposes, Earth now was dead; they had been away from it for three or four years. Space was an **anesthetic;** seventy million miles of space numbed you, put memory to sleep, **depopulated** Earth, erased the past, and

© Getty Images.

VISUALIZE

Re-read lines 53–59. Take a moment to visualize the scene, and then draw it below.

VOCABULARY

conscious (kän′shəs) *adj.:* having feeling; aware.

anesthetic (an′es·thet′ik) *n.:* drug causing numbness.

depopulated (dē·päp′yə·lāt·id) *v.:* reduced the number of people.

CONNECT

When Bradbury wrote this story, people all over the world were concerned about the threat of nuclear war. What might Bradbury's message be to the readers of this story?

_____

_____

_____

_____

70 allowed these people here to go on with their work. But now, tonight, the dead were risen, Earth was reinhabited, memory awoke, a million names were spoken: What was so-and-so doing tonight on Earth? What about this one and that one? The people on the porches glanced sideways at each other's faces.

At nine o'clock Earth seemed to explode, catch fire, and burn.

The people on the porches put up their hands as if to beat the fire out.

They waited.

80 By midnight the fire was **extinguised**. Earth was still there. There was a sigh, like an autumn wind, from the porches.

"We haven't heard from Harry for a long time."

"He's all right."

"We should send a message to Mother."

"She's all right."

"*Is* she?"

"Now, don't worry."

"Will she be all right, do you think?"

90 "Of course, of course; now come to bed."

But nobody moved. Late dinners were carried out onto the night lawns and set upon collapsible tables, and they picked at these slowly until two o'clock and the light-radio message flashed from Earth. They could read the great Morse-code flashes which flickered like a distant firefly:

> AUSTRALIAN CONTINENT **ATOMIZED** IN PREMATURE EXPLO-
> SION OF ATOMIC STOCKPILE. LOS ANGELES, LONDON BOMBED.
> WAR. COME HOME. COME HOME. COME HOME.

They stood up from their tables.

100 COME HOME. COME HOME. COME HOME.

"Have you heard from your brother Ted this year?"

"You know. With mail rates five bucks a letter to Earth, I don't write much."

COME HOME.

"I've been wondering about Jane; you remember Jane, my kid sister?"

COME HOME.

At three in the chilly morning the luggage-store proprietor glanced up. A lot of people were coming down
110 the street.

"Stayed open late on purpose. What'll it be, mister?"

By dawn the luggage was gone from his shelves.

© CORBIS.

INTERPRET

Notice the words that appear in capital letters (lines 96–107). What effect does the repetition of the words "come home" have on the reader?

_____

_____

_____

_____

_____

_____

_____

_____

IDENTIFY

What happens at the end of the story? What is the resolution of the **plot**?

_____

_____

_____

_____

_____

_____

_____

_____

_____

_____

The Martian Chronicles **39**

from The Martian Chronicles

SKILLS
FOCUS

Literary Skills
Analyze setting.

Setting Circle   This story's setting directly affects the characters and story events. Fill in the middle circle with details about the setting. Then, fill in the outside circles with plot events from the story. Finally, look over your completed setting circle to see how setting and plot interconnect.

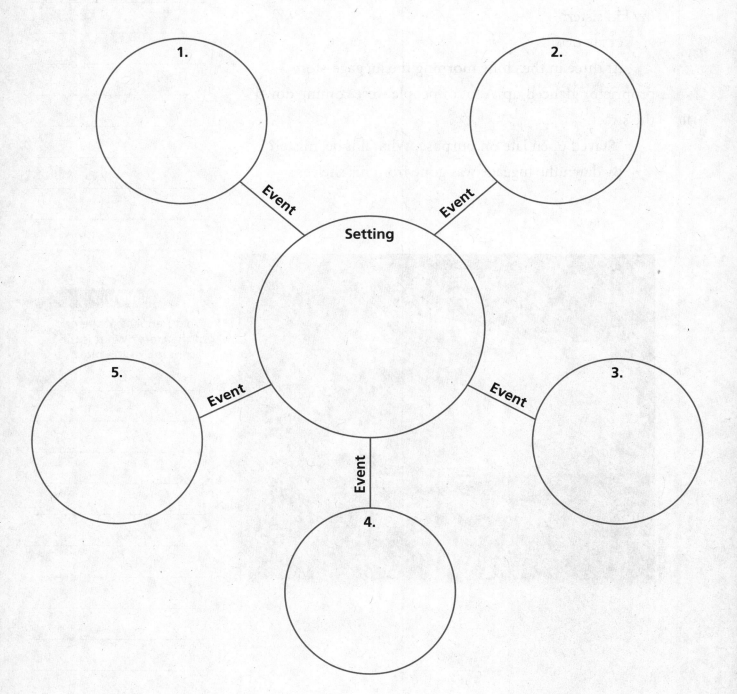

1.

2.

Event

Event

Setting

5.

3.

Event

Event

Event

4.

Skills Review

from The Martian Chronicles

VOCABULARY AND COMPREHENSION

A. Clarifying Word Meanings: Context   Write words from the Word Bank in the blanks to complete the paragraph. Underline context clues that helped you choose the correct word.

The force of the nuclear bomb had (1) _____ the island. There was nothing left but bits of floating wood. Days before, an escape plan had (2) _____ the island, sending most of the people to the mainland. Before they left, the people (3) _____ the fires that had burned in their fireplaces. The smoke was a(n) (4) _____ that caused everyone to feel numb and sad. Yet they were aware of what they needed to do. They made a(n) (5) _____ effort to get out quickly.

B. Reading Comprehension   Circle the letter of the correct response.

1. The **setting** of the narrative is—
   a. Earth   b. Mars   c. deep space   d. the ocean

2. The **plot** involves—
   f. a luggage shop on Mars that is visited by Father Peregrine
   g. a war on Earth as seen by Earth settlers on Mars
   h. a Martian war among settlers who have arrived from Earth
   j. getting a stranded spaceship back home

3. People came to Mars in order to—
   a. start businesses   c. escape problems on Earth
   b. live longer lives   d. grow food

4. By the end of the story, we know that the settlers—
   f. decide not to listen to any more radio reports
   g. relocate to a planet farther from Earth
   h. agree to stay on Mars
   j. still regard the Earth as their home

SKILLS FOCUS

Vocabulary Skills
Use context clues.

Characters: The People You'll Meet

COPYRIGHT, 1895
BY B.J. FALK N.Y.

COPYRIGHT
1895
BY
D. FALK

Academic Vocabulary for Collection 2

These are the terms you should know
as you read and analyze the selections in this collection.

Characters The people in a story. In some works, such as fables and folk tales, animals are characters. In fairy tales, fantastic creatures, such as ogres and dragons, are characters. In myths, gods and heroes are characters.

Characterization How the writer shows the personality of a character. We usually learn about characters by paying attention to their appearance and actions, "listening" to what they have to say, noting their thoughts and feelings, and observing how other characters react to them.

Direct Characterization Statements in a story that tell you directly what a character is like. Example: "Jennifer hated spending money, but she was generous to her friends."

Indirect Characterization "Showing" rather than telling what a character is like. With indirect characterization, you observe the character and reach your own conclusions about what kind of person the character is.

● ● ●

Plot A series of related events. Most plots include **conflict, complications, climax,** and **resolution.**

Conflict A struggle. In most stories, the main character faces a conflict.

External Conflict Struggle between a character and an outside force, such as bitter cold or a bear.

Internal Conflict Struggle within a character's mind or heart. For example, a character might struggle to overcome shyness or greed.

● ● ●

Point of View Standpoint from which a story is told.

First-Person Point of View In this point of view, one of the story's characters, using the personal pronoun *I,* is telling the story.

Before You Read

This selection also appears in *Elements of Literature.* ◆

Ta-Na-E-Ka by Mary Whitebird

LITERARY FOCUS: CHARACTER AND CONFLICT

A **character** is a person (or animal or monster or other being) in a story. Like people in real life, story characters have qualities, such as kindness or wisdom. What happens in a story depends on the way its characters respond to conflict.

Put simply, a **conflict** is a battle or struggle. A struggle between a character and an outside force, such as a competitor or a natural disaster, is an **external conflict.** A struggle within a character's mind or heart, such as a struggle with anxiety, distrust, or anger, is an **internal conflict.** Characters often face both kinds of conflict.

READING SKILLS: COMPARISON AND CONTRAST

Without even realizing it, you probably compare and contrast things every day. For example, do you compare and contrast pop music stars when you watch music videos? Do you compare and contrast styles of clothing or haircuts?

- When you **compare,** you look for ways in which things are alike.
- When you **contrast,** you look for ways in which things are different.

As you read "Ta-Na-E-Ka," compare and contrast its characters and how they respond to the challenges they face. Use the compare-and-contrast sidenotes throughout the selection to guide you.

SKILLS FOCUS

Literary Skills
Understand character and conflict.

Reading Skills
Use comparison and contrast.

Vocabulary Skills
Use context clues.

VOCABULARY DEVELOPMENT

PREVIEW SELECTION VOCABULARY

Learn these words before you read "Ta-Na-E-Ka."

loftiest (lôf′tē·əst) *adj.*: noblest; highest.

> *Grandfather described endurance as the loftiest virtue.*

shrewdest (shrōōd′əst) *adj.* used as *n.*: sharpest; most clever.

> *Only the shrewdest could survive Ta-Na-E-Ka.*

grimaced (grim′ist) *v.*: twisted the face to express pain, anger, or disgust.

> *Roger grimaced at the thought of eating grasshoppers.*

gorging (gôrj′iŋ) *v.*: filling up; stuffing.

> *During his Ta-Na-E-Ka the boy dreamed of gorging himself on hamburgers.*

audacity (ô·das′ə·tē) *n.*: boldness; daring.

> *Mary's parents were shocked at her audacity.*

CLARIFYING WORD MEANINGS: RESTATEMENT

When you come across an unfamiliar word in your reading, what do you do? Do you skip over it? Do you raise your hand and ask your teacher for help? Do you crack open a dictionary? One great way to figure out the meaning of an unfamiliar word is to search for nearby context clues. **Context clues** are words and phrases that appear near the unfamiliar word and that may help you define it. Here are some examples of context clues:

DEFINITION: Her **audacity,** *or boldness,* was known throughout the school.

RESTATEMENT: She had the **audacity**—she actually had *the nerve*—to ask for a full refund.

EXAMPLE: She has a lot of **audacity.** *She walked right up and demanded her money back.*

CONTRAST: *Unlike* her sister, who is *very timid and shy,* Mary has **audacity.**

TA-NA-E-KA

Mary Whitebird

> **BACKGROUND: Literature and Social Studies**
> This story has to do with the traditions of the Native
> Americans known as the Kaw. The Kaw are also
> known as the Kansa. Both names are forms of a
> word that means "People of the South Wind." The
> Kaw originally lived along the Kansas River.

INFER

Underline the details in lines
5–15 that tell you how the
grandfather looks, dresses,
and acts. Based on these
clues, make three inferences,
educated guesses, about his
character.

_____

_____

_____

_____

_____

_____

_____

As my birthday drew closer, I had awful nightmares about
it. I was reaching the age at which all Kaw Indians had to
participate in Ta-Na-E-Ka. Well, not all Kaws. Many of the
younger families on the reservation were beginning to give
up the old customs. But my grandfather, Amos Deer Leg,
was devoted to tradition. He still wore handmade beaded
moccasins instead of shoes and kept his iron-gray hair in
tight braids. He could speak English, but he spoke it only
with white men. With his family he used a Sioux dialect.[1]

10   Grandfather was one of the last living Indians (he died
in 1953, when he was eighty-one) who actually fought against
the U.S. Cavalry. Not only did he fight, he was wounded in
a skirmish at Rose Creek—a famous encounter in which
the celebrated Kaw chief Flat Nose lost his life. At the time,
my grandfather was only eleven years old.

---

1. **Sioux** (soo) **dialect:** one of the languages spoken by the Plains Indians,
including the Kaw.

Kaw
Homeland

Missouri R.

Iowa

Nebraska

Kansas R.

Santa Fe Trail

Missouri

Arkansas R.

Kansas

Oklahoma

Eleven was a magic word among the Kaws. It was the time of Ta-Na-E-Ka, the "flowering of adulthood." It was the age, my grandfather informed us hundreds of times, "when a boy could prove himself to be a warrior and a girl

20   took the first steps to womanhood."

"I don't want to be a warrior," my cousin, Roger Deer Leg, confided to me. "I'm going to become an accountant."

"None of the other tribes make girls go through the endurance ritual," I complained to my mother.

"It won't be as bad as you think, Mary," my mother said, ignoring my protests. "Once you've gone through it, you'll certainly never forget it. You'll be proud."

I even complained to my teacher, Mrs. Richardson, feeling that, as a white woman, she would side with me.

30   She didn't. "All of us have rituals of one kind or another," Mrs. Richardson said. "And look at it this way: How many girls have the opportunity to compete on equal terms with boys? Don't look down on your heritage."

Heritage, indeed! I had no intention of living on a reservation for the rest of my life. I was a good student. I loved school. My fantasies were about knights in armor and fair

IDENTIFY

Circle the details that tell you what Ta-Na-E-Ka is (lines 16–20). Then, read on and underline the **narrator's** name.

IDENTIFY

Pause at line 33. **External conflict** is a struggle between a character and some outside force. The older generation is on one side of the external conflict here. Which two characters are struggling against the older generation?

_____

_____

_____

IDENTIFY

At this point in the story, how does Mary feel about her Indian heritage? In lines 34–38, what else do you find out about Mary's **character** and her interests?

_____

_____

_____

_____

_____

_____

IDENTIFY

In lines 39–40, Mary says she's "always thought that the Kaw were the originators of the women's liberation movement." What does she mean? Circle the details that she gives to support her opinion.

_____

_____

_____

_____

_____

_____

_____

_____

_____

_____

_____

_____

_____

VOCABULARY

loftiest (lôf′tē·əst) *adj.*: noblest; highest.

IDENTIFY

Re-read lines 59–67. Circle the words that tell how long Ta-Na-E-Ka lasted when Grandfather was a boy.

ladies in flowing gowns being saved from dragons. It never once occurred to me that being an Indian was exciting.

40　　But I've always thought that the Kaw were the originators of the women's liberation movement. No other Indian tribe—and I've spent half a lifetime researching the subject—treated women more "equally" than the Kaw. Unlike most of the subtribes of the Sioux Nation, the Kaw allowed men and women to eat together. And hundreds of years before we were "acculturated,"[2] a Kaw woman had the right to refuse a prospective husband even if her father arranged the match.

The wisest women (generally wisdom was equated with age) often sat in tribal councils. Furthermore, most 50 Kaw legends revolve around "Good Woman," a kind of supersquaw, a Joan of Arc[3] of the high plains. Good Woman led Kaw warriors into battle after battle, from which they always seemed to emerge victorious.

And girls as well as boys were required to undergo Ta-Na-E-Ka.

The actual ceremony varied from tribe to tribe, but since the Indians' life on the plains was dedicated to survival, Ta-Na-E-Ka was a test of survival.

"Endurance is the **loftiest** virtue of the Indian," my 60 grandfather explained. "To survive, we must endure. When I was a boy, Ta-Na-E-Ka was more than the mere symbol it is now. We were painted white with the juice of a sacred herb and sent naked into the wilderness without so much as a knife. We couldn't return until the white had worn off. It wouldn't wash off. It took almost eighteen days, and during that time we had to stay alive, trapping food, eating insects

---

2. **acculturated** (ə·kul′chər·āt′id) *v.* used as *adj.*: adapted to a new or different culture.
3. **Joan of Arc** (1412–1431): French heroine who led her country's army to victory over the English in 1429.

and roots and berries, and watching out for enemies. And we did have enemies—both the white soldiers and the Omaha warriors, who were always trying to capture Kaw boys and girls undergoing their endurance test. It was an exciting time."

"What happened if you couldn't make it?" Roger asked. He was born only three days after I was, and we were being trained for Ta-Na-E-Ka together. I was happy to know he was frightened, too.

"Many didn't return," Grandfather said. "Only the strongest and **shrewdest.** Mothers were not allowed to weep over those who didn't return. If a Kaw couldn't survive, he or she wasn't worth weeping over. It was our way."

"What a lot of hooey," Roger whispered. "I'd give anything to get out of it."

"I don't see how we have any choice," I replied.

Roger gave my arm a little squeeze. "Well, it's only five days."

Five days! Maybe it was better than being painted white and sent out naked for eighteen days. But not much better.

We were to be sent, barefoot and in bathing suits, into the woods. Even our very traditional parents put their foot down when Grandfather suggested we go naked. For five days we'd have to live off the land, keeping warm as best we could, getting food where we could. It was May, but on the northernmost reaches of the Missouri River, the days were still chilly and the nights were fiercely cold.

Grandfather was in charge of the month's training for Ta-Na-E-Ka. One day he caught a grasshopper and demonstrated how to pull its legs and wings off in one flick of the fingers and how to swallow it.

VOCABULARY

shrewdest (shrōōd′əst) *adj.* used as *n.*: sharpest; most clever.

COMPARE & CONTRAST

Re-read lines 83–93. List the *differences* between the Ta-Na-E-Ka ritual planned for Mary and Roger and the Ta-Na-E-Ka that Grandfather had.

_____

_____

_____

_____

_____

_____

_____

_____

_____

_____

_____

_____

_____

_____

_____

_____

_____

I felt sick, and Roger turned green. "It's a darn good
thing it's 1947," I told Roger teasingly. "You'd make a terrible
100 warrior." Roger just **grimaced.**

I knew one thing. This particular Kaw Indian girl
wasn't going to swallow a grasshopper no matter how
hungry she got. And then I had an idea. Why hadn't I
thought of it before? It would have saved nights of bad
dreams about squooshy grasshoppers.

I headed straight for my teacher's house. "Mrs.
Richardson," I said, "would you lend me five dollars?"

"Five dollars!" she exclaimed. "What for?"

"You remember the ceremony I talked about?"

110 "Ta-Na-E-Ka. Of course. Your parents have written
me and asked me to excuse you from school so you can
participate in it."

"Well, I need some things for the ceremony," I replied, in
a half-truth. "I don't want to ask my parents for the money."

"It's not a crime to borrow money, Mary. But how can
you pay it back?"

"I'll baby-sit for you ten times."

"That's more than fair," she said, going to her purse
and handing me a crisp, new five-dollar bill. I'd never had
120 that much money at once.

"I'm happy to know the money's going to be put to a
good use," Mrs. Richardson said.

A few days later the ritual began with a long speech
from my grandfather about how we had reached the age of
decision, how we now had to fend for ourselves and prove
that we could survive the most horrendous of ordeals. All
the friends and relatives who had gathered at our house for
dinner made jokes about their own Ta-Na-E-Ka experiences.
They all advised us to fill up now, since for the next five

130 days we'd be **gorging** ourselves on crickets. Neither Roger nor I was very hungry. "I'll probably laugh about this when I'm an accountant," Roger said, trembling.

"Are you trembling?" I asked.

"What do you think?"

"I'm happy to know boys tremble, too," I said.

At six the next morning, we kissed our parents and went off to the woods. "Which side do you want?" Roger asked. According to the rules, Roger and I would stake out "territories" in separate areas of the woods, and we weren't

140 to communicate during the entire ordeal.

"I'll go toward the river, if it's OK with you," I said.

"Sure," Roger answered. "What difference does it make?"

To me, it made a lot of difference. There was a marina a few miles up the river, and there were boats moored there. At least, I hoped so. I figured that a boat was a better place to sleep than under a pile of leaves.

"Why do you keep holding your head?" Roger asked.

"Oh, nothing. Just nervous," I told him. Actually, I was afraid I'd lose the five-dollar bill, which I had tucked into

150 my hair with a bobby pin. As we came to a fork in the trail, Roger shook my hand. "Good luck, Mary."

"N'ko-n'ta," I said. It was the Kaw word for "courage."

The sun was shining and it was warm, but my bare feet began to hurt immediately. I spied one of the berry bushes Grandfather had told us about. "You're lucky," he had said. "The berries are ripe in the spring, and they are delicious and nourishing." They were orange and fat, and I popped one into my mouth.

Argh! I spat it out. It was awful and bitter, and even

160 grasshoppers were probably better tasting, although I never intended to find out.

VOCABULARY

gorging (gôrj'iŋ) *v.:* filling up; stuffing.

INFER

Pause at line 152. Which cousin do you think will need luck? Which cousin will make his or her own luck? Explain.

_____

_____

_____

_____

_____

_____

_____

_____

_____

_____

_____

_____

_____

VISUALIZE

Read lines 153–167 carefully. Circle the details that help you picture the **setting**. Notice that the narrator includes details that tell you what she sees, tastes, and feels.

Carson Baldwin, Jr./Earth Scenes.

INFER

Pause at line 170. How has Mary overcome her fear?

PREDICT

Pause at line 176. Will the man at the counter be an enemy or a friend to Mary? Tell what you think might happen next.

I sat down to rest my feet. A rabbit hopped out from under the berry bush. He nuzzled the berry I'd spat out and ate it. He picked another one and ate that, too. He liked them. He looked at me, twitching his nose. I watched a redheaded woodpecker bore into an elm tree, and I caught a glimpse of a civet cat[4] waddling through some twigs. All of a sudden I realized I was no longer frightened. Ta-Na-E-Ka might be more fun than I'd anticipated. I got up and headed toward

170   the marina.

"Not one boat," I said to myself dejectedly. But the restaurant on the shore, Ernie's Riverside, was open. I walked in, feeling silly in my bathing suit. The man at the counter was big and tough-looking. He wore a sweat shirt with the words "Fort Sheridan, 1944," and he had only three fingers on one of his hands. He asked me what I wanted.

"A hamburger and a milkshake," I said, holding the five-dollar bill in my hand so he'd know I had money.

---

4. **civet** (siv′it) **cat** n.: furry spotted skunk.

"That's a pretty heavy breakfast, honey," he murmured.

180 "That's what I always have for breakfast," I lied.

"Forty-five cents," he said, bringing me the food. (Back in 1947, hamburgers were twenty-five cents and milkshakes were twenty cents.)

"Delicious," I thought. "Better 'n grasshoppers—and Grandfather never once mentioned that I couldn't eat hamburgers."

While I was eating, I had a grand idea. Why not sleep in the restaurant? I went to the ladies' room and made sure the window was unlocked. Then I went back outside and

190 played along the riverbank, watching the water birds and trying to identify each one. I planned to look for a beaver dam the next day.

The restaurant closed at sunset, and I watched the three-fingered man drive away. Then I climbed in the unlocked window. There was a night light on, so I didn't turn on any lights. But there was a radio on the counter. I turned it on to a music program. It was warm in the restaurant, and I was hungry. I helped myself to a glass of milk and a piece of pie, intending to keep a list of what I'd

200 eaten so I could leave money. I also planned to get up early, sneak out through the window, and head for the woods before the three-fingered man returned. I turned off the radio, wrapped myself in the man's apron, and in spite of the hardness of the floor, fell asleep.

"What the heck are you doing here, kid?"

It was the man's voice.

It was morning. I'd overslept. I was scared.

"Hold it, kid. I just wanna know what you're doing here. You lost? You must be from the reservation. Your folks

210 must be worried sick about you. Do they have a phone?"

WORD STUDY

In line 184, 'n is a slangy contraction for *than*.

RETELL

Pause at line 204. Retell what has happened to Mary on her Ta-Na-E-Ka so far.

_____

_____

_____

_____

_____

_____

_____

_____

_____

_____

_____

_____

_____

_____

_____

_____

_____

INTERPRET

What **internal conflict** does Mary feel when Ernie says that Ta-Na-E-Ka is silly (lines 218–219)? Underline the details that tell how she defends the ritual.

_____

_____

_____

_____

_____

EVALUATE

What do you like most about Mary? What do you like least about her? What's your opinion of the way Mary has endured Ta-Na-E-Ka so far?

_____

_____

_____

_____

_____

_____

_____

_____

_____

_____

_____

"Yes, yes," I answered. "But don't call them."

I was shivering. The man, who told me his name was Ernie, made me a cup of hot chocolate while I explained about Ta-Na-E-Ka.

"Darnedest thing I ever heard," he said, when I was through. "Lived next to the reservation all my life and this is the first I've heard of Ta-Na-whatever-you-call-it." He looked at me, all goose bumps in my bathing suit. "Pretty silly thing to do to a kid," he muttered.

220 That was just what I'd been thinking for months, but when Ernie said it, I became angry. "No, it isn't silly. It's a custom of the Kaw. We've been doing this for hundreds of years. My mother and my grandfather and everybody in my family went through this ceremony. It's why the Kaw are great warriors."

"OK, great warrior," Ernie chuckled, "suit yourself. And, if you want to stick around, it's OK with me." Ernie went to the broom closet and tossed me a bundle. "That's the lost-and-found closet," he said. "Stuff people left on 230 boats. Maybe there's something to keep you warm."

The sweater fitted loosely, but it felt good. I felt good. And I'd found a new friend. Most important, I was surviving Ta-Na-E-Ka.

My grandfather had said the experience would be filled with adventure, and I was having my fill. And Grandfather had never said we couldn't accept hospitality.

I stayed at Ernie's Riverside for the entire period. In the mornings I went into the woods and watched the animals and picked flowers for each of the tables in Ernie's. I had 240 never felt better. I was up early enough to watch the sun rise on the Missouri, and I went to bed after it set. I ate everything I wanted—insisting that Ernie take all my money for the food. "I'll keep this in trust for you, Mary," Ernie promised, "in case you are ever desperate for five dollars." (He did, too, but that's another story.)

I was sorry when the five days were over. I'd enjoyed every minute with Ernie. He taught me how to make western omelets and to make Chili Ernie Style (still one of my favorite dishes). And I told Ernie all about the legends of

250 the Kaw. I hadn't realized I knew so much about my people.

But Ta-Na-E-Ka was over, and as I approached my house at about nine-thirty in the evening, I became nervous all over again. What if Grandfather asked me about the berries and the grasshoppers? And my feet were hardly cut. I hadn't lost a pound and my hair was combed.

"They'll be so happy to see me," I told myself hopefully, "that they won't ask too many questions."

I opened the door. My grandfather was in the front room. He was wearing the ceremonial beaded deerskin

260 shirt which had belonged to *his* grandfather. "N'g'da'ma," he said. "Welcome back."

I embraced my parents warmly, letting go only when I saw my cousin Roger sprawled on the couch. His eyes were red and swollen. He'd lost weight. His feet were an unsightly mass of blood and blisters, and he was moaning: "I made it, see. I made it. I'm a warrior. A warrior."

My grandfather looked at me strangely. I was clean, obviously well-fed, and radiantly healthy. My parents got the message. My uncle and aunt gazed at me with hostility.

270 Finally my grandfather asked, "What did you eat to keep you so well?"

I sucked in my breath and blurted out the truth: "Hamburgers and milkshakes."

"Hamburgers!" my grandfather growled.

"Milkshakes!" Roger moaned.

PREDICT

Pause at line 255. How do you think Grandfather will react when he sees Mary looking healthy? Explain.

_____

_____

_____

_____

_____

_____

_____

_____

_____

COMPARE & CONTRAST

Re-read lines 254–269. Circle the details that describe Mary's appearance. Underline the details describing Roger's.

FLUENCY

Re-read the boxed passage, and underline clues, such as "my grandfather growled," that tell you how the characters would speak. Then, read the passage aloud. Practice reading as if you were Roger, Mary's grandfather, and the narrator.

"You didn't say we *had* to eat grasshoppers," I said sheepishly.

"Tell us all about your Ta-Na-E-Ka," my grandfather commanded.

280 I told them everything, from borrowing the five dollars, to Ernie's kindness, to observing the beaver.

"That's not what I trained you for," my grandfather said sadly.

I stood up. "Grandfather, I learned that Ta-Na-E-Ka is important. I didn't think so during training. I was scared stiff of it. I handled it my way. And I learned I had nothing to be afraid of. There's no reason in 1947 to eat grasshoppers when you can eat a hamburger."

I was inwardly shocked at my own **audacity.** But I 290 liked it. "Grandfather, I'll bet you never ate one of those rotten berries yourself."

Grandfather laughed! He laughed aloud! My mother and father and aunt and uncle were all dumbfounded. Grandfather never laughed. Never.

"Those berries—they are terrible," Grandfather admitted. "I could never swallow them. I found a dead deer on the

first day of my Ta-Na-E-Ka—shot by a soldier, probably—
and he kept my belly full for the entire period of the test!"

Grandfather stopped laughing. "We should send you

300   out again," he said.

I looked at Roger. "You're pretty smart, Mary," Roger
groaned. "I'd never have thought of what you did."

"Accountants just have to be good at arithmetic," I said
comfortingly. "I'm terrible at arithmetic."

Roger tried to smile but couldn't. My grandfather
called me to him. "You should have done what your cousin
did. But I think you are more alert to what is happening to
our people today than we are. I think you would have passed
the test under any circumstances, in any time. Somehow,

310   you know how to exist in a world that wasn't made for
Indians. I don't think you're going to have any trouble
surviving."

Grandfather wasn't entirely right. But I'll tell about
that another time.

IDENTIFY

Circle the details in lines 305–312 that tell you that Mary's grandfather approves of the way she handled her Ta-Na-E-Ka.

EVALUATE

Rate this story with a number from 0 to 4, with 4 meaning excellent. Give a reason for your rating.

_____

_____

_____

_____

_____

_____

_____

_____

_____

_____

_____

_____

_____

_____

_____

Ta-Na-E-Ka

SKILLS FOCUS

Literary Skills
Analyze character and conflict.

Character-and-Conflict Chart   Fill out this Character-and-Conflict Chart after you read "Ta-Na-E-Ka." Then, analyze how Mary's personality affects the story's resolution.

Main Character

↓

Personality Traits

↓

Conflict

↓

How Traits Affect Resolution of Conflict

Skills Review

Ta-Na-E-Ka

VOCABULARY AND COMPREHENSION

A. Clarifying Word Meanings: Context Clues   Fill in each blank with the correct Word Bank word. Then, underline the context clues that helped you.

1. Last time we saw Mary, she was _____ on popcorn, eating a whole bag of it.

2. She _____ in pain when she cut her heel on a rock.

3. Never one to back down, her _____ helped her survive the tough situation.

4. If the lowest quality a person can have is cowardice, then the _____ quality must be courage.

5. That girl always finds clever solutions to hard problems. She is probably the _____ person I know.

B. Reading Comprehension   Write **T** or **F** next to each statement to tell whether it is true or false.

_____ **1.** Mary is eleven years old.

_____ **2.** Mary must go through an endurance ritual.

_____ **3.** Mary is excited about the ritual.

_____ **4.** Mary obeys the rules of the ritual.

_____ **5.** Mary's grandfather thinks that Mary failed the test.

SKILLS FOCUS

Vocabulary Skills
Use context clues.

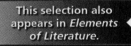

The Bracelet by Yoshiko Uchida

LITERARY FOCUS: CHARACTER AND POINT OF VIEW

The story you are about to read is told from the **first-person point of view.** The main character, Ruri, is also the narrator, who speaks as "I." You learn only what Ruri tells you. As she tells her story, Ruri reveals something about her personality. She also reveals her inner thoughts and feelings.

READING SKILLS: MAKING PREDICTIONS

Part of the fun of reading is making **predictions**—guessing what will happen next. You base your guesses on clues that the writer gives you and on what you know from your own experiences. Since predictions are guesses, some of your predictions will not prove to be correct. When this happens, simply adjust your predictions, and read on.

To keep track of your predictions, use a chart like the one below. You can copy the chart and make notes as you read. Then, after you have read the story, evaluate your predictions. Were you right most of the time?

My Prediction	My Adjusted Prediction	What Actually Happened

SKILLS FOCUS

Literary Skills
Understand character and point of view.

Reading Skills
Make predictions.

Vocabulary Skills
Clarify word meanings by recognizing word roots.

VOCABULARY DEVELOPMENT

PREVIEW SELECTION VOCABULARY

The following words are from "The Bracelet." Get to know these
words before you read the story.

evacuated (ē·vak′yoo·āt′id) *v.:* removed
from an area.

*During the war, Japanese Americans were
evacuated from the West Coast. Their removal
had tragic consequences.*

interned (in·turnd′) *v.:* imprisoned or
confined, especially during a war.

*Ruri's father was interned in a prisoner-of-war
camp.*

aliens (āl′yənz) *n.:* foreigners.

*The U.S. government treated Japanese
Americans as if they were enemy aliens.*

forsaken (fôr·sā′kən) *adj.:* abandoned;
deserted.

*The garden looked as forsaken as Ruri felt when
she had to leave home.*

CLARIFYING WORD MEANINGS: THE ROOTS OF ENGLISH

Do you ever wonder where a word comes from? Many words in
English come from Latin, the language of ancient Rome. Some words
come from Old English, the language spoken in England between
about the 400s and about 1066. Following is a chart that pairs Latin
and Old English words with vocabulary words that are listed above.

Word Origin and Meaning	Vocabulary Word
Old English: *forsacan,* "to oppose"	forsaken
Latin: *alienus,* "other"	aliens
Latin: *internus,* "inward"	interned
Latin: *vacuare,* "to make empty"	evacuated

The Bracelet

Yoshiko Uchida

> **BACKGROUND: Literature and Social Studies**
> Shortly after the United States entered World War II against Japan, more than 110,000
> people of Japanese ancestry who were living in the United States were forced to
> move to guarded camps. Most were American citizens who had been born here
> and had done nothing wrong. But the U.S. government feared that they might give
> support to Japan. When they were finally allowed to leave the camps, after the war,
> many Japanese Americans found that other people had taken over their homes and
> businesses. In 1989, the U.S. government issued a formal apology to Japanese
> Americans for the injustice that had been done to them.

IDENTIFY

Pause at line 7. Who is this story's **narrator**? Circle the clues in lines 1–6 that reveal this story has a **first-person narrator**.

_____

_____

_____

_____

_____

_____

"The Bracelet" by Yoshiko Uchida from *The Scribner Anthology for Young People*, edited by Anne Diven. Copyright © 1976 by Yoshiko Uchida. Reproduced by permission of **Atheneum Books for Young Readers**, an imprint of Simon & Schuster Children's Publishing Division.

"Mama, is it time to go?"

I hadn't planned to cry, but the tears came suddenly, and I wiped them away with the back of my hand. I didn't want my older sister to see me crying.

"It's almost time, Ruri," my mother said gently. Her face was filled with a kind of sadness I had never seen before.

I looked around at my empty room. The clothes that Mama always told me to hang up in the closet, the junk
10 piled on my dresser, the old rag doll I could never bear to part with—they were all gone. There was nothing left in my room, and there was nothing left in the rest of the house. The rugs and furniture were gone, the pictures and drapes were down, and the closets and cupboards were empty. The house was like a gift box after the nice thing inside was gone; just a lot of nothingness.

Chang Park/HRW Illustration.

It was almost time to leave our home, but we weren't moving to a nicer house or to a new town. It was April 21, 1942. The United States and Japan were at war, and every

20 Japanese person on the West Coast was being **evacuated** by the government to a concentration camp. Mama, my sister Keiko, and I were being sent from our home, and out of Berkeley, and eventually out of California.

The doorbell rang, and I ran to answer it before my sister could. I thought maybe by some miracle a messenger from the government might be standing there, tall and proper and buttoned into a uniform, come to tell us it was all a terrible mistake, that we wouldn't have to leave after all. Or maybe the messenger would have a telegram from Papa,

30 who was **interned** in a prisoner-of-war camp in Montana because he had worked for a Japanese business firm.

VOCABULARY

evacuated (ē·vak′yōō·āt′id) v.: removed from an area.

interned (in·turnd′) v.: imprisoned or confined, especially during a war.

VOCABULARY

aliens (āl′yənz) *n.*: foreigners.

INTERPRET

Re-read lines 19–38. Based on the details in these lines, describe the way Japanese Americans were treated during World War II.

_____

_____

_____

_____

_____

_____

IDENTIFY

Pause at line 51. Underline the words that tell you what Laurie gives Ruri.

CONNECT

Re-read lines 39–51. What kind of relationship do Ruri and Laurie have? How can you tell?

_____

_____

_____

_____

_____

_____

_____

The FBI had come to pick up Papa and hundreds of other Japanese community leaders on the very day that Japanese planes had bombed Pearl Harbor. The government thought they were dangerous enemy **aliens.** If it weren't so sad, it would have been funny. Papa could no more be dangerous than the mayor of our city, and he was every bit as loyal to the United States. He had lived here since 1917.

When I opened the door, it wasn't a messenger from anywhere. It was my best friend, Laurie Madison, from next door. She was holding a package wrapped up like a birthday present, but she wasn't wearing her party dress, and her face drooped like a wilted tulip.

"Hi," she said. "I came to say goodbye."

She thrust the present at me and told me it was something to take to camp. "It's a bracelet," she said before I could open the package. "Put it on so you won't have to pack it." She knew I didn't have one inch of space left in my suitcase. We had been instructed to take only what we could carry into camp, and Mama had told us that we could each take only two suitcases.

Chang Park/HRW Illustration.

"Then how are we ever going to pack the dishes and blankets and sheets they've told us to bring with us?" Keiko worried.

"I don't really know," Mama said, and she simply began packing those big impossible things into an enormous duffel bag—along with umbrellas, boots, a kettle, hot plate, and flashlight.

"Who's going to carry that huge sack?" I asked.

60 But Mama didn't worry about things like that. "Someone will help us," she said. "Don't worry." So I didn't.

Laurie wanted me to open her package and put on the bracelet before she left. It was a thin gold chain with a heart dangling on it. She helped me put it on, and I told her I'd never take it off, ever.

"Well, goodbye then," Laurie said awkwardly. "Come home soon."

"I will," I said, although I didn't know if I would ever get back to Berkeley again.

70 I watched Laurie go down the block, her long blond pigtails bouncing as she walked. I wondered who would be sitting in my desk at Lincoln Junior High now that I was gone. Laurie kept turning and waving, even walking backward for a while, until she got to the corner. I didn't want to watch anymore, and I slammed the door shut.

The next time the doorbell rang, it was Mrs. Simpson, our other neighbor. She was going to drive us to the Congregational Church, which was the Civil Control Station where all the Japanese of Berkeley were supposed

80 to report.

It was time to go. "Come on, Ruri. Get your things," my sister called to me.

It was a warm day, but I put on a sweater and my coat so I wouldn't have to carry them, and I picked up my two

INFER

What does a heart usually **symbolize**, or stand for? Why does Ruri say she will never take the bracelet off (lines 64–65)?

_____

_____

_____

_____

_____

_____

_____

_____

_____

INFER

Why does Ruri slam the door shut after Laurie leaves (lines 74–75)?

_____

_____

_____

_____

_____

_____

_____

_____

RETELL

Pause at line 87. Retell what has happened to Ruri and her family up to this point in the story.

_____

_____

_____

_____

_____

INFER

Based on lines 88–98, what inference can you make about Ruri's parents?

_____

_____

_____

VOCABULARY

forsaken (fôr·sā′kən) adj.:
abandoned; deserted.

FLUENCY

Read the boxed passage aloud. Use a voice that shows how scared Ruri feels. When you read the passage carefully, you'll notice other feelings too. For instance, Ruri's amazed to see how many Japanese people have gathered. See if your voice can capture all of Ruri's different feelings.

suitcases. Each one had a tag with my name and our family number on it. Every Japanese family had to register and get a number. We were Family Number 13453.

Mama was taking one last look around our house. She was going from room to room, as though she were trying
90 to take a mental picture of the house she had lived in for fifteen years, so she would never forget it.

I saw her take a long last look at the garden that Papa loved. The irises beside the fish pond were just beginning to bloom. If Papa had been home, he would have cut the first iris blossom and brought it inside to Mama. "This one is for you," he would have said. And Mama would have smiled and said, "Thank you, Papa San"° and put it in her favorite cut-glass vase.

But the garden looked shabby and **forsaken** now that
100 Papa was gone and Mama was too busy to take care of it. It looked the way I felt, sort of empty and lonely and abandoned.

When Mrs. Simpson took us to the Civil Control Station, I felt even worse. I was scared, and for a minute I thought I was going to lose my breakfast right in front of everybody. There must have been over a thousand Japanese people gathered at the church. Some were old and some were young. Some were talking and laughing, and some were crying. I guess everybody else was scared too. No one
110 knew exactly what was going to happen to us. We just knew we were being taken to the Tanforan Racetracks, which the army had turned into a camp for the Japanese. There were fourteen other camps like ours along the West Coast.

What scared me most were the soldiers standing at the doorway of the church hall. They were carrying guns with mounted bayonets. I wondered if they thought we would

---

° **San:** Japanese term added to names to indicate respect.

try to run away and whether they'd shoot us or come after us with their bayonets if we did.

A long line of buses waited to take us to camp. There
120 were trucks, too, for our baggage. And Mama was right; some men were there to help us load our duffel bag. When it was time to board the buses, I sat with Keiko, and Mama sat behind us. The bus went down Grove Street and passed the small Japanese food store where Mama used to order her bean-curd cakes and pickled radish. The windows were all boarded up, but there was a sign still hanging on the door that read, "We are loyal Americans."

The crazy thing about the whole evacuation was that we were all loyal Americans. Most of us were citizens
130 because we had been born here. But our parents, who had come from Japan, couldn't become citizens because there was a law that prevented any Asian from becoming a citizen. Now everybody with a Japanese face was being shipped off to concentration camps.

"It's stupid," Keiko muttered as we saw the racetrack looming up beside the highway. "If there were any Japanese spies around, they'd have gone back to Japan long ago."

"I'll say," I agreed. My sister was in high school and she ought to know, I thought.
140 When the bus turned into Tanforan, there were more armed guards at the gate, and I saw barbed wire strung around the entire grounds. I felt as though I were going into a prison, but I hadn't done anything wrong.

We streamed off the buses and poured into a huge room, where doctors looked down our throats and peeled back our eyelids to see if we had any diseases. Then we were given our housing assignments. The man in charge gave Mama a slip of paper. We were in Barrack 16, Apartment 40.

CLARIFY

Pause at line 134. Were the Japanese Americans evacuated because they were disloyal or because they were Japanese? Explain.

The Bracelet **67**

PREDICT

Pause at line 156. Do you think Ruri's "apartment" will be like her piano teacher's? Explain.

_____

_____

_____

_____

VISUALIZE

Circle the details in lines 169–173 that help you picture Apartment 40. Notice the phrases like "on each side of the door" that help you know where things are located. Draw a diagram of the apartment below.

INTERPRET

Pause at line 178. How would you describe the **character** of the narrator's mother?

_____

_____

_____

_____

150   "Mama!" I said. "We're going to live in an apartment!" The only apartment I had ever seen was the one my piano teacher lived in. It was in an enormous building in San Francisco, with an elevator and thick-carpeted hallways. I thought how wonderful it would be to have our own elevator. A house was all right, but an apartment seemed elegant and special.

   We walked down the racetrack, looking for Barrack 16. Mr. Noma, a friend of Papa's, helped us carry our bags. I was so busy looking around I slipped and almost fell on the

160   muddy track. Army barracks had been built everywhere, all around the racetrack and even in the center oval.

   Mr. Noma pointed beyond the track toward the horse stables. "I think your barrack is out there."

   He was right. We came to a long stable that had once housed the horses of Tanforan, and we climbed up the wide ramp. Each stall had a number painted on it, and when we got to 40, Mr. Noma pushed open the door.

   "Well, here it is," he said, "Apartment 40."

   The stall was narrow and empty and dark. There were

170   two small windows on each side of the door. Three folded army cots were on the dust-covered floor, and one light bulb dangled from the ceiling. That was all. This was our apartment, and it still smelled of horses.

   Mama looked at my sister and then at me. "It won't be so bad when we fix it up," she began. "I'll ask Mrs. Simpson to send me some material for curtains. I could make some cushions too, and . . . well . . ." She stopped. She couldn't think of anything more to say.

   Mr. Noma said he'd go get some mattresses for us. "I'd

180   better hurry before they're all gone." He rushed off. I think he wanted to leave so that he wouldn't have to see Mama cry. But he needn't have run off, because Mama didn't cry.

Two Japanese Folk Tales

retold by **Florence Sakade**

The Spider Weaver

Long ago there was a young farmer named Yosaku. One day
he was working in the fields and saw a snake getting ready
to eat a spider. Yosaku felt very sorry for the spider. So he
ran at the snake with his hoe and drove the snake away,
thus saving the spider's life. Then the spider disappeared
into the grass, but first it seemed to pause a minute and
bow in thanks toward Yosaku.

One morning not long after that, Yosaku was in his
house when he heard a tiny voice outside calling: "Mr.

10 Yosaku, Mr. Yosaku." He went to the door and saw a
beautiful young girl standing in the yard.

"I heard that you are looking for someone to weave
cloth for you," said the girl. "Won't you please let me live
here and weave for you?"

Yosaku was very pleased because he did need a weaving girl. So he showed the girl the weaving room and she
started to work at the loom. At the end of the day Yosaku
went to see what she'd done and was very surprised to find
that she'd woven eight long pieces of cloth, enough to make

20 eight kimonos. He'd never known anyone could weave so
much in just a single day.

IDENTIFY

What amazing event is
related in the first paragraph?
Underline it.

INFER

Pause at line 7. Think over
Yosaku's actions. What kind
of person does he seem to
be? Explain.

_____

_____

_____

_____

IDENTIFY

Re-read lines 8–21. What is
mysterious about the girl
who arrives at Yosaku's
house?

_____

_____

_____

Female orb weaver.

IDENTIFY

Pause at line 25. In many folk tales a person is helped or promised something, but on some condition. What rule does the girl say Yosaku must obey?

_____

_____

_____

_____

_____

IDENTIFY

Re-read lines 26–31. Underline the text that directly describes Yosaku's **character.**

WORD STUDY

Pause at line 40. Like many folk tales, this one includes a *metamorphosis* (met′ə·môr′fə·sis), a marvelous change from one form to another. What has been transformed in this tale?

_____

_____

IDENTIFY

Re-read lines 32–40. Why did the spider take a human form? Underline the passage that tells you why.

"How ever did you weave so much?" he asked the girl.

But instead of answering him, she said a very strange thing: "You mustn't ask me that. And you must never come into the weaving room while I am at work."

But Yosaku was very curious. So one day he slipped very quietly up to the weaving room and peeped in the window. What he saw really surprised him! Because it was not the girl who was seated at the loom, but a large spider, weaving very fast with its eight legs, and for thread it was using its own spider web, which came out of its mouth.

Yosaku looked very closely and saw that it was the same spider which he'd saved from the snake. Then Yosaku understood. The spider had been so thankful that it had wanted to do something to help Yosaku. So it had turned itself into a beautiful young girl and come to weave cloth for him. Just by eating the cotton in the weaving room it could spin it into thread inside its own body, and then with its eight legs it could weave the thread into cloth very, very fast.

Yosaku was very grateful for the spider's help. He saw that the cotton was almost used up. So next morning he set out for the nearest village, on the other side of the mountains, to buy some more cotton. He bought a big bundle of cotton and started home, carrying it on his back.

Along the way a very terrible thing happened. Yosaku sat down to rest, and the same snake that he'd driven away from the spider came up and slipped inside the bundle of cotton. But Yosaku didn't know anything about this. So he
50 carried the cotton home and gave it to the weaving girl.

She was very glad to get the cotton, because she'd now used up all the cotton that was left. So she took it and went to the weaving room.

As soon as the girl was inside the weaving room, she turned back into a spider and began eating the cotton very, very fast, just as though it were something very delicious, so she could spin it into thread inside her body. The spider ate and ate and ate, and then suddenly, when it had eaten down to the bottom of the bundle—the snake jumped out
60 of the cotton. It opened its mouth wide to swallow the spider. The spider was very frightened and jumped out of the window. The snake went wriggling very fast after it. And the spider had eaten so much cotton that it couldn't run very fast. So the snake gradually caught up with the spider. Again the snake opened its mouth wide to gulp the spider down. But just then a wonderful thing happened.

Old Man Sun, up in the sky, had been watching what was happening. He knew how kind the spider had been to Yosaku and he felt very sorry for the poor little spider. So
70 he reached down with a sunbeam and caught hold of the end of the web that was sticking out of the spider's mouth, and he lifted the spider high up into the sky, where the snake couldn't reach it at all.

The spider was very grateful to Old Man Sun for saving him from the snake. So it used all the cotton that was inside its body to weave beautiful fleecy clouds up in the sky. That's the reason, they say, why clouds are soft

IDENTIFY

Pause at line 50. What new problem has come up?

_____

_____

_____

_____

_____

FLUENCY

Read aloud the boxed passage. As you read, vary your volume, rate of speech, and pitch to help your listeners feel the scene's excitement. Then, re-read the passage to improve the smoothness of your delivery.

IDENTIFY

Pause at line 73. Why did Old Man Sun save the spider?

_____

_____

_____

_____

_____

_____

_____

_____

and white like cotton, and also that is the reason why both a spider and a cloud are called by the same name 80 in Japan—*kumo*.

The Grateful Statues

Once upon a time an old man and an old woman were living in a country village in Japan. They were very poor and spent every day weaving big hats out of straw. Whenever they finished a number of hats, the old man would take them to the nearest town to sell them.

One day the old man said to the old woman: "New Year's is the day after tomorrow. How I wish we had some rice cakes to eat on New Year's Day! Even one or two little cakes would be enough. Without some rice cakes we can't 10 even celebrate New Year's."

CONNECT

What natural feature of our world is explained in "The Spider Weaver"?

_____

_____

_____

_____

_____

_____

_____

_____

_____

READ FOR DETAILS

Underline words in lines 1–10 that describe the old man. Circle passages in which he states what he wants. Box passages that tell what he does.

_____

_____

_____

_____

_____

_____

_____

_____

"Well, then," said the old woman, "after you've sold these hats, why don't you buy some rice cakes and bring them back with you?"

So early the next morning the old man took the five new hats that they had made, and went to town to sell them. But after he got to town, he was unable to sell a single hat. And to make things still worse, it began to snow very hard.

20 The old man was very sad as he began trudging wearily back toward his village. He was going along a lonesome mountain trail when he suddenly came upon a row of six stone statues of Jizo, the protector of children, all covered with snow.

"My, my! Now isn't this a pity," the old man said. "These are only stone statues of Jizo, but even so just think how cold they must be standing here in the snow."

"I know what I'll do!" the old man suddenly said to himself. "This will be just the thing."

So he unfastened the five new hats from his back and
30 began tying them, one by one, on the heads of the Jizo statues.

When he came to the last statue, he suddenly realized that all the hats were gone. "Oh, my!" he said, "I don't have enough hats." But then he remembered his own hat. So he took it off his head and tied it on the head of the last Jizo. Then he went on his way home.

When he reached his house, the old woman was waiting for him by the fire. She took one look at him and cried: "You must be frozen half to death. Quick! Come to the fire.
40 What did you do with your hat?"

The old man shook the snow out of his hair and came to the fire. He told the old woman how he had given all the

READ FOR DETAILS

Re-read lines 24–36. Circle passages that tell what the old man says. Box the passages that tell what the old man does for the statues. What do the old man's actions reveal about his **character**?

_____

_____

_____

_____

_____

_____

_____

_____

_____

PREDICT

Pause at line 40. How do you think the old woman will react to what the old man has done?

_____

_____

_____

_____

_____

_____

_____

_____

_____

_____

Pause at line 53. What "very wonderful thing" might happen?

_____

_____

_____

_____

_____

Pause at line 69. How are the old man and the old woman rewarded for their actions?

_____

_____

_____

_____

_____

new hats, and even his own hat, to the six stone Jizo. He told her he was sorry that he hadn't been able to bring any rice cakes.

"My! That was a very kind thing you did for the Jizo," said the old woman. She was very proud of the old man, and went on: "It's better to do a kind thing like that than to have all the rice cakes in the world. We'll get along without

50 any rice cakes for New Year's."

By this time it was late at night, so the old man and woman went to bed. And just before dawn, while they were still asleep, a very wonderful thing happened. Suddenly there was the sound of voices in the distance, singing:

"A kind old man walking in the snow
Gave all his hats to the stone Jizo.
So we bring him gifts with a yo-heave-ho!"

The voices came nearer and nearer, and then you could hear the sound of footsteps on the snow.

60 The sounds came right up to the house where the old man and woman were sleeping. And then all at once there was a great noise, as though something had been put down just in front of the house.

The old couple jumped out of bed and ran to the front door. When they opened it, what do you suppose they found? Well, right there at the door someone had spread a straw mat, and arranged very neatly on the mat was one of the biggest and most beautiful and freshest rice cakes the old people had ever seen.

70 "Whoever could have brought us such a wonderful gift?" they said, and looked about wonderingly.

They saw some tracks in the snow leading away from their house. The snow was all tinted with the colors of

© Royalty-Free/CORBIS.

What would you say is the "lesson" of this folk tale? Compare this lesson with the lesson in "The Spider Weaver."

_____

_____

_____

_____

_____

_____

_____

_____

_____

_____

_____

_____

_____

_____

_____

_____

_____

_____

_____

_____

_____

_____

dawn, and there in the distance, walking over the snow, were the six stone Jizo, still wearing the hats which the old man had given them.

The old man said: "It was the stone Jizo who brought this wonderful rice cake to us."

The old woman said: "You did them a kind favor when you gave them your hats, so they brought this rice cake to show their gratitude."

The old couple had a very wonderful New Year's Day celebration after all, because now they had this wonderful rice cake to eat.

80

Two Japanese Folk Tales

Character Diagram   Use the **Venn diagram** below to compare and contrast the characters in the two folk tales. Record details that show how the characters are the same and how they are different.

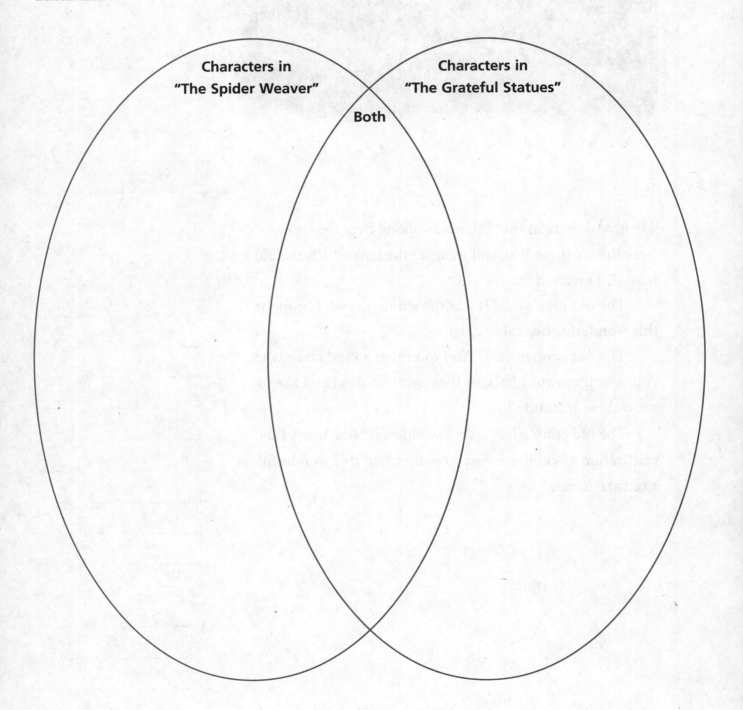

Characters in
"The Spider Weaver"

Characters in
"The Grateful Statues"

Both

Skills Review

Two Japanese Folk Tales

COMPREHENSION

Reading Comprehension   Answer each question below.

1. What kind deed does Yosaku in "The Spider Weaver" perform?

_____

_____

2. What does the spider transform into?

_____

_____

3. What does Old Man Sun do at the end of the story?

_____

_____

4. What does the old man in "The Grateful Statues" plan to do in town?

_____

_____

5. What happens to the old man's hats?

_____

_____

6. How is the couple rewarded at the story's end?

_____

_____

Theme: The Heart of the Matter

Academic Vocabulary for Collection 3

These are the terms you should know
as you read and analyze the selections in this collection.

Subject What the selection is about. You can usually describe the
subject in a word or two—friendship, growing up, happiness,
and so on.

Theme A truth about life revealed in a story or poem. Sometimes the
theme is stated directly, but more often it is implied. A theme is
not the same as a subject; instead, it *comments* on a subject.
Example: True friends stand by you even in times of trouble.

Universal Theme A theme that shows up in stories and poems from
many cultures and different times in history. Here's an example:
Kindness toward others is usually rewarded.

The All-American Slurp by Lensey Namioka

LITERARY FOCUS: SUBJECT VERSUS THEME

When you describe what a story is about, you are identifying its **subject.** When you explain what a story means, you are describing its **theme.** Although a word or two is usually enough to describe a subject, you'll need a statement to describe a theme. Here are some examples:

Subject	Theme
friendship	Friendships have ups and downs.
dogs	Dogs are more than just pets.
hiking	You can find inner peace by hiking.

When you read a story, see if you can connect its theme to your own life or experience. Also keep in mind that a story's theme can be stated in different ways.

READING SKILLS: SUMMARIZING

When you **summarize** a story, you retell its main events in your own words. Summarizing helps you remember what happens in the story. As you read "The All-American Slurp," sum up what happens in each of the story's six parts. You may want to use a chart like this one:

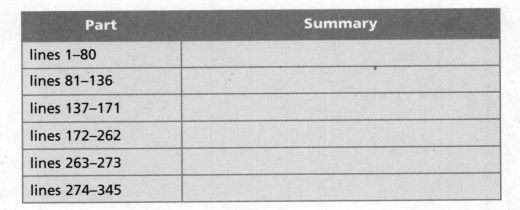

Part	Summary
lines 1–80	
lines 81–136	
lines 137–171	
lines 172–262	
lines 263–273	
lines 274–345	

SKILLS FOCUS

Literary Skills
Recognize the difference between subject and theme.

Reading Skills
Summarize plot.

Vocabulary Skills
Clarify word meanings by using context clues.

VOCABULARY DEVELOPMENT

PREVIEW SELECTION VOCABULARY

Get to know these words before you read the story.

lavishly (lav′ish·lē) *adv.:* generously; plentifully.

The table was heaped lavishly with food.

mortified (môrt′ə·fīd′) *v.* used as *adj.:* ashamed; deeply embarrassed.

Mortified by her family's behavior, she fled to the ladies' room.

spectacle (spek′tə·kəl) *n.:* remarkable sight.

The narrator fears that her noisy brother is making a spectacle of himself.

etiquette (et′i·kit) *n.:* acceptable manners and behavior.

Slurping is not proper etiquette in a fancy restaurant.

CLARIFYING WORD MEANINGS: CONTEXT CLUES

Just as detectives look for clues to solve a mystery, you can look for clues to figure out unfamiliar words. You can often find clues to the meaning of a word by looking at its **context**—the nearby words and sentences. Read each of the following sentences. In the examples below, the words in italics provide context clues for the boldface words.

- They spent money **lavishly,** *buying anything they wanted at any price.*
- **Mortified** by his mistake, Hank *hung his head in shame.*
- The *fantastic* fireworks *display* was a **spectacle** that we'll never forget.
- Some people say that *licking your fingers is not* good **etiquette.**

The All-American Slurp

Lensey Namioka

IDENTIFY

Re-read lines 1–4. Underline words and phrases that hint at the story's **subject**—what the story is about.

WORD STUDY

The words *disgraced* (line 2) and *disinfect* (line 6) both contain the prefix *dis–*, which means "not." Review the passages containing those words. Then, explain what the words mean. Note that *grace* means "bring honor or dignity."

_____

_____

_____

_____

INFER

Pause at line 13. How old do you think the narrator might be? Explain.

_____

_____

_____

_____

_____

The first time our family was invited out to dinner in America, we disgraced ourselves while eating celery. We had immigrated to this country from China, and during our early days here we had a hard time with American table manners.

In China we never ate celery raw, or any other kind of vegetable raw. We always had to disinfect the vegetables in boiling water first. When we were presented with our first relish tray, the raw celery caught us unprepared.

We had been invited to dinner by our neighbors, the
10 Gleasons. After arriving at the house, we shook hands with our hosts and packed ourselves into a sofa. As our family of four sat stiffly in a row, my younger brother and I stole glances at our parents for a clue as to what to do next.

Nancy Davis/HRW Illustration.

Copyright © by Holt Rinehart and Winston. All rights reserved

Mrs. Gleason offered the relish tray to Mother. The tray looked pretty, with its tiny red radishes, curly sticks of carrots, and long, slender stalks of pale-green celery. "Do try some of the celery, Mrs. Lin," she said. "It's from a local farmer, and it's sweet."

20 Mother picked up one of the green stalks, and Father followed suit. Then I picked up a stalk, and my brother did too. So there we sat, each with a stalk of celery in our right hand.

Mrs. Gleason kept smiling. "Would you like to try some of the dip, Mrs. Lin? It's my own recipe: sour cream and onion flakes, with a dash of Tabasco sauce."

Most Chinese don't care for dairy products, and in those days I wasn't even ready to drink fresh milk. Sour cream sounded perfectly revolting. Our family shook our heads in unison.

30 Mrs. Gleason went off with the relish tray to the other guests, and we carefully watched to see what they did. Everyone seemed to eat the raw vegetables quite happily.

Mother took a bite of her celery. *Crunch.* "It's not bad!" she whispered.

Father took a bite of his celery. *Crunch.* "Yes, it *is* good," he said, looking surprised.

I took a bite, and then my brother. *Crunch, crunch.* It was more than good; it was delicious. Raw celery has a slight sparkle, a zingy taste that you don't get in cooked celery.

40 When Mrs. Gleason came around with the relish tray, we each took another stalk of celery, except my brother. He took two.

There was only one problem: Long strings ran through the length of the stalk, and they got caught in my teeth. When I help my mother in the kitchen, I always pull the strings out before slicing celery.

PREDICT

Pause at line 29. The Lins are not used to American food. Do you think they will enjoy eating the celery? Why or why not?

_____

_____

_____

_____

_____

_____

_____

_____

_____

_____

_____

_____

_____

_____

_____

IDENTIFY

Onomatopoeia is the use of a word like *crunch* (lines 33, 35, 37), where the sound of the word imitates or suggests its meaning. Read on, and circle another example of onomatopoeia in lines 47–50.

The All-American Slurp   87

INFER

Pause at line 56. How do you think the Lins feel at this point in the evening? Explain.

_____

_____

_____

_____

_____

VOCABULARY

lavishly (lav′ish·lē) *adv.:* generously; plentifully.

mortified (môrt′ə·fīd′) *v.* used as *adj.:* ashamed; deeply embarrassed.

spectacle (spek′tə·kəl) *n.:* strange or remarkable sight.

INFER

Based on what she says to the narrator about the party (lines 73–77), what inference can you make about Meg's character?

_____

_____

_____

_____

_____

I pulled the strings out of my stalk. *Z-z-zip, z-z-zip.* My brother followed suit. *Z-z-zip, z-z-zip, z-z-zip.* To my left, my parents were taking care of their own stalks. *Z-z-zip,* 50 *z-z-zip, z-z-zip.*

Suddenly I realized that there was dead silence except for our zipping. Looking up, I saw that the eyes of everyone in the room were on our family. Mr. and Mrs. Gleason, their daughter Meg, who was my friend, and their neighbors the Badels—they were all staring at us as we busily pulled the strings of our celery.

That wasn't the end of it. Mrs. Gleason announced that dinner was served and invited us to the dining table. It was **lavishly** covered with platters of food, but we couldn't 60 see any chairs around the table. So we helpfully carried over some dining chairs and sat down. All the other guests just stood there.

Mrs. Gleason bent down and whispered to us, "This is a buffet dinner. You help yourselves to some food and eat it in the living room."

Our family beat a retreat back to the sofa as if chased by enemy soldiers. For the rest of the evening, too **mortified** to go back to the dining table, I nursed a bit of potato salad on my plate.

70 Next day, Meg and I got on the school bus together. I wasn't sure how she would feel about me after the **spectacle** our family made at the party. But she was just the same as usual, and the only reference she made to the party was, "Hope you and your folks got enough to eat last night. You certainly didn't take very much. Mom never tries to figure out how much food to prepare. She just puts everything on the table and hopes for the best."

I began to relax. The Gleasons' dinner party wasn't so different from a Chinese meal after all. My mother also puts
80   everything on the table and hopes for the best.

Meg was the first friend I had made after we came to America. I eventually got acquainted with a few other kids in school, but Meg was still the only real friend I had.

My brother didn't have any problems making friends. He spent all his time with some boys who were teaching him baseball, and in no time he could speak English much faster than I could—not better, but faster.

I worried more about making mistakes, and I spoke carefully, making sure I could say everything right before
90   opening my mouth. At least I had a better accent than my parents, who never really got rid of their Chinese accent, even years later. My parents had both studied English in school before coming to America, but what they had studied was mostly written English, not spoken.

Father's approach to English was a scientific one. Since Chinese verbs have no tense, he was fascinated by the way English verbs changed form according to whether they were in the present, past, perfect, pluperfect, future, or future perfect tense. He was always making diagrams of verbs and
100   their inflections, and he looked for opportunities to show off his mastery of the pluperfect and future perfect tenses, his two favorites. "I shall have finished my project by Monday," he would say smugly.

Mother's approach was to memorize lists of polite phrases that would cover all possible social situations. She was constantly muttering things like "I'm fine, thank you. And you?" Once she accidentally stepped on someone's

IDENTIFY

In lines 78–80, circle the similarity, or likeness, that the narrator sees between her family and the Gleason family.

COMPARE & CONTRAST

Describe the different ways the narrator's mother and father go about learning English (lines 95–111).

INFER

Why do you think the narrator wants to dress like the other girls at school (lines 112–131)?

_____

_____

_____

_____

_____

_____

_____

INFER

Pause at line 136. The narrator and Meg swap clothes. How do you think Meg likes the narrator's Chinese dresses? Explain.

_____

_____

_____

_____

_____

_____

IDENTIFY

Underline three details in lines 137–149 that help you infer that the Lins don't have much money.

foot and hurriedly blurted, "Oh, that's quite all right!" Embarrassed by her slip, she resolved to do better next time. So when someone stepped on *her* foot, she cried, "You're welcome!"

In our own different ways, we made progress in learning English. But I had another worry, and that was my appearance. My brother didn't have to worry, since Mother bought him bluejeans for school, and he dressed like all the other boys. But she insisted that girls had to wear skirts. By the time she saw that Meg and the other girls were wearing jeans, it was too late. My school clothes were bought already, and we didn't have money left to buy new outfits for me. We had too many other things to buy first, like furniture, pots, and pans.

The first time I visited Meg's house, she took me upstairs to her room, and I wound up trying on her clothes. We were pretty much the same size since Meg was shorter and thinner than average. Maybe that's how we became friends in the first place. Wearing Meg's jeans and T-shirt, I looked at myself in the mirror. I could almost pass for an American— from the back, anyway. At least the kids in school wouldn't stop and stare at me in the hallways, which was what they did when they saw me in my white blouse and navy-blue skirt that went a couple of inches below the knees.

When Meg came to my house, I invited her to try on my Chinese dresses, the ones with a high collar and slits up the sides. Meg's eyes were bright as she looked at herself in the mirror. She struck several sultry poses, and we nearly fell over laughing.

The dinner party at the Gleasons' didn't stop my growing friendship with Meg. Things were getting better for me in other ways too. Mother finally bought me some jeans at

140 the end of the month, when Father got his paycheck. She wasn't in any hurry about buying them at first, until I worked on her. This is what I did. Since we didn't have a car in those days, I often ran down to the neighborhood store to pick up things for her. The groceries cost less at a big supermarket, but the closest one was many blocks away. One day, when she ran out of flour, I offered to borrow a bike from our neighbor's son and buy a ten-pound bag of flour at the big supermarket. I mounted the boy's bike and waved to Mother. "I'll be back in five minutes!"

150 Before I started pedaling, I heard her voice behind me. "You can't go out in public like that! People can see all the way up to your thighs!"

"I'm sorry," I said innocently. "I thought you were in a hurry to get the flour." For dinner we were going to have pot stickers (fried Chinese dumplings), and we needed a lot of flour.

"Couldn't you borrow a girl's bicycle?" complained Mother. "That way your skirt won't be pushed up."

"There aren't too many of those around," I said.
160 "Almost all the girls wear jeans while riding a bike, so they don't see any point buying a girl's bike."

We didn't eat pot stickers that evening, and Mother was thoughtful. Next day we took the bus downtown and she bought me a pair of jeans. In the same week, my brother made the baseball team of his junior high school, Father started taking driving lessons, and Mother discovered rummage sales. We soon got all the furniture we needed, plus a dartboard and a 1,000-piece jigsaw puzzle. (Fourteen hours later, we discovered that it was a 999-piece jigsaw puzzle.)
170 There was hope that the Lins might become a normal American family after all.

SUMMARIZE

Explain how the narrator gets her mother to buy jeans for her (lines 137–164).

_____

_____

_____

_____

_____

_____

_____

_____

_____

_____

_____

_____

_____

_____

_____

_____

_____

IDENTIFY

Re-read lines 162–171. Underline details that describe what the narrator views as "American."

PREDICT

Pause at line 177. What do you think will happen to the Lin family at this fancy restaurant?

_____

_____

_____

_____

_____

_____

_____

_____

WORD STUDY

In line 191, the narrator describes the restaurant as *murky*, which means "dark" or "gloomy." Is that a word you would choose to describe a candlelit restaurant? Explain.

_____

_____

_____

_____

_____

_____

_____

Then came our dinner at the Lakeview restaurant. The Lakeview was an expensive restaurant, one of those places where a headwaiter dressed in tails conducted you to your seat, and the only light came from candles and flaming desserts. In one corner of the room a lady harpist played tinkling melodies.

Father wanted to celebrate because he had just been promoted. He worked for an electronics company, and
180 after his English started improving, his superiors decided to appoint him to a position more suited to his training. The promotion not only brought a higher salary but was also a tremendous boost to his pride.

Up to then we had eaten only in Chinese restaurants. Although my brother and I were becoming fond of hamburgers, my parents didn't care much for Western food, other than chow mein.

But this was a special occasion, and Father asked his co-workers to recommend a really elegant restaurant.
190 So there we were at the Lakeview, stumbling after the headwaiter in the murky dining room.

At our table we were handed our menus, and they were so big that to read mine, I almost had to stand up again. But why bother? It was mostly in French, anyway.

Father, being an engineer, was always systematic. He took out a pocket French dictionary. "They told me that most of the items would be in French, so I came prepared." He even had a pocket flashlight the size of a marking pen. While Mother held the flashlight over the menu, he looked
200 up the items that were in French.

"*Pâté en croûte,*" he muttered. "Let's see . . . *pâté* is paste . . . *croûte* is crust . . . hmmm . . . a paste in crust."

Nancy Davis/HRW Illustration.

The waiter stood looking patient. I squirmed and died at least fifty times.

At long last Father gave up. "Why don't we just order four complete dinners at random?" he suggested.

"Isn't that risky?" asked Mother. "The French eat some rather peculiar things, I've heard."

"A Chinese can eat anything a Frenchman can eat,"
210   Father declared.

The soup arrived in a plate. How do you get soup up from a plate? I glanced at the other diners, but the ones at the nearby tables were not on their soup course, while the more distant ones were invisible in the darkness.

Fortunately my parents had studied books on Western **etiquette** before they came to America. "Tilt your plate," whispered my mother. "It's easier to spoon the soup up that way."

Notes _____

_____

_____

_____

_____

_____

_____

_____

_____

_____

INTERPRET

What does the narrator mean when she says she "squirmed and died at least fifty times" (lines 203–204)? Circle two of her father's actions that cause her to squirm.

_____

_____

_____

_____

_____

_____

_____

_____

VOCABULARY

etiquette (et'i·kit) *n.:* acceptable manners and behavior.

IDENTIFY

Circle the word in line 222 that is an example of **onomatopoeia**.

INFER

Pause at line 241. Why does the narrator leave the table so abruptly?

_____
_____
_____
_____
_____
_____
_____
_____
_____
_____
_____
_____
_____
_____
_____

VISUALIZE

Re-read lines 225–247. Circle the details that help you picture—and hear—what is happening.

220   She was right. Tilting the plate did the trick. But the etiquette book didn't say anything about what you did after the soup reached your lips. As any respectable Chinese knows, the correct way to eat your soup is to slurp. This helps to cool the liquid and prevent you from burning your lips. It also shows your appreciation.

We showed our appreciation. *Shloop*, went my father. *Shloop*, went my mother. *Shloop, shloop*, went my brother, who was the hungriest.

The lady harpist stopped playing to take a rest. And in the silence, our family's consumption of soup suddenly
230   seemed unnaturally loud. You know how it sounds on a rocky beach when the tide goes out and the water drains from all those little pools? They go *shloop, shloop, shloop*. That was the Lin family eating soup.

At the next table a waiter was pouring wine. When a large *shloop* reached him, he froze. The bottle continued to pour, and red wine flooded the table top and into the lap of a customer. Even the customer didn't notice anything at first, being also hypnotized by the *shloop, shloop, shloop*.

It was too much. "I need to go to the toilet," I mum-
240   bled, jumping to my feet. A waiter, sensing my urgency, quickly directed me to the ladies' room.

I splashed cold water on my burning face, and as I dried myself with a paper towel, I stared into the mirror. In this perfumed ladies' room, with its pink-and-silver wallpaper and marbled sinks, I looked completely out of place. What was I doing here? What was our family doing in the Lakeview restaurant? In America?

The door to the ladies' room opened. A woman came in and glanced curiously at me. I retreated into one of the
250   toilet cubicles and latched the door.

Time passed—maybe half an hour, maybe an hour. Then I heard the door open again, and my mother's voice. "Are you in there? You're not sick, are you?"

There was real concern in her voice. A girl can't leave her family just because they slurp their soup. Besides, the toilet cubicle had a few drawbacks as a permanent residence. "I'm all right," I said, undoing the latch.

Mother didn't tell me how the rest of the dinner went, and I didn't want to know. In the weeks following, I managed to push the whole thing into the back of my mind, where it jumped out at me only a few times a day. Even now, I turn hot all over when I think of the Lakeview restaurant.

But by the time we had been in this country for three months, our family was definitely making progress toward becoming Americanized. I remember my parents' first PTA meeting. Father wore a neat suit and tie, and Mother put on her first pair of high heels. She stumbled only once. They met my homeroom teacher and beamed as she told them that I would make honor roll soon at the rate I was going. Of course Chinese etiquette forced Father to say that I was a very stupid girl and Mother to protest that the teacher was showing favoritism toward me. But I could tell they were both very proud.

The day came when my parents announced that they wanted to give a dinner party. We had invited Chinese friends to eat with us before, but this dinner was going to be different. In addition to a Chinese American family, we were going to invite the Gleasons.

"Gee, I can hardly wait to have dinner at your house," Meg said to me. "I just *love* Chinese food."

SUMMARIZE

Pause at line 262. Tell what happens at the restaurant that, years later, still makes the narrator feel embarrassed.

_____
_____
_____
_____
_____
_____
_____
_____
_____

INFER

Circle Father's and Mother's comments at the PTA meeting (lines 270–273). Why did they make such comments?

_____
_____
_____
_____
_____
_____
_____
_____
_____

PREDICT

Pause at line 283. What do you think will happen at this dinner party?

_____

_____

_____

_____

_____

_____

_____

_____

_____

_____

IDENTIFY

In lines 301–311, circle the mistakes that Meg and her mother make when they eat Chinese food.

FLUENCY

Read the boxed passage several times aloud. Remember to pause slightly whenever you see a colon (:) or a comma. Come to a longer stop when you see a period. When you get to the third paragraph in this passage, use your voice to show the narrator's horrified surprise.

That was a relief. Mother was a good cook, but I wasn't sure if people who ate sour cream would also eat chicken gizzards stewed in soy sauce.

Mother decided not to take a chance with chicken gizzards. Since we had Western guests, she set the table with large dinner plates, which we never used in Chinese meals. In fact we didn't use individual plates at all, but picked up food from the platters in the middle of the table and brought it directly to our rice bowls. Following the
290 practice of Chinese American restaurants, Mother also placed large serving spoons on the platters.

The dinner started well. Mrs. Gleason exclaimed at the beautifully arranged dishes of food: the colorful candied fruit in the sweet-and-sour pork dish, the noodle-thin shreds of chicken meat stir-fried with tiny peas, and the glistening pink prawns° in a ginger sauce.

At first I was too busy enjoying my food to notice how the guests were doing. But soon I remembered my duties. Sometimes guests were too polite to help themselves and
300 you had to serve them with more food.

I glanced at Meg to see if she needed more food, and my eyes nearly popped out at the sight of her plate. It was piled with food: The sweet-and-sour meat pushed right against the chicken shreds, and the chicken sauce ran into the prawns. She had been taking food from a second dish before she finished eating her helping from the first!

Horrified, I turned to look at Mrs. Gleason. She was dumping rice out of her bowl and putting it on her dinner plate. Then she ladled prawns and gravy on top of the rice
310 and mixed everything together, the way you mix sand, gravel, and cement to make concrete.

° **prawns** _n._: large shrimps.

Nancy Davis/HRW Illustration.

I couldn't bear to look any longer, and I turned to Mr. Gleason. He was chasing a pea around his plate. Several times he got it to the edge, but when he tried to pick it up with his chopsticks, it rolled back toward the center of the plate again. Finally he put down his chopsticks and picked up the pea with his fingers. He really did! A grown man!

All of us, our family and the Chinese guests, stopped eating to watch the activities of the Gleasons. I wanted to
320   giggle. Then I caught my mother's eyes on me. She frowned and shook her head slightly, and I understood the message: The Gleasons were not used to Chinese ways, and they were just coping the best they could. For some reason I thought of celery strings.

When the main courses were finished, Mother brought out a platter of fruit. "I hope you weren't expecting a sweet dessert," she said. "Since the Chinese don't eat dessert, I didn't think to prepare any."

"Oh, I couldn't possibly eat dessert!" cried Mrs. Gleason.
330   "I'm simply stuffed!"

INFER

Notice that Mr. Gleason is trying to eat with chopsticks (lines 312–317). Why do you think he didn't ask the Lins for a fork?

_____

_____

_____

_____

_____

_____

COMPARE & CONTRAST

Pause at line 324. How is this incident like the celery-string incident on pages 87–88?

_____

_____

_____

_____

_____

_____

_____

_____

INTERPRET

What has the narrator come to realize about life at the story's end? What **theme** is revealed by her experience?

_____
_____
_____
_____
_____
_____
_____
_____
_____
_____
_____
_____
_____
_____
_____
_____
_____
_____
_____
_____
_____
_____
_____
_____
_____
_____
_____

Meg had different ideas. When the table was cleared, she announced that she and I were going for a walk. "I don't know about you, but I feel like dessert," she told me, when we were outside. "Come on, there's a Dairy Queen down the street. I could use a big chocolate milkshake!"

Although I didn't really want anything more to eat, I insisted on paying for the milkshakes. After all, I was still hostess.

340   Meg got her large chocolate milkshake and I had a small one. Even so, she was finishing hers while I was only half done. Toward the end she pulled hard on her straws and went _shloop, shloop._

"Do you always slurp when you eat a milkshake?" I asked, before I could stop myself.

Meg grinned. "Sure. All Americans slurp."

The All-American Slurp

Theme Pyramid   Complete this pyramid. In the top section, write a word from the story that you think is a key word. (More than one choice is possible.) In the next section, tell how this word relates to the characters and their actions. In the bottom section of the pyramid, identify the theme—the idea about life—that is revealed in the story.

SKILLS FOCUS

Literary Skills
Analyze theme.

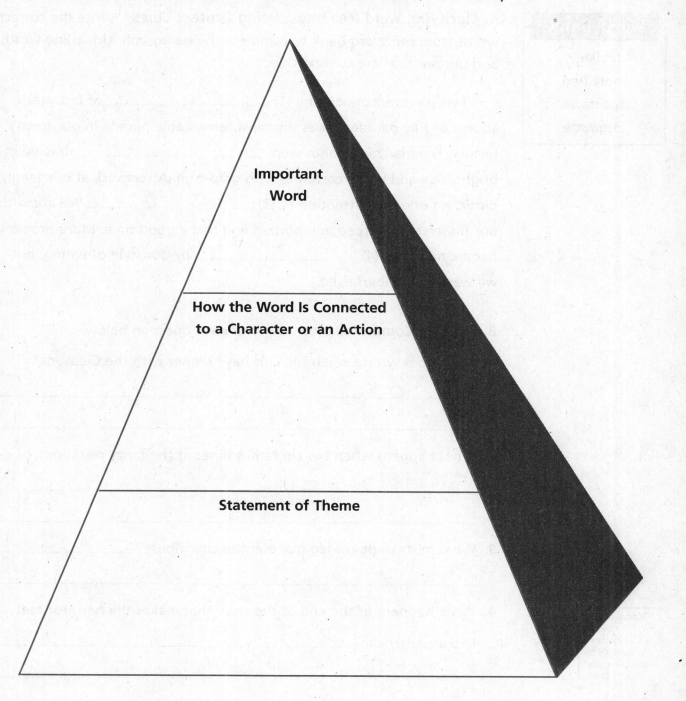

Important Word

How the Word Is Connected to a Character or an Action

Statement of Theme

Skills Review

The All-American Slurp

VOCABULARY AND COMPREHENSION

Word Bank

lavishly

mortified

spectacle

etiquette

A. Clarifying Word Meanings: Using Context Clues   Write the correct words from the Word Bank to complete the paragraph. Underline words and phrases that are context clues.

Everyone remembers the (1) _____ of last year's Fourth of July parade. It was the most remarkable parade in our town's history. The marching bands were (2) _____ dressed in bright blue and white costumes with gold trim. Afterward, at our family picnic, no one paid attention to (3) _____. We ate with our fingers and slurped and burped and had a good time. More proper people might be (4) _____ by our style of eating, but we were not embarrassed.

B. Reading Comprehension   Answer each question below.

1. What goes wrong when the Lins have dinner with the Gleasons?

_____

_____

2. What happens when the Lin family dines at the fancy restaurant?

_____

_____

3. What mistake does Meg make at the Lins' house? _____

_____

4. What happens at the end of the story that makes the narrator feel like an American? _____

_____

SKILLS FOCUS

Vocabulary Skills
Clarify word meanings by using context clues.

This selection also appears in *Elements of Literature.*

The Emperor's New Clothes

by Hans Christian Andersen

LITERARY FOCUS: THEME—GETTING THE MESSAGE

You know that most stories contain a **plot,** a series of related events. Did you also know that most stories contain messages? These messages about life, called **themes,** help us connect what we read with our observations about real life. Most times, writers don't come out and directly state a story's theme. Instead, you think about the characters and their experiences to come up with a statement of theme. As you read "The Emperor's New Clothes," look for its theme, or message about life.

READING SKILLS: MAKING GENERALIZATIONS

You've probably made or heard **generalizations** such as "Most kids like sports" or "Most TV shows are a waste of time." A generalization is a broad statement that is based on examples or evidence. To come up with the theme of a story, it's useful to use the skill of generalizing. Here's how to do it:

- Think about the main events and conflicts in the story.
- Decide what the characters have discovered by the end of the story.
- State the idea in a general way so that it applies not just to the story but to real life.

SKILLS FOCUS

Literary Skills
Recognize the difference between theme and plot.

Reading Skills
Make generalizations.

The Emperor's New Clothes

Hans Christian Andersen

INFER

Pause at line 7. Underline the emperor's biggest interest in life. What does that major interest reveal about the type of person the emperor is?

_____

_____

_____

_____

_____

_____

WORD STUDY

A swindler (line 9) is a person who cheats or tricks others. What **context clue** in lines 9–11 helps you understand that swindlers are untrustworthy?

_____

_____

_____

_____

_____

_____

_____

Many years ago there lived an Emperor who was so fond of new clothes that he spent all his money on them. He did not care for his soldiers, or for the theater, or for driving in the woods, except to show off his new clothes. He had an outfit for every hour of the day, and just as they say of a king, "He is in the council chamber," so they always said of him, "The Emperor is in his dressing room."

The great city where he lived was very lively, and every day many strangers came there. One day two swindlers
10 came. They claimed that they were weavers and said they could weave the finest cloth imaginable. Their colors and patterns, they said, were not only exceptionally beautiful, but the clothes made of this material possessed the wonderful quality of being invisible to any man who was unfit for his office, or who was hopelessly stupid.

"Those must be wonderful clothes," thought the Emperor. "If I wore them, I should be able to find out which men in my empire were unfit for their posts, and I could tell the clever from the stupid. Yes, I must have this
20 cloth woven for me without delay." So he gave a lot of money to the two swindlers in advance, so that they could set to work at once.

They set up two looms[1] and pretended to be very hard at work, but they had nothing on the looms. They asked for the finest silk and the most precious gold, all of which they

---

1. **looms** _n.:_ machines used for weaving thread into cloth.

Suzanne Duranceau/HRW Illustration.

put into their own bags, and worked at the empty looms till late into the night.

"I should very much like to know how they are getting on with the cloth," thought the Emperor. But he felt rather

30 uneasy when he remembered that whoever was not fit for his office could not see it. He believed, of course, that he had nothing to fear for himself, yet he thought he would send somebody else first to see how things were progressing.

Everybody in the town knew what a wonderful property the cloth possessed, and all were anxious to see how bad or stupid their neighbors were.

"I will send my honest old minister to the weavers," thought the Emperor. "He can judge best how the cloth looks, for he is intelligent, and nobody is better fitted for

40 his office than he."

So the good old minister went into the room where the two swindlers sat working at the empty looms. "Heaven help us!" he thought, and opened his eyes wide. "Why, I cannot see anything at all," but he was careful not to say so.

INFER

Pause at line 33. Write three words that describe what you know about the emperor's **character** so far.

_____

_____

_____

_____

_____

_____

_____

_____

PREDICT

Pause at line 40. Will the minister be able to see the cloth? What will he tell the emperor about it?

_____

_____

_____

_____

_____

_____

_____

_____

_____

IDENTIFY

Circle and number the two questions that the minister asks himself before he decides he must lie (lines 45–53).

INFER

Pause at line 58. Why do you think the old minister never questions the weavers' honesty?

Both swindlers bade him be so good as to step closer and asked him if he did not admire the exquisite pattern and the beautiful colors. They pointed to the empty looms, and the poor old minister opened his eyes even wider, but he could see nothing, for there was nothing to be seen.

50 "Good Lord!" he thought, "can I be so stupid? I should never have thought so, and nobody must know it! Is it possible that I am not fit for my office? No, no, I must not tell anyone that I couldn't see the cloth."

"Well, have you got nothing to say?" said one, as he wove.

"Oh, it is very pretty—quite enchanting!" said the old minister, peering through his glasses. "What a pattern, and what colors! I shall tell the Emperor that I am very much pleased with it."

"Well, we are glad of that," said both the weavers, and

60 they described the colors to him and explained the curious pattern. The old minister listened carefully, so that he might tell the Emperor what they said.

Now the swindlers asked for more money, more silk, and more gold, which they required for weaving. They kept it all for themselves, and not a thread came near the loom, but they continued, as before, working at the empty looms.

Soon afterward the Emperor sent another honest official to the weavers to see how they were getting on and if the cloth was nearly finished. Like the old minister, he

70 looked and looked but could see nothing, as there was nothing to be seen.

"Is it not a beautiful piece of cloth?" said the two swindlers, showing and explaining the magnificent pattern, which, however, was not there at all.

"I am not stupid," thought the man, "so it must be that I am unfit for my high post. It is ludicrous,[2] but I must not let anyone know it." So he praised the cloth, which he did

---

2. **ludicrous** (loo′di·krəs) *adj.*: ridiculous; laughable.

not see, and expressed his pleasure at the beautiful colors and the fine pattern. "Yes, it is quite enchanting," he said to the Emperor.

Everybody in the whole town was talking about the beautiful cloth. At last the Emperor wished to see it himself while it was still on the loom. With a whole company of chosen courtiers, including the two honest councilors who had already been there, he went to the two clever swindlers, who were now weaving away as hard as they could but without using any thread.

"Is it not magnificent?" said both the honest statesmen. "Look, Your Majesty, what a pattern! What colors!" And they pointed to the empty looms, for they imagined the others could see the cloth.

"What is this?" thought the Emperor. "I do not see anything at all. This is terrible! Am I stupid? Am I unfit to be Emperor? That would indeed be the most dreadful thing that could happen to me!"

"Yes, it is very beautiful," said the Emperor. "It has our highest approval," and nodding contentedly, he gazed at the empty loom, for he did not want to say that he could see nothing. All the attendants who were with him looked and looked, and, although they could not see anything more than the others, they said, just like the Emperor, "Yes, it is very fine." They all advised him to wear the new magnificent clothes at a great procession that was soon to take place. "It is magnificent! beautiful, excellent!" went from mouth to mouth, and everybody seemed delighted. The Emperor awarded each of the swindlers the cross of the order of knighthood to be worn in their buttonholes, and the title of Imperial Court Weavers.

RETELL

Pause at line 80. Describe the important events that have happened in the story since the strangers came to town.

_____

_____

_____

_____

_____

_____

PREDICT

Pause at line 108. What will the emperor do when it's time to wear his new clothes? Will anyone dare to tell him the truth?

_____

_____

_____

_____

FLUENCY

As you read the boxed passage aloud, imagine that you're the emperor reacting to the "invisible cloth."

Notes _____

_____

_____

_____

_____

_____

_____

_____

_____

_____

VISUALIZE

Re-read lines 109–121. Circle
the words and phrases that
help you "see" the swindlers
as they trick everyone into
believing they are working.
Underline the comment that
is the swindlers' answer to a
question that no one dares
to ask. What is that question?

_____

_____

_____

_____

_____

_____

_____

Throughout the night preceding the procession, the
swindlers were up working, and they had more than sixteen
candles burning. People could see how busy they were, getting the Emperor's new clothes ready. They pretended to
take the cloth from the loom, they snipped the air with big
scissors, they sewed with needles without any thread, and at
last said: "Now the Emperor's new clothes are ready!"

The Emperor, followed by all his noblest courtiers,
then came in. Both the swindlers held up one arm as if they
held something, and said: "See, here are the trousers! Here
is the coat! Here is the cloak!" and so on. "They are all as
light as a cobweb! They make one feel as if one had nothing
on at all, but that is just the beauty of it."

"Yes!" said all the courtiers, but they could not see anything, for there was nothing to see.

"Will it please Your Majesty graciously to take off your
clothes?" said the swindlers. "Then we may help Your
Majesty into the new clothes before the large mirror!"

The Emperor took off all his clothes, and the swindlers
pretended to put on the new clothes, one piece after another.
Then the Emperor looked at himself in the glass from every
angle.

"Oh, how well they look! How well they fit!" said all. "What a pattern! What colors! Magnificent indeed!"

"They are waiting outside with the canopy which is to be borne over Your Majesty in the procession," announced the master of ceremonies.

"Well, I am quite ready," said the Emperor. "Doesn't my suit fit me beautifully?" And he turned once more to the mirror so that people would think he was admiring his garments.

140 The chamberlains, who were to carry the train, fumbled with their hands on the ground as if they were lifting up a train. Then they pretended to hold something up in their hands. They didn't dare let people know that they could not see anything.

And so the Emperor marched in the procession under the beautiful canopy, and all who saw him in the street and out of the windows exclaimed: "How marvelous the Emperor's new suit is! What a long train he has! How well it fits him!" Nobody would let the others know that he saw nothing, for then he would have been shown to be unfit for 150 his office or too stupid. None of the Emperor's clothes had ever been such a success.

"But he has nothing on at all," said a little child.

"Good heavens! Hear what the innocent child says!" said the father, and then each whispered to the other what the child said: "He has nothing on—a little child says he has nothing on at all!" "He has nothing on at all," cried all the people at last. And the Emperor too was feeling very worried, for it seemed to him that they were right, but he thought to himself, "All the same, I must go through with 160 the procession." And he held himself stiffer than ever, and the chamberlains walked on, holding up the train which was not there at all.

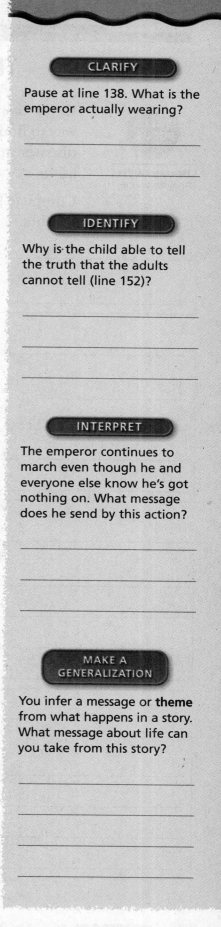

CLARIFY

Pause at line 138. What is the emperor actually wearing?

_____

_____

IDENTIFY

Why is the child able to tell the truth that the adults cannot tell (line 152)?

_____

_____

_____

INTERPRET

The emperor continues to march even though he and everyone else know he's got nothing on. What message does he send by this action?

_____

_____

_____

MAKE A GENERALIZATION

You infer a message or **theme** from what happens in a story. What message about life can you take from this story?

_____

_____

_____

_____

The Emperor's New Clothes

SKILLS FOCUS

Literary Skills
Analyze theme.

Theme Chart   A truth about life revealed in a story is its **theme.** One way to find a story's theme is to examine what we and the characters discover in the course of the story. That discovery is usually the same as the story's theme.

Complete this graphic organizer after you read "The Emperor's New Clothes."

Main character(s):

_____

↓

Key experiences:

_____

_____

_____

_____

↓

What we discover from those experiences:

_____

_____

_____

↓

Statement of theme:

_____

_____

_____

Skills Review

The Emperor's New Clothes

COMPREHENSION

Reading Comprehension   Write numbers from 1 to 10 to show the order in which the events happened in "The Emperor's New Clothes." Some numbers have already been filled in.

___3___ The Emperor sends an old minister to see how the weavers are progressing.

_____ An honest official assumes that he is unfit for his post because he could not see the cloth.

___8___ The Emperor awards the swindlers special honors for their service.

_____ The Emperor gives the swindlers money to weave new clothes.

_____ A child says that the Emperor has nothing on.

___9___ The Emperor marches under a beautiful canopy.

_____ The Emperor brings his courtiers and ministers to see the cloth.

_____ The swindlers ask the old minister to admire the cloth.

___7___ The Emperor's attendants advise him to wear his new clothes at a procession.

_____ Before beginning their task, the swindlers ask for fine silk and gold for their looms.

Atalanta and Hippomenes

retold by Margaret Evans Price

LITERARY FOCUS: UNIVERSAL THEMES

All people, no matter where or when they live, share certain basic emotions and ideas about life. In literature these types of experiences are explored through universal themes. A **universal theme** is a message or truth about life that goes beyond time and place. Examples of universal themes include "Money does not always buy happiness" and "Hard work will lead to success."

The story you are about to read is a **myth** about Atalanta (at′ə·lan′tə) and Hippomenes (hi·päm′i·nēz′). As you read, try to identify the universal theme it explores.

READING SKILLS: PARAPHRASING

When you **paraphrase** a text, you put it into your own words. Paraphrasing is a good way to check how well you understand what you've read. Here are the steps:

• Follow the author's order of ideas.
• Carefully reword each line or sentence, keeping the author's meaning and important details.

Original Text	Paraphrase
I was angry with my friend:	I was mad at my friend.
I told my wrath, my wrath did end.	I told my friend I was mad, which made my anger go away.
I was angry with my foe: I told it not, my wrath did grow. —William Blake *from* "A Poison Tree"	I was mad at my enemy, and I kept my feelings inside. I became more and more mad.

SKILLS FOCUS

Literary Skills
Understand universal themes.

Reading Skills
Paraphrase text.

Vocabulary Skills
Recognize words with multiple meanings.

VOCABULARY DEVELOPMENT

PREVIEW SELECTION VOCABULARY

Get to know these words before you read "Atalanta and Hippomenes."

suitors (soŏt'ərz) *n.*: men who are courting, or wish to marry, a woman.

Atalanta had many suitors because she was beautiful.

scorn (skôrn) *n.*: feeling that someone or something is worthless, or not worthy of notice.

Hippomenes, who was to judge the runners, felt scorn for them.

envious (en'vē·əs) *adj.*: jealous; wanting something that someone else has.

He changed his mind and became envious of the men racing Atalanta.

penalty (pen'əl·tē) *n.*: punishment.

Everyone who lost the race faced the penalty of death.

stooped (stoŏpt) *v.*: bent over.

When she saw the golden apple, Atalanta stooped to pick it up.

CLARIFYING WORD MEANINGS: MULTIPLE MEANINGS

Many words in English have more than one meaning. Take the word *bat,* for example. You probably know at least two different meanings for that word. When you read, you use **context clues** to figure out which meaning of a word is intended. Read these examples:

At the zoo we watched a **seal** dive from a platform.
Seal the envelope after you write the address on it.

In which sentence does *seal* mean "to fasten" or "to glue shut"? In which sentence does *seal* mean "a mammal that lives in water"? What context clues helped you tell the difference?

As you read "Atalanta and Hippomenes," use context clues to figure out the meanings of words with multiple meanings.

Atalanta and Hippomenes

a Greek Myth *retold by* Margaret Evans Price

DECODING TIP

Many names in Greek myths are difficult to pronounce. *Zephyr* will be easier to read if you remember that *ph* makes the *f* sound. Try breaking difficult names into syllables and sounding them out. For example, At/a/lan/ta or Hip/pom/e/nes.

IDENTIFY

Circle the words in the first two paragraphs that describe an important characteristic of Atalanta.

VOCABULARY

suitors (sōōt′ərz) *n.:* men who are courting, or wish to marry, a woman.

scorn (skôrn) *n.:* feeling that someone or something is worthless, or not worthy of notice.

FLUENCY

Improve your fluency by reading the boxed passage aloud. Read it once slowly and carefully. Then, read it again, with more speed. Read it a third time, and add expression to the description of Atalanta.

Atalanta was a Greek maiden who could run faster than anyone on earth. She could outrun the winds, Boreas and Zephyr. Only Mercury, with his winged sandals, ran more swiftly.

Besides being so fleet-footed, Atalanta was very beautiful, and many Greek youths from every part of the kingdom wished to marry her. But Atalanta did not wish to marry anyone and turned them all away, saying, "I shall be the bride only of him who shall outrun me in the race,

10 but death must be the penalty of all who try and fail."

In spite of this hard condition there still were a few brave **suitors** willing to risk their lives for a chance of winning Atalanta.

For one of the races the runners chose the youth Hippomenes for judge.

Hippomenes felt both pity and **scorn** for the runners. He thought they were foolish to risk their lives, and bade them go home. He reminded them that the land was full of lovely maidens who were kinder and more gentle than

20 Atalanta.

"But you have not yet seen Atalanta," said one of the suitors to Hippomenes. "You do not know all her beauty and loveliness. See, she comes!"

Hippomenes looked, and saw Atalanta as she drew near. She laid aside her cloak and made ready for the race. For a moment she stood poised like a graceful white bird about to fly.

The suitors who stood beside her trembled with fear and eagerness.

30 At a word from Hippomenes the runners were off, but at the first step Atalanta flew ahead. Her tunic fluttered behind her like a banner. Her hair, loosened from its ribbon, blew about her shoulders in bright waves.

As she ran, Hippomenes thought her very beautiful and became **envious** of the runner who might win her. He shouted praises when she reached the goal far ahead of her poor suitors.

Hippomenes forgot that the **penalty** of failure was death. He did not remember the advice he had given the
40 other runners to go home and forget the loveliness of Atalanta. He knew only that he loved her and must himself race with her.

Raising his head toward Mount Olympus, he prayed to Venus, the goddess of love, and asked her to help him.

Hippomenes races against Atalanta.

VOCABULARY

envious (en′vē·əs) *adj.:* jealous; wanting something that someone else has.

penalty (pen′əl·tē) *n.:* punishment.

PARAPHRASE

Restate, in your own words, what happens in lines 30–42.

_____
_____
_____
_____
_____
_____
_____
_____
_____
_____
_____
_____
_____
_____
_____
_____
_____
_____
_____
_____

Atalanta and Hippomenes 113

IDENTIFY

Pause at line 49. What does Venus tell Hippomenes to do with the golden apples?

_____

_____

_____

_____

_____

_____

VOCABULARY

stooped (stoopt) *v.*: bent over.

PARAPHRASE

Pause at line 78. In your own words, explain how Atalanta is tricked.

_____

_____

_____

_____

_____

_____

_____

_____

_____

_____

As he stood beside Atalanta, waiting for the signal for the race to start, Venus appeared to him and slipped three golden apples into his hands.

"Throw them one by one in Atalanta's path," whispered Venus.

50   The goddess was invisible to everyone but Hippomenes. No one saw her as she gave him the apples, nor heard her as she told him what to do with them.

Atalanta looked pityingly at the handsome youth as he stood ready to run. She was sorry for him, and for a moment she hesitated and almost wished that he might win the race.

The signal was given, and Atalanta and Hippomenes flew swiftly over the sand. Atalanta was soon ahead, but Hippomenes, sending up a prayer to Venus, tossed one of

60   his golden apples so that it fell directly in front of Atalanta.

Astonished at the beautiful apple which seemed to fall from nowhere, she **stooped** to pick it up.

That instant Hippomenes passed her, but Atalanta, holding the apple firmly in her hand, at once darted ahead. Again she outdistanced Hippomenes. Then he threw the second apple.

Atalanta could not pass without picking it up, and then, because of the apple in her other hand, paused a moment longer. When she looked up, Hippomenes was

70   far ahead.

But gaining, she overtook and passed him. Then, just before she reached the goal, he threw the third apple.

"I can win easily," thought Atalanta, "even though I stoop for this other apple." As she was already holding an apple in each hand, she paused just for an instant as she wondered how to grasp the third.

That moment Hippomenes shot past, reaching the goal before Atalanta.

Amid the wild shouts of those who watched, he wrapped the maiden's cloak around her shoulders and led her away. Hippomenes was so happy that he forgot to thank the goddess Venus, who followed them to the marriage feast.

Invisible, she moved among the wedding guests. She saw Atalanta place the golden apples in a bowl of ivory and admire their beauty, but Hippomenes, in his delight, thought no more of the apples or of the goddess who had given them to him.

Venus was angry with Hippomenes for being so thoughtless, and instead of blessing the lovers she caused them to be changed into a lion and a lioness, doomed forever to draw the chariot of Cybele,° the mother of Jupiter, through the heavens and over the earth.

EVALUATE

Although Hippomenes wins the race, has he really outrun Atalanta? Explain.

_____

_____

_____

_____

_____

_____

_____

_____

_____

_____

INTERPRET

Underline the word *thoughtless* in line 90, used to describe Hippomenes. What important **theme** in the myth is reflected in this word?

_____

_____

_____

_____

_____

_____

_____

_____

_____

_____

_____

Cybele on her chariot, from *Le Costume Ancien ou Moderne* by Jules Ferrario, engraved by A. Biasioli, c. 1820 (aquatint).

Bibliotheque des Arts Decoratifs, Paris, France/ Archives Charmet/Bridgeman Art Library.

° **Cybele** (sib′ə·lē′).

Atalanta and Hippomenes

SKILLS FOCUS

Literary Skills
Recognize universal themes.

Word-and-Theme Diagram   Use this word-and-theme diagram to record important ideas from "Atalanta and Hippomenes." First, select three words from the myth you think are important. Then, explain how each word helps reveal a theme in the myth.

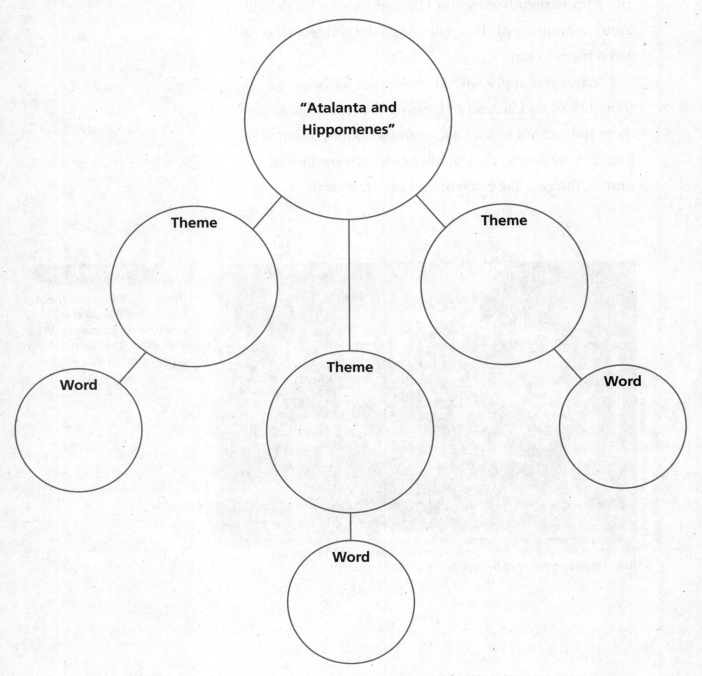

"Atalanta and Hippomenes"

Theme

Theme

Theme

Word

Word

Word

Skills Review

Atalanta and Hippomenes

VOCABULARY AND COMPREHENSION

A. Clarifying Word Meanings: Multiple Meanings   Write words from the Word Bank to complete the paragraph. Then, circle the words in the paragraph that have multiple meanings.

Princess Ora (1) _____ to pick up the flowers that had been thrown at her feet. Once again, one of her many (2) _____ had tried to win her attention. But she had nothing but (3) _____ for most of them because she thought they were beneath her. Prince Zandar was the only one who might have a chance. He would need to show his mental might in a contest. If he lost, the (4) _____ would surely be something painful. Meanwhile, other women in the court were (5) _____ of Ora—they wanted what she had.

B. Reading Comprehension   Circle the letter of the correct response.

1. The characters in the myth include all of the following *except*—
   a. Atalanta   b. Hippomenes   c. Jupiter   d. Venus

2. Why does Hippomenes pray to Venus?
   f. She is queen of the gods.   h. She is very beautiful.
   g. She protects maidens.   j. She can help him win Atalanta.

3. Atalanta and Hippomenes are turned into—
   a. three golden apples   c. a lion and a lioness
   b. Greek gods   d. two invisible cloaks

4. The **theme** of the myth might be—
   f. Hard work brings success.
   g. Beauty is all that matters.
   h. Don't forget to thank those who help you.
   j. Love is worth dying for.

SKILLS FOCUS

Vocabulary Skills
Recognize words with multiple meanings.

Forms of Fiction

Academic Vocabulary for Collection 4

These are the terms you should know
as you read and analyze the selections in this collection.

———————

Fiction A story that is made up instead of being true. The term *fiction* usually refers to short stories and novels. Fiction can take many forms, including adventure, mystery, fantasy, science fiction, and historical fiction.

Novel A long fictional story. Novels usually have complex plots and deal with more than one theme.

Novella A story that is shorter than a novel but longer than a short story.

Short Story A story that is much shorter than a novel. It is usually between five and twenty pages long.

Myth A story that usually explains something about the world and involves gods and superheroes. **Origin myths,** or **creation myths,** explain how something in the world began or was created.

Fable A brief story in prose or verse that teaches a **moral,** or lesson about how to succeed in life.

Legend A story that has been handed down from one generation to the next. It is usually based on some fact from history.

Folk Tale A story with no known author, originally passed down from one generation to another by word of mouth. The main characters of many folk tales are **tricksters.** One type of folk tale is called a **fairy tale.**

> This selection also appears in *Elements of Literature*. ◆

La Bamba by Gary Soto

LITERARY FOCUS: THE SHORT STORY

You can tell by its name that a **short story** is not long. It is usually between five and twenty pages long. A short story is a fictional prose narrative, which is another way of saying it is made up, is not a poem, and consists of a series of events. The short story was invented in the nineteenth century, when magazines began printing them. They quickly became popular and are still popular today.

STORY AND STRUCTURE

How does a writer put together a short story? The diagram below shows the building blocks of short stories. You can use this chart to analyze the structure of most stories, but keep in mind that a short story usually has just one or two main characters and a simple plot. In fact, most short stories can be read in just one sitting.

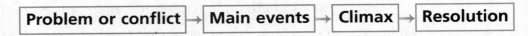

| Problem or conflict | → | Main events | → | Climax | → | Resolution |

READING SKILLS: SEQUENCING—WHAT HAPPENED WHEN?

Most of the stories you read are written in **chronological** order. The events are told in the order in which they happen. Time clues such as *last Wednesday, at the same time,* and *later* help you keep track of the order of events. Sometimes the time order of a story is interrupted to tell you of events that happened earlier. This kind of break in the story line is called a **flashback.**

Keep these questions in mind as you read "La Bamba":
- What are the story's key events?
- When did each event happen?
- What happened afterward?
- Did one event cause another event to happen?

SKILLS FOCUS

Literary Skills
Understand forms of fiction: the short story.

Reading Skills
Understand sequence.

LA BAMBA

Gary Soto

Manuel was the fourth of seven children and looked like a lot of kids in his neighborhood: black hair, brown face, and skinny legs scuffed from summer play. But summer was giving way to fall: The trees were turning red, the lawns brown, and the pomegranate trees were heavy with fruit. Manuel walked to school in the frosty morning, kicking leaves and thinking of tomorrow's talent show. He was still amazed that he had volunteered. He was going to pretend to sing Ritchie Valens's[1] "La Bamba" before the entire school.

10   Why did I raise my hand? he asked himself, but in his heart he knew the answer. He yearned for the limelight. He wanted applause as loud as a thunderstorm and to hear his friends say, "Man, that was bad!" And he wanted to impress the girls, especially Petra Lopez, the second-prettiest girl in his class. The prettiest was already taken by his friend Ernie. Manuel knew he should be reasonable since he himself was not great-looking, just average.

    Manuel kicked through the fresh-fallen leaves. When he got to school, he realized he had forgotten his math
20 workbook. If the teacher found out, he would have to stay after school and miss practice for the talent show. But fortunately for him, they did drills that morning.

    During lunch Manuel hung around with Benny, who was also in the talent show. Benny was going to play the trumpet in spite of the fat lip he had gotten playing football.

---

1. **Ritchie Valens** (1941–1959), the professional singer mentioned in the story, was the first Mexican American rock star. In 1959, when he was only seventeen, Valens was killed in a plane crash.

IDENTIFY

Underline the words in the opening paragraph (lines 1–9) that describe the **character** Manuel. Circle words that describe the **setting**.

WORD STUDY

Limelight, in line 11, refers to a brilliant light created by burning lime. This type of lighting was used in the nineteenth century in theaters to cast light on the actors onstage. Although limelights are not used anymore, the term has come to mean "being spotlighted in public." When Manuel longs for the limelight, he is longing to star onstage.

RETELL

Re-read lines 10–17. Why has Manuel volunteered for the talent show?

_____

_____

_____

_____

_____

_____

The word *pantomime* in line
27 comes from a Greek word
meaning "all-imitating." In
ancient Rome, a pantomime
was an actor who used only
actions and gestures, no
words. Today the word *pantomime* refers to an act or a
show without words. In line
27, Manuel is pantomiming,
or lip-syncing, the words to
the song.

PREDICT

Pause at line 40. Do you
think the record player will
be fixed in time for the talent show? Explain.

_____

_____

_____

_____

_____

_____

_____

_____

_____

_____

_____

_____

_____

_____

"How do I look?" Manuel asked. He cleared his throat
and started moving his lips in pantomime. No words came
out, just a hiss that sounded like a snake. Manuel tried to
look emotional, flailing his arms on the high notes and
30   opening his eyes and mouth as wide as he could when he
came to "Para bailar la baaaaammmba."[2]

After Manuel finished, Benny said it looked all right
but suggested Manuel dance while he sang. Manuel
thought for a moment and decided it was a good idea.

"Yeah, just think you're like Michael Jackson or someone like that," Benny suggested. "But don't get carried away."

During rehearsal, Mr. Roybal, nervous about his debut
as the school's talent co-ordinator, cursed under his breath
when the lever that controlled the speed on the record
40   player jammed.

"Darn," he growled, trying to force the lever. "What's
wrong with you?"

"Is it broken?" Manuel asked, bending over for a closer
look. It looked all right to him.

Mr. Roybal assured Manuel that he would have a good
record player at the talent show, even if it meant bringing
his own stereo from home.

Manuel sat in a folding chair, twirling his record on his
thumb. He watched a skit about personal hygiene, a mother-
50   and-daughter violin duo, five first-grade girls jumping rope,
a karate kid breaking boards, three girls singing "Like a
Virgin," and a skit about the pilgrims. If the record player
hadn't been broken, he would have gone after the karate
kid, an easy act to follow, he told himself.

As he twirled his forty-five record, Manuel thought
they had a great talent show. The entire school would be
amazed. His mother and father would be proud, and his

---

2. **para bailar la bamba** (pä′rä bī′lär lä bäm′bä): Spanish for "to dance
the bamba."

© Royalty-Free/CORBIS.

brothers and sisters would be jealous and pout. It would be a night to remember.

60   Benny walked onto the stage, raised his trumpet to his mouth, and waited for his cue. Mr. Roybal raised his hand like a symphony conductor and let it fall dramatically. Benny inhaled and blew so loud that Manuel dropped his record, which rolled across the cafeteria floor until it hit a wall. Manuel raced after it, picked it up, and wiped it clean.

    "Boy, I'm glad it didn't break," he said with a sigh.

    That night Manuel had to do the dishes and a lot of homework, so he could only practice in the shower. In bed he prayed that he wouldn't mess up. He prayed that it

70 wouldn't be like when he was a first-grader. For Science Week he had wired together a C battery and a bulb and told everyone he had discovered how a flashlight worked. He was so pleased with himself that he practiced for hours pressing the wire to the battery, making the bulb wink a dim, orangish light. He showed it to so many kids in his neighborhood that when it was time to show his class how

IDENTIFY

Pause at line 59. What are Manuel's hopes for the talent show?

CLARIFY

Re-read lines 67–80. What does this **flashback** tell you about Manuel?

_____

_____

_____

_____

_____

_____

_____

_____

_____

_____

_____

_____

_____

_____

VISUALIZE

Take time to picture the scene described in lines 92–109. Underline words that help you see what is happening.

WORD STUDY

Ado (ə·dōō′), in line 105, is not commonly used anymore. It means "fuss" or "trouble."

a flashlight worked, the battery was dead. He pressed the wire to the battery, but the bulb didn't respond. He pressed until his thumb hurt and some kids in the back started

80   snickering.

But Manuel fell asleep confident that nothing would go wrong this time.

The next morning his father and mother beamed at him. They were proud that he was going to be in the talent show.

"I wish you would tell us what you're doing," his mother said. His father, a pharmacist who wore a blue smock with his name on a plastic rectangle, looked up from the newspaper and sided with his wife. "Yes, what are you doing in the talent show?"

90   "You'll see," Manuel said, with his mouth full of Cheerios.

The day whizzed by, and so did his afternoon chores and dinner. Suddenly he was dressed in his best clothes and standing next to Benny backstage, listening to the commotion as the cafeteria filled with school kids and parents. The lights dimmed, and Mr. Roybal, sweaty in a tight suit and a necktie with a large knot, wet his lips and parted the stage curtains.

"Good evening, everyone," the kids behind the curtain

100   heard him say. "Good evening to you," some of the smart-alecky kids said back to him.

"Tonight we bring you the best John Burroughs Elementary has to offer, and I'm sure that you'll be both pleased and amazed that our little school houses so much talent. And now, without further ado, let's get on with the show." He turned and, with a swish of his hand, commanded, "Part the curtain." The curtains parted in jerks. A girl dressed as a toothbrush and a boy dressed as a dirty gray tooth walked onto the stage and sang:

110 *Brush, brush, brush*
Floss, floss, floss
Gargle the germs away—hey! hey! hey!

After they finished singing, they turned to Mr. Roybal, who dropped his hand. The toothbrush dashed around the stage after the dirty tooth, which was laughing and having a great time until it slipped and nearly rolled off the stage.

Mr. Roybal jumped out and caught it just in time. "Are you OK?"

The dirty tooth answered, "Ask my dentist," which
120 drew laughter and applause from the audience.

The violin duo played next, and except for one time when the girl got lost, they sounded fine. People applauded, and some even stood up. Then the first-grade girls maneuvered onto the stage while jumping rope. They were all smiles and bouncing ponytails as a hundred cameras flashed at once. Mothers "awhed" and fathers sat up proudly.

The karate kid was next. He did a few kicks, yells, and chops, and finally, when his father held up a board, punched it in two. The audience clapped and looked at each other,
130 wide-eyed with respect. The boy bowed to the audience, and father and son ran off the stage.

Manuel remained behind the stage, shivering with fear. He mouthed the words to "La Bamba" and swayed left to right. Why did he raise his hand and volunteer? Why couldn't he have just sat there like the rest of the kids and not said anything? While the karate kid was onstage, Mr. Roybal, more sweaty than before, took Manuel's forty-five record and placed it on a new record player.

"You ready?" Mr. Roybal asked.
140 "Yeah . . ."

CONNECT

In lines 99–131, Manuel waits his turn to perform. The order of events helps to build **suspense**—you can hardly wait to find out what happens next. How might you feel if you were Manuel?

_____

_____

_____

_____

_____

_____

_____

_____

IDENTIFY

What **internal conflict** is Manuel having in lines 132–138?

_____

_____

_____

_____

_____

_____

_____

_____

_____

Mr. Roybal walked back on stage and announced that Manuel Gomez, a fifth-grader in Mrs. Knight's class, was going to pantomime Ritchie Valens's classic hit "La Bamba."

The cafeteria roared with applause. Manuel was nervous but loved the noisy crowd. He pictured his mother and father applauding loudly and his brothers and sister also clapping, though not as energetically.

Manuel walked on stage and the song started immediately. Glassy-eyed from the shock of being in front of so 150 many people, Manuel moved his lips and swayed in a made-up dance step. He couldn't see his parents, but he could see his brother Mario, who was a year younger, thumb-wrestling with a friend. Mario was wearing Manuel's favorite shirt; he would deal with Mario later. He saw some other kids get up and head for the drinking fountain, and a baby sitting in the middle of an aisle sucking her thumb and watching him intently.

What am I doing here? thought Manuel. This is no fun at all. Everyone was just sitting there. Some people were 160 moving to the beat, but most were just watching him, like they would a monkey at the zoo.

But when Manuel did a fancy dance step, there was a burst of applause and some girls screamed. Manuel tried another dance step. He heard more applause and screams and started getting into the groove as he shivered and snaked like Michael Jackson around the stage. But the record got stuck, and he had to sing

Para bailar la bamba

Para bailar la bamba

170 *Para bailar la bamba*

Para bailar la bamba

again and again.

IDENTIFY

In lines 144–172, the writer is really helping you get inside Manuel's skin. Underline details that tell you what Manuel is doing, seeing, and thinking.

PREDICT

Pause at line 172. How do you think the audience will react to what happens?

Manuel couldn't believe his bad luck. The audience began to laugh and stand up in their chairs. Manuel remembered how the forty-five record had dropped from his hand and rolled across the cafeteria floor. It probably got scratched, he thought, and now it was stuck, and he was stuck dancing and moving his lips to the same words over and over. He had never been so embarrassed. He would 180 have to ask his parents to move the family out of town.

After Mr. Roybal ripped the needle across the record, Manuel slowed his dance steps to a halt. He didn't know what to do except bow to the audience, which applauded wildly, and scoot off the stage, on the verge of tears. This was worse than the homemade flashlight. At least no one laughed then; they just snickered.

© Royalty-Free/CORBIS.

Manuel thinks the audience is laughing at him because he has made a fool of himself (lines 173–174). Why do you think they are laughing?

_____

_____

_____

_____

_____

_____

_____

IDENTIFY

Pause at line 180. What probably caused the record to skip?

_____

_____

_____

_____

_____

_____

_____

_____

FLUENCY

Read the boxed passage aloud at least twice. As you read, use your voice to show Manuel's surprise and confusion when people congratulate him.

WORD STUDY

Jargon (line 215) is the special language of people who work in the same profession. Why does Manuel use jargon here?

Manuel stood alone, trying hard to hold back the tears as Benny, center stage, played his trumpet. Manuel was jealous because he sounded great, then mad as he recalled that

190   it was Benny's loud trumpet playing that made the forty-five record fly out of his hands. But when the entire cast lined up for a curtain call, Manuel received a burst of applause that was so loud it shook the walls of the cafeteria. Later, as he mingled with the kids and parents, everyone patted him on the shoulder and told him, "Way to go. You were really funny."

Funny? Manuel thought. Did he do something funny?

Funny. Crazy. Hilarious. These were the words people said to him. He was confused but beyond caring. All he knew was that people were paying attention to him, and his

200   brother and sisters looked at him with a mixture of jealousy and awe. He was going to pull Mario aside and punch him in the arm for wearing his shirt, but he cooled it. He was enjoying the limelight. A teacher brought him cookies and punch, and the popular kids who had never before given him the time of day now clustered around him. Ricardo, the editor of the school bulletin, asked him how he made the needle stick.

"It just happened," Manuel said, crunching on a star-shaped cookie.

210   At home that night his father, eager to undo the buttons on his shirt and ease into his La-Z-Boy recliner, asked Manuel the same thing, how he managed to make the song stick on the words "Para bailar la bamba."

Manuel thought quickly and reached for scientific jargon he had read in magazines. "Easy, Dad. I used laser tracking with high optics and low functional decibels per channel." His proud but confused father told him to be quiet and go to bed.

"Ah, que niños tan truchas,"[3] he said as he walked to the kitchen for a glass of milk. "I don't know how you kids nowadays get so smart."

Manuel, feeling happy, went to his bedroom, undressed, and slipped into his pajamas. He looked in the mirror and began to pantomime "La Bamba," but stopped because he was tired of the song. He crawled into bed. The sheets were as cold as the moon that stood over the peach tree in their backyard.

He was relieved that the day was over. Next year, when they asked for volunteers for the talent show, he wouldn't raise his hand. Probably.

PREDICT

Re-read the final paragraph. Do you think Manuel will end up volunteering for next year's talent show? Tell why or why not.

_____

_____

_____

_____

_____

_____

EVALUATE

Do you think the events of the story are realistic? Explain.

_____

_____

_____

_____

_____

_____

_____

_____

_____

3. **que niños tan truchas** (kā nēn'yōs tän trōō'chäs): Spanish for "what smart kids."

La Bamba

Short Story Map   Mapping the building blocks of a short story can help
you understand its form. Complete the following short story map with
details from Gary Soto's "La Bamba."

Title:	Setting:
Author:	
Main Character:	

Problem

Event 1

Event 2

Event 3

Event 4 (Climax)

Resolution

Skills Review

La Bamba

COMPREHENSION

Reading Comprehension   Ten events from "La Bamba" are listed below. Number these events in the correct sequence, or chronological order. Some numbers have already been filled in.

_____ Manuel drops his record.

___7___ Benny plays his trumpet for the audience.

_____ Manuel's father asks how Manuel made the needle stick.

_____ The karate kid punches a board in two.

_____ Manuel does a fancy dance step to the music.

_____ Benny suggests that Manuel dance while he pantomimes the song.

___9___ A teacher brings Manuel cookies and punch.

_____ Manuel receives a loud burst of applause.

_____ During rehearsal the record player jams.

___5___ Mr. Roybal places the record on a new record player.

Medusa's Head *retold by* Olivia Coolidge

LITERARY FOCUS: MYTHIC HEROES

If you invented a hero, what powers would you give him or her? In **myths,** heroes have amazing strength and courage. They perform marvelous feats. Heroes in myths are often helped by gods. Sometimes they are gods themselves. These superheroes usually have magical powers, and they always face great challenges, such as slaying monsters.

The myth you are going to read is about Perseus, a hero who goes on a difficult and exciting quest. A **quest** is a dangerous journey for an important goal.

READING SKILLS: DIALOGUE WITH THE TEXT

A **dialogue** is a conversation between people. In the course of a conversation, you might ask questions, exclaim over something surprising, and challenge the other person's ideas. When you dialogue with a text, you do the same thing, only you "converse" with the text and its ideas.

As you read the following myth, you may want to dialogue using this method:

- Put a question mark next to text you disagree with or find puzzling.
- Place an exclamation mark next to passages you find interesting or surprising.
- Underline ideas in the text you find important.

SKILLS FOCUS

Literary Skills
Identify forms of fiction: myths.

Reading Skills
Dialogue with the text.

Vocabulary Skills
Clarify word meanings.

VOCABULARY DEVELOPMENT

PREVIEW SELECTION VOCABULARY

Before you read "Medusa's Head," get to know these words
from the myth.

descended (dē·send′id) *v.:* moved to a lower
place; came down.

*Out of pity, Zeus, king of the Greek gods,
descended to the imprisoned girl.*

perplexity (pər·plek′sə·tē) *n.:* bewilderment;
confusion.

In his perplexity, Perseus turned to Athene.

perpetual (pər·pech′ōō·əl) *adj.:* permanent;
constant.

*Medusa's sisters live in a place of perpetual
twilight, where there is neither day nor night.*

recesses (rē′ses·əz) *n.:* inner places.

*The sisters scrambled to the recesses of the cave
after Perseus stole their sight.*

hovered (huv′ərd) *v.:* remained suspended
in the air.

*Wearing the winged sandals, Perseus hovered
high above the rocks.*

CLARIFYING WORD MEANINGS: SYNONYMS

Synonyms are words or phrases that share meaning. *Road* and *street,*
for example, are synonyms. So are *candy* and *sweets.* When you learn
a new word, it's also useful to learn its synonyms. In the following passages, a synonym for each boldface word appears in parentheses:

- The sun **descended** (sank); then darkness fell.
- Her **perplexity** (confusion) was caused by the mislabeled map.
- The young boy was in **perpetual** (constant) motion.
- She searched the **recesses** (corners) of her mind for clues.
- The eagle **hovered** (floated) in the air directly over its prey.

MEDUSA'S HEAD

Greek myth, *retold by* Olivia Coolidge

Characters and Places

King Acrisios (ə·crē′sē·ōs′) **of Argos** (är′gäs′): Argos was an ancient city and kingdom in southern Greece. Also spelled *Acrisius*.

Proitos (prō·ē′tōs): brother of King Acrisios.

Danae (dan′ā·ē′): daughter of King Acrisios. She bears Zeus's son Perseus.

Apollo: Greek god of light, medicine, poetry, and prophecy. The oracle of Apollo was a priest or priestess through whom the god was believed to speak.

Zeus (zo͞os): king of the Greek gods.

Dictys (dic′tis): fisherman, brother of Polydectes. He and Polydectes live on the island of Seriphos. Also spelled *Seriphus*.

Polydectes (päl′ē·dek′tēz): king of Seriphos.

Perseus (pʉr′sē·əs): son of Danae and Zeus.

Gorgons: three fearsome sisters with brass hands, gold wings, and serpent-like scales. Medusa, the youngest Gorgon, has snakes for hair and a face so terrible that it turns to stone anyone who looks at it.

Athene (ə·thē′nē): Greek goddess of crafts, war, and wisdom. Her name is also spelled *Athena*.

Phorcides (fôr′sə·dēz): three sisters who live in a cave and have only one eye and one tooth between them.

Hermes (hʉr′mēz′): messenger of the gods.

Cepheus (sē′fē·əs): king of Ethiopia.

Cassiopeia (kas′ē·ō·pē′ə): queen of Ethiopia.

Andromeda (an·dräm′ə·də): daughter of King Cepheus and Queen Cassiopeia. She has been chained to a rock near the sea to calm the anger of the god Poseidon.

Nereus (nir′ē·əs): a minor sea god.

Poseidon (pō·sī′dən): god of the sea.

Exterior view of the Parthenon at the Acropolis in Athens, Greece.

King Acrisios of Argos was a hard, selfish man. He hated his brother, Proitos, who later drove him from his kingdom, and he cared nothing for his daughter, Danae. His whole heart was set on having a son who should succeed him, but since many years went by and still he had only the one daughter, he sent a message to the oracle of Apollo to ask whether he should have more children of his own. The answer of the oracle was terrible. Acrisios should have no son, but his daughter, Danae, would bear him a grandchild

10 who should grow up to kill him. At these words Acrisios was beside himself with fear and rage. Swearing that Danae should never have a child to murder him, he had a room built underground and lined all through with brass. Thither he conducted Danae and shut her up, bidding her spend the rest of her life alone.

It is possible to thwart the plans of mortal men, but never those of the gods. Zeus himself looked with pity on the unfortunate girl, and it is said he **descended** to her through the tiny hole that gave light and air to her

20 chamber, pouring himself down into her lap in the form of a shower of gold.

Circle two words in the first paragraph that describe Acrisios. Then, come up with another adjective, not in this paragraph but based on its details, to describe him.

_____

_____

_____

IDENTIFY

Re-read lines 7–10. What does the oracle tell Acrisios? List and number the three parts of the oracle's answer below.

_____

_____

_____

_____

_____

_____

_____

_____

VOCABULARY

descended (dē·send′id) v.: moved to a lower place; came down.

IDENTIFY

People in **myths** are often helped by gods. Underline the details that tell how the gods help Danae when she and her son are cast away (lines 31–33).

RETELL

Pause at line 44. Since the action in this plot is moving so quickly, take a minute to retell the major events that have happened so far.

When word came to the king from those who brought food and drink to his daughter that the girl was with child, Acrisios was angry and afraid. He would have liked best to murder both Danae and her infant son, Perseus, but he did not dare for fear of the gods' anger at so hideous a crime. He made, therefore, a great chest of wood with bands of brass about it. Shutting up the girl and her baby inside, he cast them into the sea, thinking that they would either

30 drown or starve.

Again the gods came to the help of Danae, for they caused the planks of the chest to swell until they fitted tightly and let no water in.

The chest floated for some days and was cast up at last on an island. There Dictys, a fisherman, found it and took Danae to his brother, Polydectes, who was king of the island. Danae was made a servant in the palace, yet before many years had passed, both Dictys and Polydectes had fallen in love with the silent, golden-haired girl. She in her

40 heart preferred Dictys, yet since his brother was king, she did not dare to make her choice. Therefore she hung always over Perseus, pretending that mother love left her no room for any other, and year after year a silent frown would cross Polydectes' face as he saw her caress the child.

At last, Perseus became a young man, handsome and strong beyond the common and a leader among the youths of the island, though he was but the son of a poor servant. Then it seemed to Polydectes that if he could once get rid of Perseus, he could force Danae to become his wife,

50 whether she would or not. Meanwhile, in order to lull the young man's suspicions, he pretended that he intended to marry a certain noble maiden and would collect a wedding gift for her. Now the custom was that this gift of the bride-groom to the bride was in part his own and in part put

together from the marriage presents of his friends and relatives. All the young men, therefore, brought Polydectes a present, excepting Perseus, who was his servant's son and possessed nothing to bring. Then Polydectes said to the others, "This young man owes me more than any of you, since I took him in and brought him up in my own house, and yet he gives me nothing."

Perseus answered in anger at the injustice of the charge, "I have nothing of my own, Polydectes, yet ask me what you will, and I will fetch it, for I owe you my life."

At this Polydectes smiled, for it was what he had intended, and he answered, "Fetch me, if this is your boast, the Gorgon's head."

Now the Gorgons, who lived far off on the shores of the ocean, were three fearful sisters with hands of brass, wings of gold, and scales like a serpent. Two of them had scaly heads and tusks like the wild boar, but the third, Medusa, had the face of a beautiful woman with hair of writhing serpents, and so terrible was her expression that all who looked on it were immediately turned to stone.

Medusa by Michelangelo Caravaggio (1573–1610).

CLARIFY

How does Polydectes trick Perseus into going on a dangerous mission (lines 45–67)?

IDENTIFY

Re-read lines 81–88. Under-line and number in the text three ways the gods help (or will help) Perseus in his battle with the Gorgons.

INTERPRET

Mythic heroes often go on a **quest** (a dangerous journey) where they take on super-human tasks. What is Perseus's quest and task?

_____

_____

_____

_____

_____

PREDICT

Pause at line 95. Will Perseus follow Athene's detailed directions and succeed? What might happen next?

_____

_____

_____

_____

This much Perseus knew of the Gorgons, but of how to find or kill them, he had no idea. Nevertheless, he had given his promise, and though he saw now the satisfaction of King Polydectes, he was bound to keep his word. In his **perplexity,** he prayed to the wise goddess Athene, who
80 came to him in a vision and promised him her aid.

"First, you must go," she said, "to the sisters Phorcides, who will tell you the way to the nymphs who guard the hat of darkness, the winged sandals, and the knapsack which can hold the Gorgon's head. Then I will give you a shield, and my brother Hermes will give you a sword, which shall be made of adamant, the hardest rock. For nothing else can kill the Gorgon, since so venomous is her blood that a mortal sword, when plunged in it, is eaten away. But when you come to the Gorgons, invisible in your hat of darkness,
90 turn your eyes away from them and look only on their reflection in your gleaming shield. Thus you may kill the monster without yourself being turned to stone. Pass her sisters by, for they are immortal, but smite off the head of Medusa with the hair of writhing snakes. Then put it in your knapsack and return, and I will be with you."

The vision ended, and with the aid of Athene, Perseus set out on the long journey to seek the Phorcides. These live in a dim cavern in the far north, where nights and days are one and where the whole earth is overspread
100 with **perpetual** twilight. There sat the three old women mumbling to one another, crouched in a dim heap together, for they had but one eye and one tooth between them, which they passed from hand to hand. Perseus came quietly behind them, and as they fumbled for the eye, he put his strong, brown hand next to one of the long, yellow ones, so that the old crone thought that it was her sister's and put the eye into it. There was a high scream of anger when they

discovered the theft, and much clawing and groping in the dim **recesses** of the cavern. But they were helpless in their blindness and Perseus could laugh at them. At length, for the price of their eye, they told him how to reach the nymphs, and Perseus, laying the eye quickly in the hand of the nearest sister, fled as fast as he could before she could use it.

Again it was a far journey to the garden of the nymphs, where it is always sunshine and the trees bear golden apples. But the nymphs are friends of the wise gods and hate the monsters of darkness and the spirits of anger and despair. Therefore, they received Perseus with rejoicing and put the hat of darkness on his head, while on his feet they bound the golden, winged sandals, which are those Hermes wears when he runs down the slanting sunbeams or races along the pathways of the wind. Next, Perseus put on his back the silver sack with the gleaming tassels of gold, and flung across his shoulder the black-sheathed sword that was the gift of Hermes. On his left arm he fitted the shield that Athene gave, a gleaming silver shield like a mirror, plain without any marking. Then he sprang into the air and ran, invisible like the rushing wind, far out over the white-capped sea, across the yellow sands of the eastern desert, over strange streams and towering mountains, until at last he came to the shores of the distant ocean which flowed round all the world.

There was a gray gorge of stone by the ocean's edge, where lay Medusa and her sisters sleeping in the dim depths of the rock. All up and down the cleft, the stones took fantastic shapes of trees, beasts, birds, or serpents. Here and there, a man who had looked on the terrible Medusa stood forever with horror on his face. Far over the twilit gorge Perseus **hovered** invisible, while he loosened the pale, strange sword from its black sheath. Then, with his face

VISUALIZE

Circle the details in lines 114–132 that help you picture what Perseus sees on his journey.

IDENTIFY

Re-read lines 114–132. From whom does Perseus receive help on this part of his journey?

_____

_____

_____

_____

_____

_____

_____

_____

_____

VOCABULARY

hovered (huv′ərd) *v.:* remained suspended in the air.

PREDICT

Pause at line 149. Why is
Perseus so frightened? What
could go wrong?

_____

_____

_____

_____

_____

_____

_____

_____

_____

_____

_____

_____

_____

_____

_____

_____

_____

VISUALIZE

Lines 150–164 are filled with
imagery, language that
appeals to the senses. Circle
the images in this paragraph
that help you "see" the
Gorgons.

turned away and eyes on the silver shield, he dropped, slow
and silent as a falling leaf, down through the rocky cleft,
twisting and turning past countless strange gray shapes,
down from the bright sunlight into a chill, dim shadow
echoing and reechoing with the dashing of waves on the
tumbled rocks beneath. There on the heaped stones lay
the Gorgons sleeping together in the dimness, and even
as he looked on them in the shield, Perseus felt stiff with
horror at the sight.

150   Two of the Gorgons lay sprawled together, shaped like
women, yet scaled from head to foot as serpents are. Instead
of hands they had gleaming claws like eagles, and their feet
were dragons' feet. Skinny metallic wings like bats' wings
hung from their shoulders. Their faces were neither snake
nor woman, but part both, like faces in a nightmare. These
two lay arm in arm and never stirred. Only the blue snakes
still hissed and writhed round the pale, set face of Medusa,
as though even in sleep she were troubled by an evil dream.
She lay by herself, arms outstretched, face upwards, more
160 beautiful and terrible than living man may bear. All the
crimes and madnesses of the world rushed into Perseus' mind
as he gazed at her image in the shield. Horror stiffened his
arm as he hovered over her with his sword uplifted. Then
he shut his eyes to the vision and in the darkness struck.

There was a great cry and a hissing. Perseus groped for
the head and seized it by the limp and snaky hair. Somehow
he put it in his knapsack and was up and off, for at the
dreadful scream the sister Gorgons had awakened. Now they
were after him, their sharp claws grating against his silver
170 shield. Perseus strained forward on the pathway of the wind
like a runner, and behind him the two sisters came, smelling
out the prey they could not see. Snakes darted from their
girdles,° foam flew from their tusks, and the great wings

° **girdles** _n.:_ belts or sashes.

beat the air. Yet the winged sandals were even swifter than they, and Perseus fled like the hunted deer with the speed of desperation. Presently the horrible noise grew faint behind him, the hissing of snakes and the sound of the bat wings died away. At last the Gorgons could smell him no longer and returned home unavenged.

180   By now, Perseus was over the Libyan desert, and as the blood from the horrible head touched the sand, it changed to serpents, from which the snakes of Africa are descended.

    The storms of the Libyan desert blew against Perseus in clouds of eddying sand, until not even the divine sandals could hold him on his course. Far out to sea he was blown, and then north. Finally, whirled around the heavens like a cloud of mist, he alighted in the distant west, where the giant Atlas held up on his shoulders the heavens from the

Notes _____

_____

_____

_____

_____

_____

_____

_____

_____

_____

_____

_____

_____

_____

INFER

Why do you think Atlas wants to look at Medusa's head (lines 189–190)?

_____

_____

_____

_____

_____

IDENTIFY

Myths often explain where things came from or how they came to be. Re-read lines 180–193. What two things are explained here?

_____

_____

_____

_____

_____

PREDICT

Pause at line 216. What do you think Perseus will do now that he sees this maiden in distress?

_____

_____

_____

_____

_____

earth. There the weary giant, crushed under the load of
centuries, begged Perseus to show him Medusa's head.
Perseus uncovered for him the dreadful thing, and Atlas
was changed to the mighty mountain whose rocks rear up
to reach the sky near the gateway to the Atlantic. Perseus
himself, returning eastwards and still battling with the
wind, was driven south to the land of Ethiopia, where King
Cepheus reigned with his wife, Cassiopeia.

As Perseus came wheeling in like a gull from the ocean,
he saw a strange sight. Far out to sea the water was troubled,
seething and boiling as though stirred by a great force moving in its depths. Huge, sullen waves were starting far out
and washing inland over sunken trees and flooded houses.
Many miles of land were under water, and as he sped over
them, he saw the muddy sea lapping around the foot of a
black, upstanding rock. Here on a ledge above the water's
edge stood a young girl chained by the arms, lips parted,
eyes open and staring, face white as her linen garment. She
might have been a statue, so still she stood, while the light
breeze fluttered her dress and stirred her loosened hair. As
Perseus looked at her and looked at the sea, the water began
to boil again, and miles out a long gray scaly back of vast
length lifted itself above the flood. At that, there was a shriek
from a distant knoll where he could dimly see the forms of
people, but the girl shrank a little and said nothing. Then
Perseus, taking off the hat of darkness, alighted near the
maiden to talk to her, and she, though nearly mad with
terror, found words at last to tell him her tale.

Her name was Andromeda, and she was the only child
of the king and of his wife, Cassiopeia. Queen Cassiopeia
was exceedingly beautiful, so that all people marveled at her.
She herself was proud of her dark eyes, her white, slender
fingers, and her long black hair, so proud that she had been

heard to boast that she was fairer even than the sea nymphs, who are daughters of Nereus. At this, Nereus in wrath stirred up Poseidon, who came flooding in over the land, covering it far and wide. Not content with this, he sent a vast monster from the dark depths of the bottomless sea to ravage the whole coast of Ethiopia. When the unfortunate king and queen had sought the advice of the oracle on how to appease the god, they had been ordered to sacrifice their only daughter
230 to the sea monster Poseidon had sent. Not daring for their people's sake to disobey, they had chained her to this rock, where she now awaited the beast who should devour her.

Perseus comforted Andromeda as he stood by her on the rock, and she shrank closer against him while the great gray back writhed its half-mile length slowly towards the land. Then, bidding Andromeda hide her face, Perseus sprang once more into the air, unveiling the dreadful head of dead Medusa to the monster, which reared its dripping jaws yards high into the air. The mighty tail stiffened all of
240 a sudden, the boiling of the water ceased, and only the gentle waves of the receding ocean lapped around a long, gray ridge of stone. Then Perseus freed Andromeda and restored her to her father and beautiful mother. Thereafter, with their consent, he married her amid scenes of tremendous rejoicing, and with his bride set sail at last for the kingdom of Polydectes.

Polydectes had lost no time on the departure of Perseus. First he had begged Danae to become his wife, and then he had threatened her. Undoubtedly, he would have got his
250 way by force if Danae had not fled in terror to Dictys. The two took refuge at the altar of a temple whence Polydectes did not dare drag them away. So matters stood when Perseus returned. Polydectes was enraged to see him, for he had hoped at least that Danae's most powerful protector would

RETELL

Go back to line 165, and retell what's happened to Perseus since he cut off Medusa's head.

_____
_____
_____
_____
_____
_____
_____
_____
_____
_____
_____
_____
_____
_____
_____
_____

never return. But now, seeing him famous and with a king's daughter to wife, he could not contain himself. Openly he laughed at the tale of Perseus, saying that the hero had never killed the Gorgon, only pretended to, and that now he was claiming an honor he did not deserve. At this, Perseus, 260 enraged by the insult and by reports of his mother's persecution, said to him, "You asked me for the Gorgon's head. Behold it!" And with that he lifted it high, and Polydectes became stone.

Then Perseus left Dictys to be king of that island, but he himself went back to the Grecian mainland to seek out his grandfather, Acrisios, who was once again king of Argos. First, however, he gave back to the gods the gifts they had given him. Hermes took back the golden sandals and the hat of darkness, for both are his. But Athene took Medusa's 270 head, and she hung it on a fleece around her neck as part

Head of Medusa (detail) from a plaster cast of *Perseus Triumphant* by Antonio Canova (1757–1822).

of her battle equipment, where it may be seen in statues and portraits of the warlike goddess.

Perseus took ship for Greece, but his fame had gone before him, and King Acrisios fled secretly from Argos in terror, since he remembered the prophecy and feared that Perseus had come to avenge the wrongs of Danae. The trembling old Acrisios took refuge in Larissa, where it happened the king was holding a great athletic contest in honor of his dead father.

280   Heroes from all over Greece, among whom was Perseus, came to the games. As Perseus was competing at the discus throwing, he threw high into the air and far beyond the rest. A strong wind caught the discus as it spun, so that it left the course marked out for it and was carried into the stands. People scrambled away to right and left. Only Acrisios was not nimble enough. The heavy weight fell full on his foot and crushed his toes, and at that, the feeble old man, already weakened by his terrors, died from the shock. Thus the prophecy of Apollo was fulfilled at last;

290 Acrisios was killed by his grandson. Then Perseus came into his kingdom, where he reigned with Andromeda long and happily.

EVALUATE

One reason the Greeks created this myth was to show that no one can escape fate. What do you think of the ancient Greek idea that no one can escape fate? Give reasons for your answer.

Medusa's Head

Myth Chart   Myths, an early form of fiction, have their own unique characteristics, some of which are listed in the chart below. For each characteristic, give an example from "Medusa's Head."

Characteristics of Myths	Examples from "Medusa's Head"
Heroes often have supernatural powers.	
Gods and goddesses are characters.	
Monsters threaten the hero.	
Explanations are provided for natural occurrences.	
Metamorphoses (magical changes) take place.	
Cultural values are expressed.	

Skills Review

Medusa's Head

VOCABULARY AND COMPREHENSION

A. Clarifying Word Meanings: Synonyms   Replace each word or phrase in parentheses with its synonym from the Word Bank.

Word Bank

descended
perplexity
perpetual
recesses
hovered

1. He lit a candle and entered the dark (hollow places) _____ of the cave.

2. In his (confusion) _____ he went down the wrong tunnel.

3. Following the path, he (came down) _____ deeper into the cave.

4. The cave walls were always wet from the (constant) _____ dripping of water from the stream above.

5. It seemed as if a thousand bats (floated) _____ above his head.

B. Reading Comprehension   Answer each question below.

1. Why does Perseus set off on his dangerous journey? _____

_____

2. How does Perseus cut off the Gorgon's head? _____

_____

3. What happens to Polydectes toward the end of the story? _____

_____

4. How does King Acrisios finally meet his fate? _____

_____

Vocabulary Skills
Identify synonyms.

Little Red Riding-Hood

retold by Patricia Pierce

LITERARY FOCUS: FOLK TALES

Some of the first stories you ever heard were probably **folk tales.** Folk tales are stories that

- have no known author
- are passed from one generation to another by word of mouth
- tell of fantastic events that could never happen in real life
- have heroes or villains, called **tricksters,** who try to outwit others
- teach **morals,** or practical lessons about how to get along in the world

A **fairy tale** is one kind of folk tale. Some famous fairy tales you may have heard of are "Cinderella" and "Rumpelstiltskin." As you read "Little Red Riding-Hood," think about the elements that make it a fairy tale.

READING SKILLS: MAKING PREDICTIONS

Maybe you can't tell the future, but you can make a prediction. A **prediction** is a guess about what will happen. To make a prediction, you need just two things: information and experience. To make a prediction about a story, you take note of details and other information in the text. You connect that information with experiences you've had or observations you've made, leading you to predict how such and such a character will behave or what might happen next.

Make predictions as you read "Little Red Riding-Hood." Don't be disappointed if a prediction does not come true. Adjust your prediction, and keep on reading.

SKILLS FOCUS

Literary Skills
Understand folk tales.

Reading Skills
Make predictions.

Little Red Riding-Hood

retold by Patricia Pierce

Once upon a time there was a little village girl, the prettiest ever seen; her mother doted upon her, and so did her grandmother. She, good woman, made for her a little red hood which suited her so well, that everyone called her Little Red Riding-Hood.

One day her mother, who had just made some cakes, said to her: "My dear, you shall go and see how your grandmother is, for I have heard she is ailing; take her this cake and this little pot of butter. Go quickly, and don't talk to strangers on the way."

Little Red Riding-Hood started off at once for her grandmother's cottage, which was in another village.

While passing through a wood she walked slowly, often stopping to pick flowers. She looked back and saw a wolf approaching, so she stopped and waited. The wolf, who would very much liked to have eaten her, dared not, because some woodcutters were nearby in the forest. So he said, "Good morning, Red Riding-Hood. Where are you going?"

The poor child, who did not know it was dangerous to talk to a wolf, answered, "I am going to see my grandmother, to take her a cake and a little pot of butter that my mother sends her."

"Does she live a great way off?" said the wolf.

PREDICT

In many folk and fairy tales a warning is issued to the hero or heroine. Underline the warning in paragraph 2. Do you predict it will be obeyed? Explain.

_____

_____

_____

_____

_____

_____

IDENTIFY

In lines 20–23, what warning is Little Red Riding-Hood forgetting?

_____

_____

_____

_____

_____

_____

"Pull the bobbin, and the latch will go up!"

PREDICT

Pause at line 30. What do you predict will happen next?

"Oh, yes!" said Little Red Riding-Hood, "she lives beyond the mill you see right down there in the first house in the village."

"Well," said the wolf, "I shall go and see her too. I shall take this road, and you take that one, and let us see who

30 will get there first!"

The wolf set off at a gallop along the shortest road; but the little girl took the longest way and amused herself by gathering nuts, running after butterflies, and plucking daisies and buttercups.

The wolf soon reached her grandmother's cottage; he knocked at the door—*rap, rap.*

"Who's there?"

" 'Tis your grand-daughter, Little Red Riding-Hood," said the wolf in a shrill voice, "and I have brought you a
40 cake and a little pot of butter that my mother sends you."

The good old grandmother, who was ill in bed, called out, "Pull the bobbin, and the latch will go up!"

The wolf pulled the bobbin and the door opened. He leaped on the old woman and gobbled her up in a minute; for he had had no dinner for three days **past.**

Then he shut the door and rolled himself up in the grandmother's bed, to wait for Little Red Riding-Hood.

In a while she came knocking at the door—*rap, rap.*

"Who's there?"

50 Little Red Riding-Hood, who heard the gruff voice of the wolf, was frightened at first, but thinking that her grandmother had a cold, answered, " 'Tis your grand-daughter, Little Red Riding-Hood, and I have brought you a cake and a little pot of butter that my mother sends you."

Then the wolf called to her in as soft a voice as he could, "Pull the bobbin, and the latch will go up." Little Red Riding-Hood pulled the bobbin and the door opened.

When the wolf saw her come in, he covered himself up with the sheets, and said, "Put the cake and the little pot of
60 butter on the chest, and come and lie down beside me."

Little Red Riding-Hood went over to the bed; she was surprised to see how strange her grandmother looked in her nightcap. But she took off her cloak and hung it up, then went back and sat down by the bed. She looked at her grandmother again with great interest.

WORD STUDY

Circle the word *bobbin* (line 42), an old-fashioned term. Look at the illustration on page 150. Find the bobbin, and write a definition.

_____

_____

_____

_____

WORD STUDY

past (past) *adj.:* gone by; preceding.

Don't confuse *past* with the verb *passed. Past* refers to time that has gone by. *Passed* is the past tense of *pass,* which means "go from one place to another" or "go through a test successfully."

IDENTIFY

Pause at line 54. In what way is the wolf a **trickster,** someone who tries to outwit others?

_____

_____

_____

_____

_____

_____

_____

_____

_____

_____

_____

_____

_____

_____

_____

_____

_____

_____

_____

_____

_____

_____

She said to her, "Oh, grandmamma, grandmamma, what great arms you have got!"

"All the better to hug you with, my dear!"

70 "Oh, grandmamma, grandmamma, what great legs you have got!" she said.

"All the better to run with, my dear!"

"Oh grandmamma, grandmamma, what great ears you have got!" said the little girl.

"All the better to hear you with, my dear!"

"Oh grandmamma, grandmamma, what great eyes you have got!" she said, beginning to get frightened.

"All the better to see you with, my dear!"

"Oh, grandmamma, grandmamma, what great *teeth* you have got!" said Little Red Riding-Hood.

80 "All the better to gobble you up!" said the wicked wolf, suddenly sitting up in the bed, drooling with hunger.

Little Red Riding-Hood screamed with terror and leapt up from her chair. Then a shot from a gun was heard, and the wicked wolf dropped back in the bed—dead.

A woodcutter who was passing had heard the cries of Little Red Riding-Hood, popped his gun through the window, and shot the wolf in time to save her. The wood-cutter rushed into the cottage and picked up Little Red Riding-Hood, who was trembling with fright. She was able

90 to tell the woodcutter, between her tears, that the wolf had eaten up her grandmother. Quick as a wink, the woodcutter cut open the wolf's stomach and rescued the old lady, who soon recovered from her dreadful experience. She thanked the woodcutter for his timely arrival, and for saving both her and Little Red Riding-Hood. They both waved goodbye, when he left to go back to his work in the forest.

The old lady hugged her dear little grand-daughter and asked if she might have a cup of tea, please.

"Yes, of course," said Little Red Riding-Hood. She put
100 the kettle on and put out the cake her mother had made on
a pretty little plate. While she was waiting for the kettle to
boil, she made her grandmother comfortable once more.

All Little Red Riding-Hood really wanted to do was to
go home to her mother, for she was still very frightened by
all that had happened. So she kissed her grandmother
goodbye and ran all the way home. When she came to the
cottage, she found her mother waiting for her at the door.

The mother drew Little Red Riding-Hood in, and
listened to her story of all that had happened. She was
110 delighted to have her little girl home safely again, and
Little Red Riding-Hood was so happy to be out of danger
that she promised her mother never to be disobedient
any more.

INTERPRET

Re-read the last paragraph of
this story. What lesson does
Little Red Riding-Hood (and
all the children listening to
this tale) learn?

_____
_____
_____
_____
_____
_____
_____
_____
_____
_____
_____
_____
_____
_____
_____
_____
_____
_____
_____
_____

Little Red Riding-Hood

Literary Skills
Analyze folk tales.

Folk-Tale Grid   A **folk tale** is a story that has been passed on anonymously from generation to generation. Folk tales usually teach lessons, which is why they are often told to children. The same character types tend to show up in folk tales: the handsome prince, the all-good princess, the clever trickster, the evil giant. Complete the following graphic organizer to see how "Little Red Riding-Hood" qualifies as a folk tale.

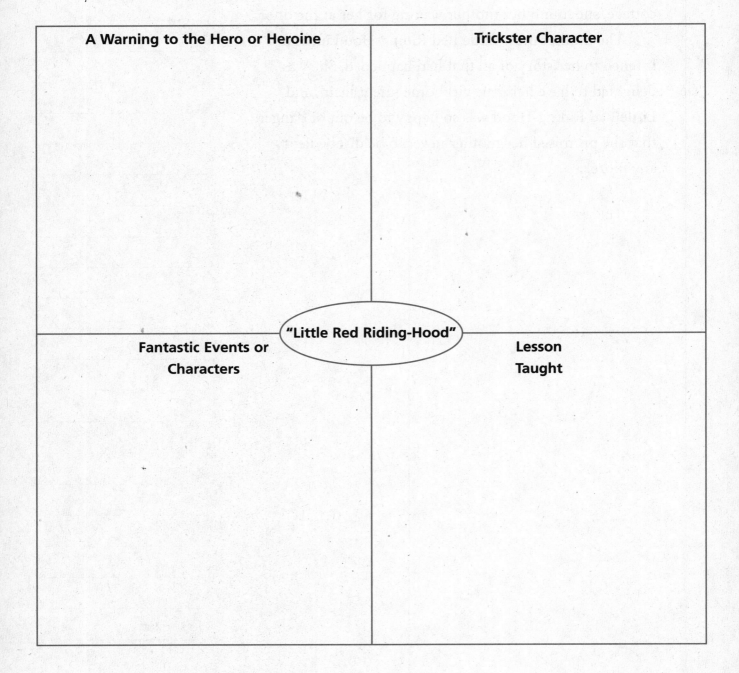

A Warning to the Hero or Heroine

Trickster Character

"Little Red Riding-Hood"

Fantastic Events or Characters

Lesson Taught

Skills Review

Little Red Riding-Hood

COMPREHENSION

Reading Comprehension   Answer the following questions.

1. What does Little Red Riding-Hood's mother tell her not to do on her journey?

   _____

   _____

   _____

2. Whom does Little Red Riding-Hood meet on her walk through the forest? _____

   _____

   _____

   _____

3. How does the wolf manage to get into the grandmother's house? What does the

   wolf do once he gets in her house? _____

   _____

   _____

   _____

4. What magical event happens after the woodcutter rescues Little Red Riding-Hood?

   _____

   _____

   _____

5. What lesson does Little Red Riding-Hood learn from her adventure? _____

   _____

   _____

   _____

Biography and Autobiography: Unforgettable Personalities

Academic Vocabulary for Collection 5

These are the terms you should know
as you read and analyze the selections in this collection.

———————

Point of View The vantage point from which a story is told. Two
common points of view are **first-person point of view** and
third-person point of view. In the **first-person point of view,**
the narrator takes part in the story and uses the personal
pronoun *I* to refer to himself or herself. In the **third-person
point of view,** the narrator stands outside the action and refers
to story characters using third-person pronouns: *his, her, their,
he, she, they,* and *them.*

● ● ●

Nonfiction Writing that deals with real people, events, and places
without changing any facts. Biography and autobiography are
forms of nonfiction.

Fiction Prose writing that is made up rather than true.

● ● ●

Autobiography The story of a person's life, written or told by
that person. Important events in the person's life are usually
presented in **chronological order.** Autobiography is written
in the **first person.**

Biography The story of a person's life, written or told by another
person. Biography is written in the **third person.** To find out
about the person, the biographer uses many sources:

- interviews with people who knew the person
- firsthand accounts, such as letters and journals
- newspaper and magazine articles that refer to the person
- historical accounts of the period

Before You Read

Storm by Gary Paulsen

LITERARY FOCUS: FIRST-PERSON POINT OF VIEW

Every story has a storyteller, or **narrator,** and is told from a point of view. When the narrator is also a story character, the story is told from the **first-person point of view.** If the narrator tells the story and never takes part in the action, the story is told from the **third-person point of view.** Once a narrator refers to himself or herself as *I,* you know immediately that the story is told in the first person. Here are some examples of types of narration:

First-Person Narration	Third-Person Narration
When the sun went down, I could barely see my hands in front of my face. It was that dark. I shivered and headed for my tent.	When the sun went down, Mike could barely see his hands in front of his face. It was that dark. Mike shivered and headed for his tent.

In "Storm," Gary Paulsen, the narrator, tells his true adventure story in the first person.

READING SKILLS: FINDING THE MAIN IDEA

The **main idea** is the most important idea in a piece of nonfiction. Sometimes a writer states the main idea directly. At other times the writer only hints at the main idea and lets the reader **infer** it, or guess what it is.

To find the main idea, follow these steps:
- Look at the **key details** or **important events** in the text.
- Look for an idea that is stated several times in different words.
- Look for **key passages** where the writer sums up the main idea.
- See if the **title** suggests the main idea.
- Create a **main idea statement** that is supported by the details. Be aware that there may be more than one main idea in a piece of writing.

SKILLS FOCUS

Literary Skills
Understand first-person point of view.

Reading Skills
Find the main idea.

Vocabulary Skills
Clarify word meanings by using prefixes.

VOCABULARY DEVELOPMENT

PREVIEW SELECTION VOCABULARY

Before you read "Storm," become familiar with these words.

disengage (dis′in·gāj′) *v.:* unfasten.

> *Before I disengage the leash, I get the dog under control.*

regain (ri·gān′) *v.:* recover.

> *I stopped to let the dog rest and regain her strength.*

emit (ē·mit′) *v.:* give out; send forth.

> *Dogs emit quick breaths when they pant.*

PREFIXES

A **prefix** is a word part added to the beginning of a word or to a base to create a new word. The chart below shows some common prefixes and how they are used. Look for prefixes as you read the story that follows.

Prefix	Meaning	Example Words
dis–	away, opposing, not	disagree, disapprove
re–	again, back, anew	react, rebuild, replay
e–	out	emotion, emigrate

from **Woodsong**

STORM

Gary Paulsen

> **BACKGROUND: Literature and Social Studies**
>
> "Storm" is taken from *Woodsong,* the true account of
> Gary Paulsen's adventures with his sled dogs in northern
> Minnesota. Paulsen later ran the Iditarod (i·dit′ə·räd),
> a dog-sled race across Alaska.

IDENTIFY

Pause at line 4. What is the
reason the **narrator,** the person telling this story, says he
is writing about "one dog"?

_____

_____

_____

_____

_____

IDENTIFY

What does the narrator reveal
about Storm's **character** in
lines 9–15? Underline those
details.

It is always possible to learn from dogs, and in fact the longer
I'm with them, the more I understand how little I know. But
there was one dog who taught me the most. Just one dog.
Storm.

First dog. . . .

Joy, loyalty, toughness, peacefulness—all of these were
part of Storm. Lessons about life and, finally, lessons about
death came from him.

He had a bear's ears. He was brindle colored[1] and built
10 like a truck, and his ears were rounded when we got him,
so that they looked like bear cub ears. They gave him a
comical look when he was young that somehow hung on
to him even when he grew old. He had a sense of humor
to match his ears, and when he grew truly old, he somehow
resembled George Burns.[2]

---

1. **brindle colored:** gray or brown and streaked or spotted with a
   dark color.
2. **George Burns** (1896–1996): American comedian and actor with
   large ears.

Excerpt (retitled "Storm") from *Woodsong* by
Gary Paulsen. Copyright © 1990 by Gary
Paulsen. Reproduced by permission of **Simon
& Schuster Books for Young Readers, an
imprint of Simon & Schuster Children's
Publishing Division.**

At peak, he was a mighty dog. He pulled like a machine. Until we retired him and used him only for training puppies, until we let him loose to enjoy his age, he pulled, his back over in the power curve, so that nothing could stop the sled.

20   In his fourth or fifth year as a puller, he started doing tricks. First he would play jokes on the dog pulling next to him. On long runs he would become bored, and when we least expected it, he would reach across the gang line and snort wind into the ear of the dog next to him. I ran him with many different dogs and he did it to all of them—chuckling when the dog jumped and shook his or her head—but I never saw a single dog get mad at him for it. Oh, there was once a dog named Fonzie who nearly took his head off, but Fonzie wasn't really mad at him so much

30   as surprised. Fonzie once nailed me through the wrist for waking him up too suddenly when he was sleeping. I'd reached down and touched him before whispering his name.

© Joe McDonald/CORBIS.

DRAW CONCLUSIONS

Based on the details in lines 28–32, how would you describe Fonzie?

IDENTIFY

Read lines 39–74 carefully. Underline key details or events. Circle repeated ideas.

_____

_____

_____

_____

_____

_____

_____

_____

_____

_____

_____

_____

_____

_____

_____

_____

_____

_____

_____

Small jokes. Gentle jokes, Storm played. He took to hiding things from me. At first I couldn't understand where things were going. I would put a bootie down while working on a dog, and it would disappear. I lost a small ladle[3] I used for watering each dog, a cloth glove liner I took off while working on a dog's feet, a roll of tape, and finally, a hat.

He was so clever.

40 When I lost the hat, it was a hot day and I had taken the hat off while I worked on a dog's harness. The dog was just ahead of Storm, and when I knelt to work on the harness—he'd chewed almost through the side of it while running—I put the hat down on the snow near Storm.

Or thought I had. When I had changed the dog's harness, I turned and the hat was gone. I looked around, moved the dogs, looked under them, then shrugged. At first I was sure I'd put the hat down; then, when I couldn't find it, I became less sure, and at last I thought perhaps I had

50 left it at home or dropped it somewhere on the run.

Storm sat quietly, looking ahead down the trail, not showing anything at all.

I went back to the sled, reached down to **disengage** the hook, and when I did, the dogs exploded forward. I was not quite on the sled when they took off, so I was knocked slightly off balance. I leaned over to the right to **regain** myself, and when I did, I accidentally dragged the hook through the snow.

And pulled up my hat.

60 It had been buried off to the side of the trail in the snow, buried neatly with the snow smoothed over the top, so that it was completely hidden. Had the snow hook not scraped down four or five inches, I never would have found it.

VOCABULARY

disengage (dis′in·gāj′) _v._: unfasten.

regain (ri·gān′) _v._: recover.

---

3. **ladle** _n._: cup-shaped spoon with a long handle for dipping out liquids.

I stopped the sled and set the hook once more. While knocking the snow out of the hat and putting it back on my head, I studied where it had happened.

Right next to Storm.

He had taken the hat, quickly dug a hole, buried the hat and smoothed the snow over it, then gone back to sitting, staring ahead, looking completely innocent.

When I stopped the sled and picked up the hat, he looked back, saw me put the hat on my head, and—I swear—smiled. Then he shook his head once and went back to work pulling.

Along with the jokes, Storm had scale eyes. He watched as the sled was loaded, carefully calculated the weight of each item, and let his disapproval be known if it went too far.

One winter a friend gave us a parlor stove with nickel trim. It was not an enormous stove, but it had some weight to it and some bulk. This friend lived twelve miles away— twelve miles over two fair hills followed by about eight miles on an old, abandoned railroad grade.[4] We needed the stove badly (our old barrel stove had started to burn through), so I took off with the team to pick it up. I left early in the morning because I wanted to get back that same day. It had snowed four or five inches, so the dogs would have to break trail. By the time we had done the hills and the railroad grade, pushing in new snow all the time, they were ready for a rest. I ran them the last two miles to where the stove was and unhooked their tugs so they could rest while I had coffee.

We stopped for an hour at least, the dogs sleeping quietly. When it was time to go, my friend and I carried the stove outside and put it in the sled. The dogs didn't move.

Except for Storm.

70

80

90

---

4. **railroad grade:** rise or elevation in a railroad track.

FLUENCY

Read the boxed text aloud. Try to capture the narrator's amused tone as he describes Storm's joke. Where might his tone change to amazement? See if you can capture that change in tone when you read the text a second or third time.

WORD STUDY

What do you think it means that the dogs will have to "break trail" (line 87)? Read on, and circle the context clue that helps you figure out what it means to break trail.

Pause at line 100. What do you think Storm will do after the stove is loaded on the sled?

_____

_____

_____

_____

_____

_____

_____

_____

What do you think Storm might be saying when he growls at the stove (lines 116 and 121)?

_____

_____

_____

_____

_____

_____

_____

_____

_____

He raised his head, opened one eye, did a perfect double take—both eyes opening wide—and sat up. He had been facing the front. Now he turned around to face the sled—so he was facing away from the direction we had to travel when we left—and watched us load the sled.

It took some time, as the stove barely fit on the sled and had to be jiggled and shuffled around to get it down between the side rails.

Through it all, Storm sat and watched us, his face a study in interest. He did not get up but sat on his back end, and when I was done and ready to go, I hooked all the dogs back in harness—which involved hooking the tugs to the rear ties on their harnesses. The dogs knew this meant we were going to head home, so they got up and started slamming against the tugs, trying to get the sled to move.

All of them, that is, but Storm.

Storm sat backward, the tug hooked up but hanging down. The other dogs were screaming to run, but Storm sat and stared at the stove.

Not at me, not at the sled, but at the stove itself. Then he raised his lips, bared his teeth, and growled at the stove.

When he was finished growling, he snorted twice, stood, turned away from the stove, and started to pull. But each time we stopped at the tops of the hills to let the dogs catch their breath after pulling the sled and stove up the steep incline, Storm turned and growled at the stove.

The enemy.

The weight on the sled.

I do not know how many miles Storm and I ran together. Eight, ten, perhaps twelve thousand miles. He was one of the first dogs and taught me the most, and as we worked together, he came to know me better than perhaps even my

own family. He could look once at my shoulders and tell how I was feeling, tell how far we were to run, how fast we had to run—knew it all.

130　　When I started to run long, moved from running a work team, a trap line team, to training for the Iditarod, Storm took it in stride, changed the pace down to the long trot, matched what was needed, and settled in for the long haul.

He did get bored, however, and one day while we were running a long run, he started doing a thing that would stay with him—with us—until the end. We had gone forty or fifty miles on a calm, even day with no bad wind. The

Notes

PREDICT

Pause at line 144. What might happen next?

_____

_____

_____

_____

_____

_____

VISUALIZE

Circle the details in lines 136–148 that help you picture the **setting**. Underline the details that help you see each of Storm's actions.

INFER

What do Storm's actions with the stick in lines 150–165 tell you about him?

_____

_____

_____

_____

_____

VOCABULARY

emit (ē·mit′) v.: give out; send forth.

140 temperature was a perfect ten below zero. The sun was bright, everything was moving well, and the dogs had settled into the rhythm that could take them a hundred or a thousand miles.

And Storm got bored.

At a curve in the trail, a small branch came out over the path we were running, and as Storm passed beneath the limb, he jumped up and grabbed it, broke a short piece off— about a foot long—and kept it in his mouth.

All day.

150 And into the night. He ran, carrying the stick like a toy, and when we stopped to feed or rest, he would put the stick down, eat, then pick it up again. He would put the stick down carefully in front of him, or across his paws, and sleep, and when he awakened, he would pick up the stick, and it soon became a thing between us, the stick.

He would show it to me, making a contact, a connection between us, each time we stopped. I would pet him on top of the head and take the stick from him—he would **emit** a low, gentle growl when I took the stick. I'd "examine" it closely,
160 nod and seem to approve of it, and hand it back to him.

Each day we ran, he would pick a different stick. And each time I would have to approve of it, and after a time, after weeks and months, I realized that he was using the sticks as a way to communicate with me, to tell me that everything was all right, that I was doing the right thing.

Once, when I pushed them too hard during a pre-Iditarod race—when I thought it was important to compete and win (a feeling that didn't last long)—I walked up to Storm, and as I came close to him, he pointedly dropped
170 the stick. I picked it up and held it out, but he wouldn't take it. He turned his face away. I put the stick against his

lips and tried to make him take it, but he let it fall to the ground. When I realized what he was doing, I stopped and fed and rested the team, sat on the sled, and thought about what I was doing wrong. After four hours or so of sitting— watching other teams pass me—I fed them another snack, got ready to go, and was gratified to see Storm pick up the stick. From time forward I looked for the stick always, knew when I saw it out to the sides of his head that I was doing the right thing. And it was always there.

180

Through storms and cold weather, on the long runs, the long, long runs where there isn't an end to it, where only the sled and the winter around the sled and the wind are there, Storm had the stick to tell me it was right, all things were right.

IDENTIFY

This story is true. It is told from the **first-person point of view**—by the person who experienced these events. What has the narrator of this story learned about himself and his dogs?

Storm

Literary Skills
Analyze point
of view.

Point-of-View Questionnaire   Understanding the characteristics of an
autobiography or a biography helps you focus on what you read. Use the
following questionnaire to help you analyze "Storm."

1. **Who is the narrator of this story?**

The author, Gary Paulsen

2. **What does the narrator tell you about the main characters?**

got along really well

3. **Does the narrator tell you what the characters think and feel? Explain.**

Yes, with Storm and the other guy
they used a/the stick to communicate.

4. **From which point of view is this story told?**

1st person (author/narrator)

5. **Does the narrator use the pronoun / to refer to himself?**

Yes

6. **What do you think is the relationship between the narrator and the writer of this story?**

they are the same person, so I
don't really know if there really is a
relationship between the same person.

7. **This story is an example of** ___autobiographical___ **writing.**
   (circle one)   biographical   (autobiographical)

Skills Review

Storm

VOCABULARY AND COMPREHENSION

A. Prefixes   Write the meaning of each prefix below. Then, write the Word Bank word that contains each prefix.

Prefix	Prefix Meaning	Word with Prefix
e–	out	emit
dis–	undo	disengage
re–	again	regain

B. Reading Comprehension   Write **T** or **F** next to each statement to show whether it is true or false.

F **1.** Storm blew in his teammates' ears in order to upset them.

T **2.** Storm hid the narrator's hat in the snow.

F **3.** Storm was pleased to pull the stove on the sled.

F **4.** Storm used a scale to measure the weight of the stove.

T **5.** Storm used a stick to communicate with the narrator.

SKILLS FOCUS

Vocabulary Skills
Understand prefixes.

A Glory over Everything by Ann Petry

LITERARY FOCUS: THIRD-PERSON POINT OF VIEW

A **biography** is the true story of a person's life written by somebody else. Suppose you wrote a biography of George Washington. You, the narrator, would not be part of the story, and you would use pronouns like *he, she,* and *they* to refer to the story characters. This type of writing is described as being from the **third-person point of view.**

"A Glory over Everything" is from a biography about Harriet Tubman, a famous conductor on the Underground Railroad. As you read, notice how the author uses third-person point of view to describe the events and what she imagines to be the characters' thoughts and feelings.

READING SKILLS: FOLLOWING THE SEQUENCE

Sequence is the order in which things happen. Most stories are written in **chronological order**—the events are related in the order in which they occur. Writers use time-order words, such as *first, later, then,* and *when,* to tell you when events occur.

As you read "A Glory over Everything," complete a chart like the one below to keep track of Tubman's journey. You should record at least six events. Use time-order words to show when the events occur. Three examples have been done for you.

SKILLS FOCUS

Literary Skills
Understand biography and third-person point of view.

Reading Skills
Understand sequence.

Vocabulary Skills
Clarify word meanings by using contrast.

Sequence Chart

When	What Happens
When Harriet learns that she has been sold,	she decides to escape.
While John Tubman sleeps,	Harriet takes food and a quilt and leaves the cabin.
Once she reaches the woods,	she goes to the farmhouse of a woman who gives her the names of two stops on the Underground Railroad.

VOCABULARY DEVELOPMENT

PREVIEW SELECTION VOCABULARY

You may want to preview these words before you begin reading the story.

elude (ē·lo͞od′) *v.:* escape the notice of; avoid detection by.

A runaway must elude the patrol.

inexplicable (in·eks′pli·kə·bəl) *adj.:* not explainable.

Tubman's inexplicable seizures put her at risk.

legitimate (lə·jit′ə·mət) *adj.:* here, reasonable or justified.

Runaways had a legitimate reason to fear capture.

defiant (dē·fī′ənt) *adj.:* disobedient; boldly resisting.

Harriet's defiant manner disturbed Dr. Thompson.

sinewy (sin′yo͞o·ē) *adj.:* strong; tough.

Her arms were sinewy from hard work.

CLARIFYING WORD MEANINGS: CONTRAST

When you contrast two things, you look for ways in which they are different from each other. Sometimes contrast clues can help you understand the meaning of a new word. **Contrast clues** tell you what the unknown word is *not*. In the sentence below, the words in italics provide a contrast clue to the meaning of *restrain*.

At first, Pia used a leash to restrain her puppy. Now that the puppy is trained, she lets him *walk freely* by her side.

Read each sentence below, and underline the word or words that show a contrast with the boldface word. Refer to the definitions above for help.

1. The meat in the stew was **sinewy,** but the vegetables were soft and mushy.

2. Her **inexplicable** poem confused everyone. Later, she explained it, and everyone got the message.

3. The cat's **defiant** movements rattled the cage. It became well behaved again when Huey gave it some catnip.

from Harriet Tubman: Conductor on
the Underground Railroad

A Glory over Everything

Ann Petry

IDENTIFY

Pause at line 6. What type of **narrator** is telling this story? (Remember that it's a biography—a story of a person's life told by someone else.)

_____

_____

One day in 1849, when Harriet was working in the fields near the edge of the road, a white woman wearing a faded sunbonnet went past, driving a wagon. She stopped the wagon and watched Harriet for a few minutes. Then she spoke to her, asked her what her name was, and how she had acquired the deep scar on her forehead.

© Royalty-Free/CORBIS.

Harriet told her the story of the blow she had received when she was a girl. After that, whenever the woman saw her in the fields, she stopped to talk to her. She told Harriet that she lived on a farm near Bucktown. Then one day she said, not looking at Harriet but looking instead at the overseer[1] far off at the edge of the fields, "If you ever need any help, Harriet, ever need any help, why, you let me know."

That same year the young heir to the Brodas estate[2] died. Harriet mentioned the fact of his death to the white woman in the faded sunbonnet the next time she saw her. She told her of the panic-stricken talk in the quarter, told her that the slaves were afraid that the master, Dr. Thompson, would start selling them. She said that Doc Thompson no longer permitted any of them to hire their time.[3] The

---

1. **overseer** *n.:* person who supervises workers; in this case, a slave driver.
2. **Brodas estate:** Edward Brodas, the previous owner of the plantation, died in 1849 and left his property to his heir, who was not yet old enough to manage it. In the meantime the plantation was placed in the hands of the boy's guardian, Dr. Thompson.
3. **hire their time:** Some slaveholders allowed the people they held in slavery to hire themselves out for pay to other plantation owners who needed extra help. In such cases the workers were permitted to keep their earnings.

What kind of help do you think the white woman might be referring to (lines 12–13)?

_____

_____

_____

_____

_____

_____

Sequence is the order of events in a story. Time-order words and phrases like *soon, next,* and *that night* signal the order of events and the time that has passed. Circle five time-order words or phrases that you find in the first three paragraphs.

_____

_____

_____

_____

_____

_____

_____

_____

IDENTIFY

Re-read lines 27–32. Circle the reason Tubman doesn't want to travel alone.

COMPARE & CONTRAST

Re-read lines 33–49. In what way is Harriet's attitude different from her brothers'?

_____
_____
_____
_____
_____
_____
_____
_____
_____
_____
_____
_____

woman nodded her head, clucked to the horse, and drove off, murmuring, "If you ever need any help—"

The slaves were right about Dr. Thompson's intention. He began selling slaves almost immediately. Among the first ones sold were two of Harriet Tubman's sisters. They went south with the chain gang[4] on a Saturday.

When Harriet heard of the sale of her sisters, she knew that the time had finally come when she must leave the plantation. She was reluctant to attempt the long trip north 30 alone, not because of John Tubman's threat to betray her[5] but because she was afraid she might fall asleep somewhere along the way and so would be caught immediately.

She persuaded three of her brothers to go with her. Having made certain that John was asleep, she left the cabin quietly and met her brothers at the edge of the plantation. They agreed that she was to lead the way, for she was more familiar with the woods than the others.

The three men followed her, crashing through the underbrush, frightening themselves, stopping constantly 40 to say, "What was that?" or "Someone's coming."

She thought of Ben[6] and how he had said, "Any old body can go through a woods crashing and mashing things down like a cow." She said sharply, "Can't you boys go quieter? Watch where you're going!"

One of them grumbled, "Can't see in the dark. Ain't got cat's eyes like you."

"You don't need cat's eyes," she retorted. "On a night like this, with all the stars out, it's not black dark. Use your own eyes."

---

4. **chain gang** *n.*: group of prisoners chained together.
5. Harriet's husband, John Tubman, was a free man who was content with his life. He violently disapproved of his wife's plan to escape and threatened to tell the master if she carried it out.
6. **Ben**: Harriet Tubman's father. Her mother is called Old Rit.

50 　　She supposed they were doing the best they could, but they moved very slowly. She kept getting so far ahead of them that she had to stop and wait for them to catch up with her, lest they lose their way. Their progress was slow, uncertain. Their feet got tangled in every vine. They tripped over fallen logs, and once one of them fell flat on his face. They jumped, startled, at the most ordinary sounds: the murmur of the wind in the branches of the trees, the twittering of a bird. They kept turning around, looking back.

60 　　They had not gone more than a mile when she became aware that they had stopped. She turned and went back to them. She could hear them whispering. One of them called out, "Hat!"

　　"What's the matter? We haven't got time to keep stopping like this."

　　"We're going back."

　　"No," she said firmly. "We've got a good start. If we move fast and move quiet—"

　　Then all three spoke at once. They said the same thing, over and over, in frantic hurried whispers, all talking at 70 once:

　　They told her that they had changed their minds. Running away was too dangerous. Someone would surely see them and recognize them. By morning the master would know they had "took off." Then the handbills advertising them would be posted all over Dorchester County. The patterollers[7] would search for them. Even if they were lucky enough to **elude** the patrol, they could not possibly hide from the bloodhounds. The hounds would be baying after them, snuffing through the swamps and the underbrush,

---

7. **patterollers** *n.:* patrollers.

PREDICT

Pause at line 58. Tubman's brothers seem fearful about going on. What do you think might happen next?

_____

_____

_____

_____

_____

_____

IDENTIFY

What is the reason Tubman's brothers want to go back (lines 71–82)?

_____

_____

_____

_____

_____

_____

VOCABULARY

elude (ē·lood′) *v.:* escape the notice of; avoid detection by.

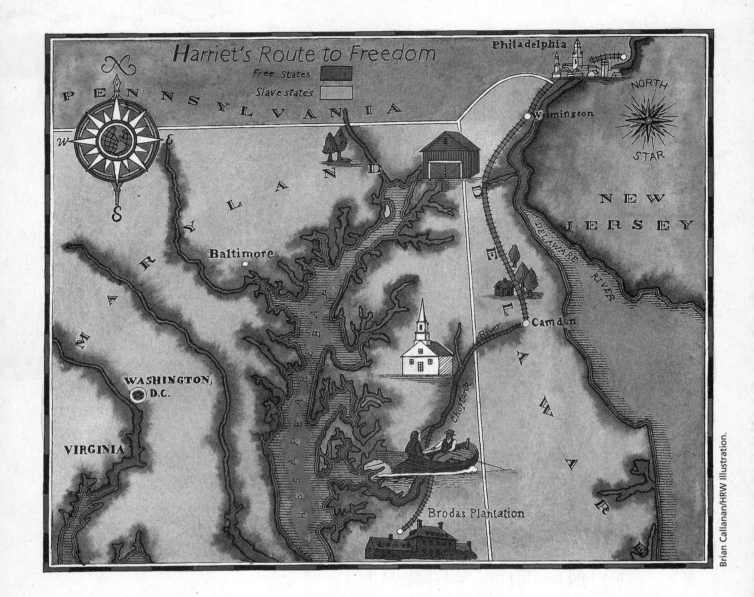

Harriet's Route to Freedom

Free States
Slave states

PENNSYLVANIA

Philadelphia

Wilmington

NORTH STAR

MARYLAND

NEW JERSEY

Baltimore

DELAWARE

DELAWARE RIVER

Choptank River

Camden

WASHINGTON, D.C.

CHESAPEAKE BAY

VIRGINIA

Brodas Plantation

Brian Callanan/HRW Illustration.

Brian Callanan/HRW Illustration.

Notes

80 zigzagging through the deepest woods. The bloodhounds
would surely find them. And everyone knew what happened
to a runaway who was caught and brought back alive.

　　She argued with them. Didn't they know that if they
went back they would be sold, if not tomorrow, then the
next day, or the next? Sold south. They had seen the chain
gangs. Was that what they wanted? Were they going to be
slaves for the rest of their lives? Didn't freedom mean anything to them?

"You're afraid," she said, trying to shame them into
action. "Go on back. I'm going north alone."

Instead of being ashamed, they became angry. They
shouted at her, telling her that she was a fool and they would
make her go back to the plantation with them. Suddenly
they surrounded her, three men, her own brothers, jostling
her, pushing her along, pinioning[8] her arms behind her.
She fought against them, wasting her strength, exhausting
herself in a furious struggle.

She was no match for three strong men. She said, pant-
ing, "All right. We'll go back. I'll go with you."

She led the way, moving slowly. Her thoughts were
bitter. Not one of them was willing to take a small risk in
order to be free. It had all seemed so perfect, so simple, to
have her brothers go with her, sharing the dangers of the
trip together, just as a family should. Now if she ever went
north, she would have to go alone.

Two days later, a slave working beside Harriet in the fields
motioned to her. She bent toward him, listening. He said
the water boy had just brought news to the field hands, and
it had been passed from one to the other until it reached
him. The news was that Harriet and her brothers had been
sold to the Georgia trader and that they were to be sent
south with the chain gang that very night.

Harriet went on working but she knew a moment of
panic. She would have to go north alone. She would have
to start as soon as it was dark. She could not go with the
chain gang. She might die on the way because of those
inexplicable sleeping seizures. But then she—how could
she run away? She might fall asleep in plain view along
the road.

---

8. **pinioning** (pin'yən·iŋ) v.: pinning.

INFER

Pause at line 99. Why do you
think Tubman's brothers prevent her from continuing
without them?

_____

_____

_____

RETELL

Briefly retell, in correct
sequence, what has happened in Tubman's life since
her sisters were sold (line 25).

_____

_____

_____

_____

_____

_____

_____

_____

_____

_____

VOCABULARY

inexplicable (in·eks'pli·kə·bəl)
adj.: not explainable.

FLUENCY

Read the boxed passage aloud until you can read it smoothly. Look for clues in the text, such as the word "murmured," that indicate how Tubman spoke.

VOCABULARY

legitimate (lə·jit′ə·mət) *adj.:* here, reasonable or justified.

defiant (dē·fī′ənt) *adj.:* disobedient; openly and boldly resisting.

INFER

Pause at line 143. Why do you think Tubman wanted someone to know she was leaving?

120　　　But even if she fell asleep, she thought, the Lord would take care of her. She murmured a prayer, "Lord, I'm going to hold steady on to You, and You've got to see me through."

　　　Afterward, she explained her decision to run the risk of going north alone in these words: "I had reasoned this out in my mind; there was one of two things I had a *right* to, liberty or death; if I could not have one, I would have the other; for no man should take me alive; I should fight for my liberty as long as my strength lasted, and when the time came for me to go, the Lord would let them take me."

130　　　At dusk, when the work in the fields was over, she started toward the Big House.[9] She had to let someone know that she was going north, someone she could trust. She no longer trusted John Tubman and it gave her a lost, lonesome feeling. Her sister Mary worked in the Big House, and she planned to tell Mary that she was going to run away, so someone would know.

　　　As she went toward the house, she saw the master, Doc Thompson, riding up the drive on his horse. She turned aside and went toward the quarter. A field hand

140　had no **legitimate** reason for entering the kitchen of the Big House—and yet—there must be some way she could leave word so that afterward someone would think about it and know that she had left a message.

　　　As she went toward the quarter, she began to sing. Dr. Thompson reined in his horse, turned around, and looked at her. It was not the beauty of her voice that made him turn and watch her, frowning; it was the words of the song that she was singing and something **defiant** in her manner that disturbed and puzzled him.

---

9. **Big House:** plantation owner's house.

150   *When that old chariot comes,*
              I'm going to leave you,
       I'm bound for the promised land,
              Friends, I'm going to leave you.

       I'm sorry, friends, to leave you,
              Farewell! Oh, farewell!
       But I'll meet you in the morning,
              Farewell! Oh, farewell!

       I'll meet you in the morning,
              When I reach the promised land;
160   *On the other side of Jordan,*
              For I'm bound for the promised land.

That night when John Tubman was asleep and the fire
had died down in the cabin, she took the ash cake that had
been baked for their breakfast and a good-sized piece of
salt herring and tied them together in an old bandanna. By
hoarding this small stock of food, she could make it last a
long time, and with the berries and edible roots she could
find in the woods, she wouldn't starve.

She decided that she would take the quilt[10] with her,
170 too. Her hands lingered over it. It felt soft and warm to her
touch. Even in the dark, she thought she could tell one color
from another because she knew its pattern and design so well.

Then John stirred in his sleep, and she left the cabin
quickly, carrying the quilt carefully folded under her arm.

Once she was off the plantation, she took to the woods,
not following the North Star, not even looking for it, going
instead toward Bucktown. She needed help. She was going
to ask the white woman who had stopped to talk to her so

DRAW
CONCLUSIONS

Why does Tubman choose to sing this particular song (lines 150–161)? Circle the details in the song that are clues for you—and for Tubman's sister.

_____
_____
_____
_____
_____
_____
_____
_____
_____
_____
_____
_____
_____
_____

IDENTIFY

Re-read lines 162–180. Underline words and phrases that reveal the **sequence** of events.

---

10. the quilt: Tubman had painstakingly stitched together a quilt before her wedding.

_____

_____

_____

_____

_____

_____

_____

_____

_____

_____

_____

_____

_____

_____

180 often if she would help her. Perhaps she wouldn't. But she would soon find out.

When she came to the farmhouse where the woman lived, she approached it cautiously, circling around it. It was so quiet. There was no sound at all, not even a dog barking or the sound of voices. Nothing.

She tapped on the door, gently. A voice said, "Who's there?" She answered, "Harriet, from Dr. Thompson's place."

When the woman opened the door, she did not seem at all surprised to see her. She glanced at the little bundle that Harriet was carrying, at the quilt, and invited her in.

190 Then she sat down at the kitchen table and wrote two names on a slip of paper and handed the paper to Harriet.

She said that those were the next places where it was safe for Harriet to stop. The first place was a farm where there was a gate with big white posts and round knobs on top of them. The people there would feed her, and when they thought it was safe for her to go on, they would tell her how to get to the next house or take her there. For these were the first two stops on the Underground Railroad— going north, from the eastern shore of Maryland.

200 Thus Harriet learned that the Underground Railroad that ran straight to the North was not a railroad at all. Neither did it run underground. It was composed of a loosely organized group of people who offered food and shelter, or a place of concealment, to fugitives who had set out on the long road to the North and freedom.

Harriet wanted to pay this woman who had befriended her. But she had no money. She gave her the patchwork quilt, the only beautiful object she had ever owned.

That night she made her way through the woods,
210 crouching in the underbrush whenever she heard the sound of horses' hoofs, staying there until the riders passed. Each

time, she wondered if they were already hunting for her. It would be so easy to describe her, the deep scar on her forehead like a dent, the old scars on the back of her neck, the husky speaking voice, the lack of height, scarcely five feet tall. The master would say she was wearing rough clothes when she ran away, that she had a bandanna on her head, that she was muscular and strong.

220   She knew how accurately he would describe her. One of the slaves who could read used to tell the others what it said on those handbills that were nailed up on the trees along the edge of the roads. It was easy to recognize the handbills that advertised runaways because there was always a picture in one corner, a picture of a black man, a little running figure with a stick over his shoulder and a bundle tied on the end of the stick.

     Whenever she thought of the handbills, she walked faster. Sometimes she stumbled over old grapevines, gnarled and twisted, thick as a man's wrist, or became

230 entangled in the tough **sinewy** vine of the honeysuckle. But she kept going.

     In the morning she came to the house where her friend had said she was to stop. She showed the slip of paper that she carried to the woman who answered her knock at the back door of the farmhouse. The woman fed her and then handed her a broom and told her to sweep the yard.

     Harriet hesitated, suddenly suspicious. Then she decided that with a broom in her hand, working in the yard, she would look as though she belonged on the place;

240 certainly no one would suspect that she was a runaway.

     That night the woman's husband, a farmer, loaded a wagon with produce. Harriet climbed in. He threw some blankets over her, and the wagon started.

VISUALIZE

Underline the details in lines 213–218 that help you picture what Tubman looked like.

INFER

Why does thinking of the handbills make Tubman walk faster (lines 227–228)?

_____
_____
_____
_____
_____
_____
_____
_____
_____
_____
_____
_____
_____
_____
_____
_____

VOCABULARY

sinewy (sin′yo͞o·ē) *adj.:* strong; firm; tough.

_____

_____

_____

_____

_____

_____

_____

_____

INFER

Pause at line 272. Why is Tubman amazed that white people would be willing to help her?

_____

_____

_____

_____

_____

_____

_____

_____

_____

_____

It was dark under the blankets and not exactly comfortable. But Harriet decided that riding was better than walking. She was surprised at her own lack of fear, wondered how it was that she so readily trusted these strangers who might betray her. For all she knew, the man driving the wagon might be taking her straight back to the master.

250 She thought of those other rides in wagons, when she was a child, the same clop-clop of the horses' feet, creak of the wagon, and the feeling of being lost because she did not know where she was going. She did not know her destination this time either, but she was not alarmed. She thought of John Tubman. By this time he must have told the master that she was gone. Then she thought of the plantation and how the land rolled gently down toward the river, thought of Ben and Old Rit, and that Old Rit would be inconsolable because her favorite daughter was missing. "Lord," she

260 prayed, "I'm going to hold steady onto You. You've got to see me through." Then she went to sleep.

The next morning, when the stars were still visible in the sky, the farmer stopped the wagon. Harriet was instantly awake.

He told her to follow the river, to keep following it to reach the next place where people would take her in and feed her. He said that she must travel only at night and she must stay off the roads because the patrol would be hunting for her. Harriet climbed out of the wagon. "Thank you,"

270 she said simply, thinking how amazing it was that there should be white people who were willing to go to such lengths to help a slave get to the North.

When she finally arrived in Pennsylvania, she had traveled roughly ninety miles from Dorchester County. She had slept on the ground outdoors at night. She had been rowed

for miles up the Choptank River by a man she had never seen before. She had been concealed in a haycock[11] and had, at one point, spent a week hidden in a potato hole in a cabin which belonged to a family of free Negroes.
280 She had been hidden in the attic of the home of a Quaker. She had been befriended by stout German farmers, whose guttural[12] speech surprised her and whose well-kept farms astonished her. She had never before seen barns and fences, farmhouses and outbuildings, so carefully painted. The cattle and horses were so clean they looked as though they had been scrubbed.

When she crossed the line into the free state of Pennsylvania, the sun was coming up. She said, "I looked at my hands to see if I was the same person now I was free.
290 There was such a glory over everything, the sun came like gold through the trees and over the fields, and I felt like I was in heaven."

© Royalty-Free/CORBIS.

---

11. **haycock:** pile of hay in a field.
12. **guttural** *adj.:* harsh, rasping.

Pause at line 286. Retell the events of Tubman's escape from slavery. Be sure you present the events in their proper **sequence**.

A Glory over Everything

Biography Chart   Most of the details in a biography are facts that can be proved true. But a biography sometimes contains details that cannot be proved true or false. These details are **inferences** the biographer makes after doing careful research.

In the chart below, identify two kinds of details in "A Glory over Everything." In the left-hand column, list details that can be proved true. In the right-hand column, list details that are probably based on the author's educated guesswork. Two examples have been done for you.

Details That Can Be Proved True	Details Inferred by the Author
In 1849, Harriet Tubman meets a woman who offers to give help.	"The woman nodded her head, clucked to the horse, and drove off, murmuring. . . ."

Skills Review

A Glory over Everything

VOCABULARY AND COMPREHENSION

A. Clarifying Word Meanings: Contrast   Fill in the blanks with words from the Word Bank that contrast with the italicized words.

Word Bank

elude
inexplicable
legitimate
defiant
sinewy

1. Ben thought he had a(n) _____ reason to skip the

   test. His teacher, however, said a stomachache was *not a good excuse.*

2. At first the people *obeyed* the unfair laws; then their actions became

   _____.

3. Joann left a(n) _____ note. Days later it *became*

   clear why she had decided to go.

4. The fish seemed to _____ my attempts to

   catch them.

5. Because my muscles were *flabby and weak,* I began working out.

   Now my muscles are strong and _____.

B. Reading Comprehension   Answer each question below.

1. Why did Harriet Tubman decide to escape alone? _____

   _____

2. Why did Tubman sing a song outside the Big House? _____

   _____

3. How did people on the Underground Railroad help Tubman? _____

   _____

4. Where was Tubman when she finally felt free? _____

   _____

SKILLS FOCUS

Vocabulary Skills
Clarify word meanings by using contrast.

Maya Angelou by Joyce Hansen
Life Doesn't Frighten Me by Maya Angelou

LITERARY FOCUS: NARRATOR AND POINT OF VIEW

Point of view is the standpoint from which a story is told. When a story's narrator is part of the story and uses the pronoun *I* to refer to himself or herself, the story is told from the **first-person point of view.** When a story's narrator is not part of the story and uses pronouns such as *he, she,* or *they* to refer to the story characters, the story is told from the **third-person point of view.**

The first selection that follows is from a biography of Maya Angelou. Like all biographies, it is written from the third-person point of view. The second selection is a poem written by Maya Angelou. The poem is written in the first person; its speaker tells her own story using the pronoun *I* to refer to herself.

READING SKILLS: MAKING INFERENCES

When you make an **inference,** you read between the lines. You use clues to figure out what a writer suggests but does not state directly. An inference is an educated guess.

Here is an example of an inference you could make while reading "A Glory over Everything" (page 172).

SKILLS FOCUS

Literary Skills
Understand narrator and point of view.

Reading Skills
Make inferences.

Vocabulary Skills
Clarify word meanings by using context clues.

Clues from the Selection	Possible Inference
"Then one day she said . . ., 'If you ever need any help, Harriet, ever need any help, why, you let me know.'"	The woman is kind, caring, and interested in Harriet.

As you read the next two selections, use text clues to draw inferences about Maya Angelou's character.

VOCABULARY DEVELOPMENT

PREVIEW SELECTION VOCABULARY

Get to know the following words before you read the selections that follow.

perceptive (pər·sep′tiv) *adj.:* able to comprehend through insight or intuition.

Maya was helped by a perceptive teacher who recognized her abilities.

segregated (seg′rə·gāt′id) *adj.:* set apart or separated according to race.

When Maya was growing up, schools in Stamps, Arkansas, were segregated.

redefined (rē′dē·fīnd′) *v.:* changed the nature of; reinvented.

Maya redefined herself by her own standards rather than those of society.

inauguration (in·ô′gyə·rā′shən) *n.:* ceremony that signifies the formal or official beginning of the U.S. president's term.

Maya was invited to read one of her poems at the inauguration of President Clinton in 1993.

CLARIFYING WORD MEANINGS: CONTEXT CLUES

When it comes to new words, don't be clueless. Use **context clues** provided by words near the word you want to understand. In the following examples, the context clues for the boldface words appear in italics.

* The music teacher was **perceptive** enough to *realize quickly* that the student had talent.
* **Segregated** schools *kept black and white students separate* from one another.
* We all saw the *change* in Tyrell after he **redefined** himself as a serious student.
* At the **inauguration** the *new president swore to uphold the Constitution.*

from Women of Hope: African Americans Who Made a Difference

Maya Angelou

Joyce Hansen

IDENTIFY

As you begin to read the essay, circle the pronouns *I* and *she*. Whom do these pronouns refer to? What is this person's relationship to the subject of the essay?

_____

_____

_____

_____

_____

_____

_____

_____

_____

_____

_____

_____

VOCABULARY

perceptive (pər·sep'tiv) *adj.:* able to comprehend through insight or intuition.

segregated (seg'rə·gāt'id) *adj.:* set apart or separated according to race.

"I was mute for five years," Maya Angelou has said. "I wasn't cute and I didn't speak. . . . But my grandma told me all the time, 'Sister, Mama don't care what these people say about you being a moron, being a idiot. Mama don't care. Mama know, Sister, when you and the good Lord get ready, you're gonna be a preacher.'"

In *I Know Why the Caged Bird Sings,* the first of her five autobiographies, Maya Angelou begins to chronicle her life. She was a little girl with a poet's heart. But when she 10 was seven, her song was silenced by a terrible experience and she stopped speaking. With the help of her grandmother who raised her in Stamps, Arkansas, the close-knit black community there, and a **perceptive** teacher who recognized her literary gifts and introduced her to literature, Maya found her voice again. She graduated from her **segregated** school at the top of her eighth-grade class.

She left Arkansas at thirteen to go to California to live with her mother. By sixteen, she had a child of her own to raise. "The greatest gift I've ever had was the birth of my 20 son. . . . When he was small, I knew more than he did, I expected to be his teacher. So because of him I educated myself. When he was four . . . I taught him to read. But then he'd ask questions, and I didn't have the answers, so I started my lifelong love affair with libraries. . . ."

She also refused to be controlled by a society that defined her as inferior because she was black and female.

"I decided many years ago to invent myself. I had obviously been invented by someone else—by a whole society—and I didn't like their invention." Maya Angelou

30 **redefined** herself. When she was in her twenties, she studied dance and was in a musical that toured Europe and Africa. Angelou also used her talents to try to help make the world a better place. In 1960, she and another performer wrote, produced, and appeared in the revue *Cabaret for Freedom* to raise money for the civil rights movement. She also spent time in Ghana, West Africa, working as a journalist in the 1960s. She has written, produced, directed, and acted in theater, movie, and television productions. She was nominated for an Emmy Award for her performance in

40 the television miniseries *Roots* and was nominated for the Pulitzer Prize in poetry. Maya Angelou also has twelve honorary doctorates.

Millions of Americans saw and heard her recite her poem "On the Pulse of Morning" for President Clinton's **inauguration** in 1993.

The message she brings through the example of her life and her art is clear. "All of my work is meant to say, you may encounter many defeats, but you must not be defeated."

50 Maya Angelou continues to rise, and we soar with her.

VOCABULARY

redefined (rē′dē·fīnd′) v.: changed the nature of; reinvented.

Redefined is used in an unusual way here. Draw a box around the context clue in line 29 that helps you figure out the sense in which the word *redefined* is used.

inauguration (in·ô′gyə·rā′shən) n.: ceremony that signifies the formal or official beginning of the U.S. president's term.

IDENTIFY

Underline the activities Angelou has participated in, as well as the jobs or careers she has had. These details reveal some important decisions that Angelou has made. What do these details reveal about Angelou?

_____

_____

_____

_____

_____

_____

_____

_____

_____

_____

_____

_____

_____

Life Doesn't Frighten Me

Maya Angelou

FLUENCY

Read the boxed stanza silently at first, circling the words you think are the most important. Then, read the stanza aloud.

WORD STUDY

The word *counterpane* in line 11 means "bedspread." This word is rarely used anymore.

IDENTIFY

Pause at line 12. From what **point of view** is the poem told? How do you know?

Shadows on the wall
Noises down the hall
Life doesn't frighten me at all
Bad dogs barking loud
5   Big ghosts in a cloud
Life doesn't frighten me at all.

Mean old Mother Goose
Lions on the loose
They don't frighten me at all
10 Dragons breathing flame
On my counterpane
That doesn't frighten me at all.

I go boo
Make them shoo
15 I make fun
Way they run
I won't cry
So they fly
I just smile
20 They go wild
Life doesn't frighten me at all.

Tough guys in a fight

All alone at night

Life doesn't frighten me at all.

25 Panthers in the park

Strangers in the dark

No, they don't frighten me at all.

That new classroom where

Boys pull all my hair

30 (Kissy little girls

With their hair in curls)

They don't frighten me at all.

Don't show me frogs and snakes

And listen for my scream.

35 If I'm afraid at all

It's only in my dreams.

I've got a magic charm

That I keep up my sleeve,

I can walk the ocean floor

40 And never have to breathe.

Life doesn't frighten me at all

Not at all

Not at all

Life doesn't frighten me at all.

INFER

What do you think the speaker means by "Kissy little girls" (line 30)?

_____

_____

_____

_____

INFER

Pause at line 32. How old do you think the narrator of this poem is? Do you think this speaker is the poet or someone else?

_____

_____

_____

_____

INTERPRET

Do you think that despite her brave remarks, this little girl is not really so brave? Explain.

_____

_____

_____

_____

_____

Maya Angelou / Life Doesn't Frighten Me

SKILLS FOCUS

Literary Skills
Understand narrator and point of view.

Comparison Chart   When you compare, you look for ways in which two or more people or things are alike. When you contrast, you look for differences. Fill in the chart to compare and contrast the two selections you've just read.

"Maya Angelou" by Joyce Hansen	"Life Doesn't Frighten Me" by Maya Angelou
Who is the subject of the biographical essay?	Who is the speaker in the poem?
Who is the narrator?	Do you think the speaker is the same as the poet? Tell why or why not.
What is the narrator's point of view? How do you know?	What pronouns does the speaker use to refer to herself?
Describe Maya Angelou's character, based on the essay.	Describe the speaker's character, based on the poem.

Skills Review

Maya Angelou / Life Doesn't Frighten Me

VOCABULARY AND COMPREHENSION

A. Clarifying Word Meanings: Context Clues   Write the correct words from the Word Bank on the lines below. The context clues in each passage should help you.

Word Bank

perceptive
segregated
redefined
inauguration

1. Maya Angelou grew up in a society that treated her as inferior. She

   _____ herself by changing her life and becoming

   a world-famous writer.

2. "Life Doesn't Frighten Me" is about a _____ child

   who uses her insight to protect herself from a frightening world.

3. When Angelou was growing up, schools in the South were still

   _____. It would be years before black children and

   white children attended school together.

4. At the _____ of President Kennedy in 1961,

   Robert Frost recited a poem called "The Gift Outright."

B. Reading Comprehension   Answer each question below.

1. Who are the two people who helped Angelou find her voice?

   _____

2. How does Angelou learn to love libraries? _____

   _____

3. Why does Angelou decide to reinvent herself? _____

   _____

4. In "Life Doesn't Frighten Me," what are some things the speaker says

   she does to overcome her fears? _____

   _____

The Writer's Craft: Metaphors, Symbols, and Images

Academic Vocabulary for Collection 6

Here are the terms you should know
as you read and analyze the selections in this collection.

Imagery Language that appeals to the senses—sight, hearing, touch, taste, and smell. Some images appeal to several senses at once.

● ● ●

Figurative Language The general term for similes, metaphors, personification, and symbols. Figurative language always involves a comparison of seemingly different things.

Simile A comparison between two unlike things, using a connecting word such as *like, as, than,* or *resembles.* Example: "The paint was as thick as molasses."

Metaphor A comparison between two unlike things that is made without the use of a connecting word such as *like, as, than,* or *resembles.* Example: "The ocean was an angry god."

Personification A **figure of speech** in which a nonhuman or nonliving thing or quality is described as if it were human or alive. Example: "The jars stood at attention on the top shelf."

● ● ●

Symbol A person, a place, a thing, or an event that has its own meaning and stands for something beyond itself. The dove, for example, is a symbol of peace.

This selection also appears in *Elements of Literature.*

The Mysterious Mr. Lincoln

by Russell Freedman

LITERARY FOCUS: METAPHOR

Suppose someone describes you as "a tiger." You've just been described by means of a metaphor. A **metaphor** is an imaginative way to compare two things that on the surface appear to be very different. A metaphor says that something *is* something else: "You *are* a tiger." Metaphor is one kind of **figurative language.** Writers use metaphors to help us see ordinary things in new and fresh ways. You'll find metaphors in all kinds of writing. As you read "The Mysterious Mr. Lincoln," look for the use of metaphor.

READING SKILLS: USING PRIOR KNOWLEDGE

Prior knowledge is what you already know about a subject before you begin reading. Your prior knowledge can help you to understand a text better. Here's how to get the most from your storehouse of knowledge:

- Preview the selection you're about to read. Quickly look at the title, headings, photographs, and captions.
- Take note of the ideas and questions that pop into your mind as you preview.
- Use a **KWL** chart to record what you Know, what you Want to know, and what you Learn as you read. You can use a chart like the one below as you read "The Mysterious Mr. Lincoln."

K What I **K**now	W What I **W**ant to Know	L What I **L**earned
Lincoln was president during the Civil War.	Why is Lincoln "mysterious"?	

SKILLS FOCUS

Literary Skills
Understand the use of metaphor in nonfiction.

Reading Skills
Use prior knowledge.

Vocabulary Skills
Understand synonyms.

VOCABULARY DEVELOPMENT

PREVIEW SELECTION VOCABULARY

Before you read "The Mysterious Mr. Lincoln," get to know these words.

gawky (gô′kē) *adj.:* clumsy; awkward.

> *As a youth, Lincoln was tall and gawky.*

repose (ri·pōz′) *n.:* state of rest or inactivity.

> *He sometimes looked sad in repose.*

listless (list′lis) *adj.:* lifeless; lacking in interest or energy.

> *When he was silent, he seemed gloomy and listless.*

animation (an′i·mā′shən) *n.:* liveliness; life.

> *Although he was often quiet, Lincoln spoke with animation.*

defy (dē·fī′) *v.:* resist; oppose.

> *Lincoln's appearance seemed to defy description.*

reticent (ret′ə·sənt) *adj.:* reserved; tending to speak little.

> *Lincoln's law partner described him as secretive and reticent.*

melancholy (mel′ən·käl′ē) *adj.:* mournful; gloomy.

> *Although he loved telling stories and jokes, at heart Lincoln was a melancholy man.*

omens (ō′mənz) *n.:* things believed to be signs of future events.

> *Although he had a logical mind, Lincoln had a superstitious belief in omens.*

paramount (par′ə·mount′) *adj.:* main; most important.

> *Preserving the Union was his paramount concern.*

crusade (krōō·sād′) *n.:* struggle for a cause or belief.

> *The war became a crusade for both sides.*

CLARIFYING WORD MEANINGS: SYNONYMS

Synonyms (sin′ə·nimz) are words with the same or nearly the same meaning. Getting to know synonyms of words you already know will increase your vocabulary and make it more lively. Also, when you learn a difficult word, it helps to learn its synonyms. In the following examples, synonyms for the boldface words appear in parentheses.

- The newborn colt was **gawky** (clumsy).
- If you **defy** (disobey) the rules of the club, you will be asked to resign.
- We all noticed that the new student was **reticent** (quiet).

The Mysterious Mr. Lincoln

Russell Freedman

VISUALIZE

Underline the words and phrases in lines 1–21 that help you picture how Lincoln looked.

VOCABULARY

gawky (gô′kē) *adj.:* clumsy; awkward.

Abraham Lincoln wasn't the sort of man who could lose himself in a crowd. After all, he stood six feet four inches tall, and to top it off, he wore a high silk hat.

His height was mostly in his long, bony legs. When he sat in a chair, he seemed no taller than anyone else. It was only when he stood up that he towered above other men.

At first glance most people thought he was homely. Lincoln thought so too, referring once to his "poor, lean, lank face." As a young man he was sensitive about his
10 **gawky** looks, but in time, he learned to laugh at himself. When a rival called him "two-faced" during a political debate, Lincoln replied: "I leave it to my audience. If I had another face, do you think I'd wear this one?"

Lawrence Migdale/Stock, Boston.

According to those who knew him, Lincoln was a man of many faces. In **repose** he often seemed sad and gloomy. But when he began to speak, his expression changed. "The dull, **listless** features dropped like a mask," said a Chicago newspaperman. "The eyes began to sparkle, the mouth to smile; the whole countenance[1] was wreathed in **animation,** so that a stranger would have said, "Why, this man, so angular and solemn a moment ago, is really handsome!"

Lincoln was the most photographed man of his time, but his friends insisted that no photo ever did him justice. It's no wonder. Back then, cameras required long exposures. The person being photographed had to "freeze" as the seconds ticked by. If he blinked an eye, the picture would be blurred. That's why Lincoln looks so stiff and formal in his photos. We never see him laughing or joking.

Artists and writers tried to capture the "real" Lincoln that the camera missed, but something about the man always escaped them. His changeable features, his tones, gestures, and expressions, seemed to **defy** description.

Today it's hard to imagine Lincoln as he really was. And he never cared to reveal much about himself. In company he was witty and talkative, but he rarely betrayed his inner feelings. According to William Herndon, his law partner, he was "the most secretive—**reticent**—shut-mouthed man that ever lived."

In his own time, Lincoln was never fully understood even by his closest friends. Since then, his life story has been told and retold so many times he has become as much a legend as a flesh-and-blood human being. While the legend is based on truth, it is only partly true. And it hides the man behind it like a disguise.

The legendary Lincoln is known as Honest Abe, a humble man of the people who rose from a log cabin to

1. **countenance** (koun′tə·nəns) *n.:* face.

VOCABULARY

repose (ri·pōz′) *n.:* state of rest or inactivity.

listless (list′lis) *adj.:* lifeless; lacking in interest or energy.

animation (an′i·mā′shən) *n.:* liveliness; life.

CLARIFY

Pause at line 28. Why does Lincoln look so stiff and formal in his photographs?

_____

_____

_____

VOCABULARY

defy (dē·fī′) *v.:* resist; oppose.

reticent (ret′ə·sənt) *adj.:* reserved; tending to speak little.

INFER

What do you think Lincoln was like? Do you think he was an easy man to get to know? Circle details in lines 29–44 that support your opinion.

_____

_____

_____

_____

_____

_____

_____

_____

_____

_____

_____

the White House. There's no doubt that Lincoln was a poor boy who made good. And it's true that he carried his folksy manners and homespun speech to the White House with
50 him. He said "howdy" to visitors and invited them to "stay a spell." He greeted diplomats while wearing carpet slippers, called his wife "mother" at receptions, and told bawdy[2] jokes at cabinet meetings.

Lincoln may have seemed like a common man, but he wasn't. His friends agreed that he was one of the most ambitious people they had ever known. Lincoln struggled hard to rise above his log-cabin origins, and he was proud of his achievements. By the time he ran for president he was a wealthy man, earning a large income from his law
60 practice and his many investments. As for the nickname Abe, he hated it. No one who knew him well ever called him Abe to his face. They addressed him as Lincoln or Mr. Lincoln.

Lincoln is often described as a sloppy dresser, careless about his appearance. In fact, he patronized the best tailor in Springfield, Illinois, buying two suits a year. That was at a time when many men lived, died, and were buried in the same suit.

It's true that Lincoln had little formal "eddication," as
70 he would have pronounced it. Almost everything he "larned" he taught himself. All his life he said "thar" for *there*, "git" for *get*, "kin" for *can*. Even so, he became an eloquent public speaker who could hold a vast audience spellbound and a great writer whose finest phrases still ring in our ears. He was known to sit up late into the night, discussing Shakespeare's plays with White House visitors.

He was certainly a humorous man, famous for his rollicking stories. But he was also moody and **melancholy,**

---

2. **bawdy** *adj.*: humorous but crude.

tormented by long and frequent bouts of depression. Humor was his therapy. He relied on his yarns,[3] a friend observed, to "whistle down sadness."

80

He had a cool, logical mind, trained in the courtroom, and a practical, commonsense approach to problems. Yet he was deeply superstitious, a believer in dreams, **omens,** and visions.

We admire Lincoln today as an American folk hero. During the Civil War, however, he was the most unpopular president the nation had ever known. His critics called him a tyrant, a hick,[4] a stupid baboon who was unfit for his office. As commander in chief of the armed forces, he was denounced as a bungling amateur who meddled in military affairs he knew nothing about. But he also had his supporters. They praised him as a farsighted statesman, a military mastermind who engineered the Union victory.

90

Lincoln is best known as the Great Emancipator, the man who freed the slaves. Yet he did not enter the war with that idea in mind. "My **paramount** object in this struggle *is* to save the Union," he said in 1862, "and is *not* either to save or destroy slavery." As the war continued, Lincoln's attitude changed. Eventually he came to regard the conflict as a moral **crusade** to wipe out the sin of slavery.

100

No black leader was more critical of Lincoln than the fiery abolitionist[5] writer and editor Frederick Douglass. Douglass had grown up as a slave. He had won his freedom by escaping to the North. Early in the war, impatient with Lincoln's cautious leadership, Douglass called him "preeminently the white man's president, entirely devoted to the

---

3. **yarns** *n.:* entertaining stories filled with exaggeration. Storytellers like Lincoln could be said to "spin" yarns.
4. **hick** *n.:* awkward, inexperienced person from the country.
5. **abolitionist** *n.:* person who supported abolishing, or ending, slavery in the United States.

VOCABULARY

omens (ōʹmənz) *n.:* things believed to be signs of future events.

CLARIFY

Re-read lines 95–101. How did Lincoln's attitude change during the war?

_____

_____

_____

_____

_____

_____

_____

_____

_____

_____

_____

_____

_____

_____

VOCABULARY

paramount (parʹə·mount′) *adj.:* main; most important.

crusade (krōō·sādʹ) *n.:* struggle for a cause or belief.

In one sentence, summarize what Frederick Douglass concluded was most important about Lincoln (lines 111–118).

_____

_____

_____

_____

_____

_____

_____

_____

_____

What was the most surprising, interesting, or important new thing you learned about Lincoln in this selection?

_____

_____

_____

_____

_____

_____

_____

_____

welfare of white men." Later, Douglass changed his mind and came to admire Lincoln. Several years after the war, he said this about the sixteenth president:

110

"His greatest mission was to accomplish two things: first, to save his country from dismemberment[6] and ruin; and second, to free his country from the great crime of slavery. . . . Taking him for all in all, measuring the tremendous magnitude of the work before him, considering the necessary means to ends, and surveying the end from the beginning, infinite wisdom has seldom sent any man into the world better fitted for his mission than Abraham Lincoln."

Abraham Lincoln and his son Tad. (1865)

---

6. **dismemberment** *n.:* separation into parts; division.

The Mysterious Mr. Lincoln

Metaphor Map   A **metaphor** compares two things without using a comparison word such as *like* or *as.* In each box on the right, explain what the metaphor on the left means or symbolizes.

SKILLS FOCUS

Literary Skills
Analyze the use of metaphor in nonfiction.

Metaphor	Meaning
A rival called Lincoln "two-faced."	
Lincoln was a man of many faces.	
His critics called him a stupid baboon.	

Skills Review

The Mysterious Mr. Lincoln

VOCABULARY AND COMPREHENSION

Word Bank

gawky
repose
listless
animation
defy
reticent
melancholy
omens
paramount
crusade

A. Clarifying Word Meanings: Synonyms   Match each Word Bank word with its synonym. Write the letter of the correct answer next to each word.

_____ 1. reticent   **a.** warnings

_____ 2. repose   **b.** quiet

_____ 3. omens   **c.** main

_____ 4. crusade   **d.** rest

_____ 5. defy   **e.** mission

_____ 6. gawky   **f.** lifeless

_____ 7. melancholy   **g.** liveliness

_____ 8. listless   **h.** oppose

_____ 9. paramount   **i.** clumsy

_____ 10. animation   **j.** gloomy

B. Reading Comprehension   Answer each question below.

1. What qualities made Lincoln mysterious? _____

_____

2. Why does Lincoln look so stiff and formal in photographs? _____

_____

3. At first, what was Lincoln's chief objective in the Civil War? _____

_____

4. What was Lincoln's main goal toward the end of the Civil War?

_____

_____

SKILLS FOCUS

Vocabulary Skills
Recognize synonyms.

Before You Read

Eleven by Sandra Cisneros

This selection also appears in *Elements of Literature.*

LITERARY FOCUS: IMAGERY

Your mind is full of images—memories of things you've seen, heard, touched, tasted, and smelled. **Imagery** is language that appeals to your senses: sight, hearing, smell, taste, and touch. Through the use of imagery, writers can rekindle those images in your mind or even create new ones.

The poem in the left-hand column below contains lots of imagery. Look at the right-hand column to see which senses the images in each line of the poem appeal to.

Lines of Poem	Senses the Lines Appeal To
Unwarmed by any sunset light	touch, sight
The gray day darkened into night.	sight
A hard, dull bitterness of cold	touch, taste
The shrieking of mindless wind—	hearing
like the odors blown	smell

READING SKILLS: MAKING INFERENCES

If a writer were to tell you every little thing about every single character and each one of his or her thoughts, things would get pretty boring. Part of the fun of reading is making inferences, or guesses, as you go along. To make an **inference,** look for clues the writer gives you. Connect those clues with what you already know. Then, make an educated guess—your inference. As you read "Eleven," pause from time to time to make inferences about what the author is telling you.

Literary Skills
Identify imagery in fiction.

Reading Skills
Make inferences.

Eleven

Sandra Cisneros

INTERPRET

In lines 16–19, Rachel, the narrator, compares growing old to three things. Underline those things. Then, explain in your own words Rachel's idea about growing older.

What they don't understand about birthdays and what they never tell you is that when you're eleven, you're also ten, and nine, and eight, and seven, and six, and five, and four, and three, and two, and one. And when you wake up on your eleventh birthday you expect to feel eleven, but you don't. You open your eyes and everything's just like yesterday, only it's today. And you don't feel eleven at all. You feel like you're still ten. And you are—underneath the year that makes you eleven.

Like some days you might say something stupid, and
10 that's the part of you that's still ten. Or maybe some days you might need to sit on your mama's lap because you're scared, and that's the part of you that's five. And maybe one day when you're all grown up maybe you will need to cry like if you're three, and that's okay. That's what I tell Mama when she's sad and needs to cry. Maybe she's feeling three.

Because the way you grow old is kind of like an onion or like the rings inside a tree trunk or like my little wooden dolls that fit one inside the other, each year inside the next one. That's how being eleven years old is.

20 You don't feel eleven. Not right away. It takes a few days, weeks even, sometimes even months before you say Eleven when they ask you. And you don't feel smart eleven, not until you're almost twelve. That's the way it is.

Only today I wish I didn't have only eleven years rattling inside me like pennies in a tin Band-Aid box. Today I wish I was one hundred and two instead of eleven because if I was one hundred and two I'd have known what to say when Mrs. Price put the red sweater on my desk. I would've known how to tell her it wasn't mine instead of just sitting there with that look on my face and nothing coming out of my mouth.

"Whose is this?" Mrs. Price says, and she holds the red sweater up in the air for all the class to see. "Whose? It's been sitting in the coatroom for a month."

"Not mine," says everybody. "Not me."

"It has to belong to somebody," Mrs. Price keeps saying, but nobody can remember. It's an ugly sweater with red plastic buttons and a collar and sleeves all stretched out like you could use it for a jump-rope. It's maybe a thousand years old and even if it belonged to me I wouldn't say so.

Maybe because I'm skinny, maybe because she doesn't like me, that stupid Sylvia Saldívar says, "I think it belongs to Rachel." An ugly sweater like that, all raggedy and old, but Mrs. Price believes her. Mrs. Price takes the sweater and puts it right on my desk, but when I open my mouth nothing comes out.

"That's not, I don't, you're not . . . Not mine," I finally say in a little voice that was maybe me when I was four.

"Of course it's yours," Mrs. Price says. "I remember you wearing it once." Because she's older and the teacher, she's right and I'm not.

Not mine, not mine, not mine, but Mrs. Price is already turning to page thirty-two, and math problem number four. I don't know why but all of a sudden I'm feeling sick inside, like the part of me that's three wants to come out of my eyes, only I squeeze them shut tight and bite down on my teeth real hard and try to remember today I am eleven, eleven. Mama is making a cake for me for tonight, and when Papa comes home everybody will sing Happy birthday, happy birthday to you.

30

40

50

60

INFER

Pause at line 31. What can you infer about Rachel from how she describes herself and her actions?

_____

_____

_____

_____

_____

VISUALIZE

Underline the words in lines 36–40 that help you picture the sweater.

INFER

Pause at line 60. Why does Rachel keep trying to focus on her birthday celebration?

_____

_____

_____

_____

_____

_____

_____

_____

_____

RETELL

Pause at line 66. Retell what's happened to Rachel up to this point in the story.

_____

_____

_____

_____

_____

_____

_____

_____

_____

_____

_____

_____

_____

_____

_____

_____

_____

_____

But when the sick feeling goes away and I open my eyes, the red sweater's still sitting there like a big red mountain. I move the red sweater to the corner of my desk with my ruler. I move my pencil and books and eraser as far from it as possible. I even move my chair a little to the right. Not mine, not mine, not mine.

In my head I'm thinking how long till lunchtime, how long till I can take the red sweater and throw it over the schoolyard fence, or leave it hanging on a parking meter, 70 or bunch it up into a little ball and toss it in the alley. Except when math period ends Mrs. Price says loud and in front of everybody, "Now, Rachel, that's enough," because she sees I've shoved the red sweater to the tippy-tip corner of my desk and it's hanging all over the edge like a waterfall, but I don't care.

"Rachel," Mrs. Price says. She says it like she's getting mad. "You put that sweater on right now and no more nonsense."

"But it's not—"

80 "Now!" Mrs. Price says.

This is when I wish I wasn't eleven, because all the years inside of me—ten, nine, eight, seven, six, five, four, three, two, and one—are pushing at the back of my eyes when I put one arm through one sleeve of the sweater that smells like cottage cheese, and then the other arm through the other and stand there with my arms apart like if the sweater hurts me and it does, all itchy and full of germs that aren't even mine.

That's when everything I've been holding in since this morning, since when Mrs. Price put the sweater on my desk, finally lets go, and all of a sudden I'm crying in front of everybody. I wish I was invisible but I'm not. I'm eleven and it's my birthday today and I'm crying like I'm three in front of everybody. I put my head down on the desk and bury my face in my stupid clown-sweater arms. My face all hot and spit coming out of my mouth because I can't stop the little animal noises from coming out of me, until there aren't any more tears left in my eyes, and it's just my body shaking like when you have the hiccups and my whole head hurts like when you drink milk too fast.

But the worst part is right before the bell rings for lunch. That stupid Phyllis Lopez, who is even dumber than Sylvia Saldívar, says she remembers the red sweater is hers! I take it off right away and give it to her, only Mrs. Price pretends like everything's okay.

Today I'm eleven. There's a cake Mama's making for tonight, and when Papa comes home from work we'll eat it. There'll be candles and presents and everybody will sing Happy birthday, happy birthday to you, Rachel, only it's too late.

I'm eleven today. I'm eleven, ten, nine, eight, seven, six, five, four, three, two, and one, but I wish I was one hundred and two. I wish I was anything but eleven, because I want today to be far away already, far away like a runaway balloon, like a tiny *o* in the sky, so tiny-tiny you have to close your eyes to see it.

FLUENCY

Read the boxed paragraph a couple of times to yourself. Notice the words and phrases that help you understand Rachel's feelings. Read the passage aloud, and try to convey Rachel's feelings to your listeners.

INFER

Pause at line 105. What can you infer about how Mrs. Price feels about Rachel?

_____

_____

_____

_____

_____

_____

INTERPRET

What does Rachel mean when she says "it's too late" (lines 108–110)?

_____

_____

_____

_____

_____

_____

Eleven

Literary Skills
Analyze the use of imagery in fiction.

Imagery Grid   **Imagery** is language that appeals to the senses. Images describe sights, smells, tastes, sounds, and the way things feel when you touch them. Writers use imagery to help us share an experience. Fill in the imagery chart below with images that Sandra Cisneros uses throughout "Eleven." Then, answer the questions.

Sight	Touch

Sound	Taste	Smell

Questions

1. Which sense from the diagram had the most images?

_____

2. Which had the least?

_____

3. Which image from the story do you like the most? Why?

_____

Skills Review

Eleven

COMPREHENSION

Reading Comprehension   Answer each question below.

1. Rachel is eleven, but what age does she feel? _____

   _____

2. Why does Rachel want to be 102 years old? _____

   _____

3. Who does Mrs. Price think the red sweater belongs to? _____

   _____

4. Why is Rachel upset when Mrs. Price puts the sweater on her desk? ____

   _____

5. What does Rachel want to do with the sweater? _____

   _____

6. Why does Rachel want to be invisible? _____

   _____

7. What happens just before the bell rings for lunch? _____

   _____

8. Will Rachel be happy at her birthday party? Tell why or why not. _____

   _____

   _____

from **The Autobiography of a Kid**

by Jerry Spinelli

LITERARY FOCUS: IMAGERY AND FIGURATIVE LANGUAGE

You have your own style of dressing and talking. Style involves making choices and arranging things in a certain way—clothes, furniture, words, and so on. Writers have style, too. Every writer develops his or her own writing style by

- using or avoiding **imagery,** language that appeals to the senses
- using or avoiding literary devices such as **simile** and **metaphor**
- using or avoiding slang or sentence fragments

As you read the excerpt from "The Autobiography of a Kid," look for the special way in which Jerry Spinelli uses language.

READING SKILLS: SUMMARIZING

When you **summarize** a text, you restate the author's main points in your own words. Your summary should include only the most important ideas and details. The chart below lists sections of the story you might want to summarize as you read.

Story Section	Summary
Cereal boxes and comics, lines 1–24	
Sports, lines 25–46	
Books, lines 47–81	
Words, lines 82–110	
Conclusion, lines 111–137	

SKILLS FOCUS

Literary Skills
Understand imagery and figurative language.

Reading Skills
Summarize events.

Vocabulary Skills
Identify context clues.

VOCABULARY DEVELOPMENT

PREVIEW SELECTION VOCABULARY

Get to know the following words before you read the story that follows.

subscription (səb·skrip′shən) *n.:* agreement to pay for a magazine or newspaper for a certain period of time.

Instead of buying comics at newsstands, he decided to get a subscription.

curriculum (kə·rik′yōō·ləm) *n.:* courses offered at a school.

The curriculum did not offer exciting books to read.

blithely (blīth′lē) *adv.:* in a carefree way; casually.

He was totally bored by words and blithely said so.

CLARIFYING WORD MEANINGS: CONTEXT

When you get lost, what's the first thing you do? One good idea is to look around you to see if there are familiar landmarks to guide you. The same sort of strategy works when you get muddled while reading. Stop and look for clues to help you sort out meaning. These kinds of clues are called **context clues.** In the examples below, the words in italics provide context clues for the boldface words.

- I'm so glad I got a magazine **subscription.** I look forward to reading the magazine *each month.*

- The **curriculum** our school offered was pretty ordinary: *English, math, science, and social studies.*

- The argument *didn't bother* Bess at all. She **blithely** said, "See you," and left the room.

from The Autobiography of a Kid

Jerry Spinelli

IDENTIFY

Pause at line 6. What do you think Spinelli is going to talk about?

_____

_____

VOCABULARY

subscription (səb·skrip′shən) *n.:* agreement to pay for a magazine or newspaper for a certain period of time.

FLUENCY

Read the boxed passage aloud twice. Experiment with your tone and speed to produce a comic effect.

SUMMARIZE

Pause at line 24. Sum up what Spinelli has told you so far about his reading.

_____

_____

_____

_____

I did not read. Not books, anyway. Now, cereal boxes—that was another story. Every morning I pored over boxes of Wheaties and Cheerios at the breakfast table. I looked forward to new cereals as much for a change in reading material as for a change in breakfast fare.

And comics. I read them by the hundreds.

Mostly I read cowboy and war comics. I bought them at corner stores and newsstands. Then when I was twelve, I got serious. I decided the comic should come to me. I got 10 my first **subscription:** *Bugs Bunny.* Once a month, accompanied by the metallic flapping of the front door mail slot, the postman delivered Bugs's latest adventures to me.

My favorite comic character of all, however, was neither man nor rabbit. In fact, I'm still not sure what it was. All I know is that it was called the Heap, and it looked something like a haystack. The Heap never spoke, and the reader never saw it move, but the Heap appeared on the scene when people were having problems. Somehow or other the Heap managed to solve the problem, though it 20 never got credit. As far as most of the people knew, it was just another haystack in the field.

Of course, I read the newspaper comics too. While I never missed "Dick Tracy," "Little Lulu," and "Mandrake the Magician," my favorite of all was "Alley Oop."

Another part of the newspaper got my attention as well: sports.

Mostly I read the sports pages of the *Times Herald.* I especially liked the clever writing of sports editor Red McCarthy in his daily column. Until then I had thought

30 there was only one English language—the language I spoke and heard in the West End of Norristown. I was happily surprised to discover that there was more than one way to say something, that the words and their arrangement could be as interesting as the thing they said.

From April to September in the Sunday *Philadelphia Inquirer,* I read the major league baseball batting statistics. They were printed in small type in a long box, row after row of numbers and names, hundreds of them—every player in the majors. To the non-baseball fan, they were as

40 boring as a page in a phone book. I loved it. I wallowed in the numbers. What was Ted Williams's batting average this week? Stan Musial's? Richie Ashburn's? Was Ralph Kiner still the leader in home runs? Who had the most RBIs? Did Mantle have a shot at the Triple Crown? Or Mays? It was like peeking at a race once every seven days, watching the lead change places from week to week.

IDENTIFY

Based on information in lines 25–26, what is Spinelli going to talk about next?

_____

_____

_____

_____

INTERPRET

The sentence "I wallowed in the numbers" (lines 40–41) is an **idiom.** The writer did not really roll around in numbers. What might this **figurative expression** mean? Why did Spinelli choose to use this expression?

_____

_____

_____

_____

_____

_____

_____

_____

_____

_____

_____

_____

© Bettmann/CORBIS.

Ted Williams.

_____

_____

_____

_____

_____

_____

_____

_____

_____

_____

_____

_____

_____

_____

_____

Cereal boxes, comics, baseball stats—that was my reading. As for books, I read maybe ten of them, fifteen tops, from the day I entered first grade until graduation from high school. I remember reading a few Bobbsey Twins adventures, and in junior high, sports stories about Chip Hilton, a fictional high school hotshot athlete. I read *The Adventures of Robin Hood,* a Sherlock Holmes mystery, and *Kon-Tiki,* the true story of a man who crossed the Pacific in a raft. That's about it.

Why didn't I read more?

I could blame it on my grade school, which had no library. I could blame it on the **curriculum,** which limited my classroom reading to "See Dick run. See Jane run. See Spot do something on the rug." I could blame it on history, for enrolling me in life and school before the time of book fairs and author visits. I could blame it on my friends, because like me, the only books they read were comic books.

But I can't do that.

It's always handy to blame things on one's parents, but I can't do that either. My father had his books on display in the dining room. Thirty times a day I passed his collection of histories and Ellery Queen mysteries. Some of my earliest memories are of my mother reading to me, stories like *Babar* and *The Little Engine That Could.* My parents steered me in the right direction.

And the fact is, on those few occasions when I actually did read a book, I enjoyed it. Yet for some reason I would not admit this to myself. Instead of saying, Hey, that was good, that was fun, I think I'll read another—I would dump my baseball glove into my bike basket and head out the path to the Little League field, and months would go

Cover of THE LITTLE ENGINE THAT COULD (Original Classic Edition) by Watty Piper, illustrated by George & Doris Hauman, copyright Penguin Group (USA) Inc. The Little Engine That Could, engine design and I Think I Can are trademarks of Penguin Group (USA) Inc. Used with permission.

by before I picked up a book again. Reading a book was
80   for times when I was totally bored and lacking anything
else to do.

And what about words, which, packed together, made
up a book as cells made up my body? I liked them. Yet this
was such a naturally occurring, unachieved sort of thing
that if someone had asked me in those days, "Do you like
words?" I probably would have shrugged and **blithely**
answered, "No."

Still, whether I knew it or not, words were claiming
me. When I visited Hartenstine Printing, where my father
90   worked as a typesetter, I saw words being created letter by
letter, one thin slug of lead at a time.

Once, in a comic book, someone with a bad heart was
described as having a bum ticker. That tickled me to no
end. I kept whispering "bum ticker" to myself for days.

Except for the Heap, my favorite comic book
characters were Bugs Bunny and Daffy Duck. I liked them

IDENTIFY

To what does Spinelli compare words in a book in lines
82–83?

IDENTIFY

Re-read lines 82–91.
Underline the **imagery**
that appeals to your sense
of sight.

VOCABULARY

blithely (blīth'lē) adv.: in a
carefree way; casually.

How would you describe the
difference between blithe
and careless?

A gossoon (gä·sōōn′)
(line 106) is a young boy.
The word is used mainly
in Ireland.

INTERPRET

What does Spinelli's **metaphor**
"the Popsicles and penknives
and bike tires of my days"
(lines 114–115) mean?

_____

_____

_____

_____

_____

_____

PREDICT

Pause at line 123. What do
you think happened when
Spinelli wrote a poem?

_____

_____

_____

_____

_____

_____

_____

_____

_____

as much for their words as their ways. For me, the highlight
of a scene was not what happened, but what Bugs or Daffy
said about what happened. This is probably why Mickey
100   Mouse never much appealed to me. His speech was too
bland for my taste.

Occasionally I had to look up a word in the dictionary.
Sometimes my eye would stray to the surrounding words.
Invariably it stopped at an interesting one, and I read the
definition. In one such instance I discovered that I was a
gossoon. I clearly remember two feelings attached to these
moments: (1) surprise that a dictionary could be so
interesting, and (2) a notion to sit down and look through
more pages. I never did.

110   And then of course there was my success in spelling.

All of these items were indicators of an early leaning
toward language, but I failed to see them as such. The tickle
of a rabbit's wit, the rattle of alphabet in a compositor's
drawer—they simply took their place among the Popsicles
and penknives and bike tires of my days.

With one exception.

In sixth grade our teacher assigned us a project: Make
a scrapbook of Mexico. I found pictures of Mexico in
National Geographic and other magazines and pasted them
120   in my scrapbook, for which my father made a professional-
looking cover at the print shop. Then I did something
extra. It wasn't part of the assignment. I just did it.

I wrote a poem.

Three stanzas about Mexico, ending with a touristy
come-on: "Now, isn't that where you would like to be?" I
wrote it in pencil, longhand, my best penmanship, on a
piece of lined classroom paper. I pasted it neatly on the last
page of my scrapbook and turned in my project.

Several days later my mother walked the three blocks to my school. She met with my teacher, who told her she did not believe that my poem about Mexico was my own work. She thought I copied it from a book. (Hah! If she only knew how few books I read, and never one with poetry.) I was suspected of plagiarism.

I don't know what my mother said to her, but by the time she walked out I was in the clear, legally at least. Five years would pass before I wrote another poem.

© Michael Pole/CORBIS.

130

WORD STUDY

Plagiarism (plā′jə·riz′əm), in line 134, means "taking someone else's ideas and passing them off as if they are your own." For example, a plagiarist might steal a plot or a passage from another writer. *Plagiarize* comes from a Latin word for "kidnapper."

INFER

Why do you suppose the teacher thought Spinelli had plagiarized the poem?

_____

_____

_____

_____

_____

_____

_____

_____

_____

_____

_____

_____

_____

from The Autobiography of a Kid

SKILLS FOCUS

Literary Skills
Analyze a
writer's use of
imagery and
figurative
language.

Language Chart   The particular way a writer uses language is called
style. Fill in the chart below with examples from "The Autobiography of
a Kid." If you cannot find an example of something, write *None* in the
space provided. Review your finished chart, and then describe Jerry
Spinelli's use of language in the box below.

> **Writer's Style**

Use of Imagery

Use of Simile or Metaphor

Use of Repetition

Use of Slang or Fragments

Description of Spinelli's Writing

Skills Review

from The Autobiography of a Kid

VOCABULARY AND COMPREHENSION

A. Clarifying Word Meanings: Context Clues   Write the correct words from the Word Bank in the blanks below. Use context clues to help you.

There I was, relaxing and (1)_____ paging through the latest copy of my magazine. I didn't have a care in the world. Suddenly it dawned on me that my (2) _____ was about to run out! It was crazy of me to forget to send money for a renewal. This magazine really helps me with the current-events part of the (3) _____ at my school.

B. Reading Comprehension   Answer each question below.

1. How does Spinelli describe his reading habits at the beginning of the story? _____

_____

2. Why does Spinelli find joy in reading the *Philadelphia Inquirer*?

_____

3. Does Spinelli blame his parents for his lack of interest in reading? Explain. _____

_____

4. What does Spinelli's teacher think of the poem he wrote? _____

_____

5. Why do you think Spinelli let five years pass before he wrote another poem? _____

_____

SKILLS FOCUS

Vocabulary Skills
Use context clues.

Poetry

Academic Vocabulary for Collection 7

These are the terms you should know
as you read and analyze the poems in this collection.

_____

Free Verse Poetry that does not have a regular meter and rhyme scheme. Through use of free verse, poets strive to capture the natural rhythms of ordinary speech.

Rhyme The repetition of accented vowel sounds and all sounds following them. *School* and *tool* rhyme, as do *handle* and *candle*. The repeated sounds sometimes occur at the ends of lines and sometimes within a line of a poem.

End Rhyme Rhyme that comes at the end of lines. Example: "If you give a boy a *horn* / He will blow it night and *morn*. . . ."

Internal Rhyme Rhyme that occurs within a line. Example: "'Leave me *alone*,' said the rock to the *stone* / 'Or trouble will follow you surely. . . .'"

Rhyme Scheme The pattern of rhyming sounds at the ends of lines in a poem.

Meter A regular pattern of accented and unaccented syllables that gives poetry its beat.

Scanning Analyzing lines of poetry for accented and unaccented syllables to figure out the meter.

Refrain A word, phrase, line, or group of lines repeated regularly in a poem or song, usually at the end of a stanza.

Repetition The repeated use of a word, phrase, sound, or pattern. Alliteration, rhyme, and refrain are all forms of repetition.

Alliteration The repetition of the same or similar consonant sounds in words that are close together. Example: "The **b**ar**b**er was as **b**usy as a **b**ee."

Onomatopoeia (ăn′ō·mat′ō·pē′ə) The use of a word whose sound imitates or suggests its meaning. Examples include *hoot* and *splat.*

This selection also appears in *Elements of Literature*.

The Sneetches

by Dr. Seuss (Theodor Geisel)

LITERARY FOCUS: RHYME AND METER

You probably know lots of rhymes from games, commercials, and songs. **Rhymes** are two or more words that have the same chiming sounds, like *heat* and *sheet*. In the poem you're about to read, Dr. Seuss sometimes makes up words to rhyme with real words. For example, he rhymes the real word *stars* with the made-up word *thars*.

A pattern of rhymes is called a **rhyme scheme.** Patterns of rhymes are indicated by letters of the alphabet. For example, a stanza with an *abab* pattern has two rhymes. The first line (*a*) rhymes with the third line; the second line (*b*) rhymes with the fourth line.

The **meter** of a poem is its beat. To determine a poem's meter, you must **scan** it. Here's how: Read the poem aloud, and mark each stressed sylla-ble with the symbol ′ and each unstressed syllable with the symbol ◡.

Here are the first four lines of "The Sneetches" with the rhyme scheme and meter marked:

Now, the Star-Belly Sneetches   *a*

Had bellies with stars.   *b*

The Plain-Belly Sneetches   *a*

Had none upon thars.   *b*

READING SKILLS: READING POETRY ALOUD

"The Sneetches" has a bouncy rhythm and humorous rhymes. To fully appreciate Dr. Seuss's clever use of language, pause from time to time to read passages of the poem aloud. Listen for rhymes and rhythms, and let the playfulness of the language come through.

SKILLS FOCUS

Literary Skills
Understand rhyme and rhyme scheme.

Reading Skills
Read poetry aloud.

The Sneetches

Dr. Seuss (Theodor Geisel)

Now, the Star-Belly Sneetches
Had bellies with stars.
The Plain-Belly Sneetches
Had none upon thars.

5   Those stars weren't so big. They were really so small
You might think such a thing wouldn't matter at all.

But, because they had stars, all the Star-Belly Sneetches
Would brag, "We're the best kind of Sneetch on the beaches."
With their snoots in the air, they would sniff and they'd snort
10 "We'll have nothing to do with the Plain-Belly sort!"
And whenever they met some, when they were out walking,
They'd hike right on past them without even talking.

When the Star-Belly children went out to play ball,
Could a Plain Belly get in the game . . . ? Not at all.
15 You only could play if your bellies had stars
And the Plain-Belly children had none upon thars.

When the Star-Belly Sneetches had frankfurter roasts
Or picnics or parties or marshmallow toasts,
They never invited the Plain-Belly Sneetches.
20 They left them out cold, in the dark of the beaches.
They kept them away. Never let them come near.
And that's how they treated them year after year.

IDENTIFY

What real word does the invented word *thars* replace in line 4?

_____

_____

IDENTIFY

Re-read lines 7–10. Circle examples of **alliteration**.

CLARIFY

Pause at line 22. In what way are the Star-Belly Sneetches snobs? Give examples.

_____

_____

_____

What is the stranger's real motive (lines 27–37)?

_____

_____

_____

_____

IDENTIFY

Re-read lines 34–37 aloud. **Scan** those lines, using **ʹ** to indicate stressed syllables and ⌣ to indicate unstressed syllables.

PREDICT

What might the "peculiar machine" (line 35) do?

_____

_____

_____

_____

_____

IDENTIFY

Circle all the words that **rhyme** in lines 38–43. Underline examples of **onomatopoeia**, words that sound like their meaning.

Then ONE day, it seems . . . while the Plain-Belly Sneetches
Were moping and doping alone on the beaches,

25 Just sitting there wishing their bellies had stars . . .
A stranger zipped up in the strangest of cars!

"My friends," he announced in a voice clear and keen,
"My name is Sylvester McMonkey McBean.
And I've heard of your troubles. I've heard you're unhappy.

30 But I can fix that. I'm the Fix-it-Up Chappie.
I've come here to help you. I have what you need.
And my prices are low. And I work at great speed.
And my work is one hundred per cent guaranteed!"

Then, quickly, Sylvester McMonkey McBean

35 Put together a very peculiar machine.
And he said, "You want stars like a Star-Belly Sneetch . . . ?
My friends, you can have them for three dollars each!"

"Just pay me your money and hop right aboard!"
So they clambered inside. Then the big machine roared

40 And it klonked. And it bonked. And it jerked. And it berked
And it bopped them about. But the thing really worked!
When the Plain-Belly Sneetches popped out, they had stars!
They actually did. They had stars upon thars!

Then they yelled at the ones who had stars at the start.

45 "We're exactly like you! You can't tell us apart.

We're all just the same, now, you snooty old smarties!

And now we can go to your frankfurter parties."

"Good grief!" groaned the ones who had stars at the first.

"We're *still* the best Sneetches and they are the worst.

50 But, now, how in the world will we know," they all frowned,

"If which kind is what, or the other way round?"

Then up came McBean with a very sly wink

And he said, "Things are not quite as bad as you think.

So you don't know who's who. That is perfectly true.

55 But come with me, friends. Do you know what I'll do?

I'll make you, again, the best Sneetches on beaches

And all it will cost you is ten dollars eaches."

"Belly stars are no longer in style," said McBean.

What you need is a trip through my Star-*Off* Machine.

60 This wondrous contraption will take *off* your stars

So you won't look like Sneetches who have them on thars."

And that handy machine

Working very precisely

Removed all the stars from their tummies quite nicely.

The Sneetches 227

COMPARE & CONTRAST

In lines 52–64, how is McBean's offer to the Star-Bellies similar to the deal he reached with the Plain-Bellies? In what way is it different?

_____

_____

_____

_____

_____

INFER

Why does McBean's offer sound like a good one to the Star-Belly Sneetches (lines 55–61)?

_____

_____

_____

_____

_____

PREDICT

Pause at line 64. What will happen now that the Star-Bellies' stars have been removed?

_____

_____

_____

_____

65 Then, with snoots in the air, they paraded about
And they opened their beaks and they let out a shout,
"We know who is who! Now there isn't a doubt.
The best kind of Sneetches are Sneetches without!"

Then, of course, those with stars all got frightfully mad.
70 To be wearing a star now was frightfully bad.
Then, of course, old Sylvester McMonkey McBean
Invited *them* into his Star-Off Machine.

Then, of course from THEN on, as you probably guess,
Things really got into a horrible mess.

75 All the rest of that day, on those wild screaming beaches,
The Fix-it-Up Chappie kept fixing up Sneetches.
Off again! On again!
In again! Out again!
Through the machines they raced round and about again,
80 Changing their stars every minute or two.

They kept paying money. They kept running through
Until neither the Plain nor the Star-Bellies knew
Whether this one was that one . . . or that one was this one
Or which one was what one . . . or what one was who.

85 Then, when every last cent
Of their money was spent,
The Fix-it-Up Chappie packed up
And he went.

And he laughed as he drove
90 In his car up the beach,
"They never will learn.
No. You can't teach a Sneetch!"

But McBean was quite wrong. I'm quite happy to say
That the Sneetches got really quite smart on that day,
95 The day they decided that Sneetches are Sneetches
And no kind of Sneetch is the best on the beaches.
That day, all the Sneetches forgot about stars
And whether they had one, or not, upon thars.

FLUENCY

Read lines 75–84 aloud a few times. Note the changes in rhyme and rhythm. The ellipses (series of dots) in lines 83 and 84 indicate pauses.

INFER

Why do you think the Sneetches change their attitude (lines 93–98)?

_____

_____

_____

_____

_____

_____

_____

INTERPRET

What point is the poem making about people and the way they treat one another?

_____

_____

_____

_____

_____

_____

The Sneetches

Rhyme Chart   The words that rhyme in a poem contribute to the
poem's tone and meaning. Fill out the rhyme chart below after you read
the first seven stanzas of "The Sneetches." Circle any rhyming words that
are made up. In the bottom box, describe the **rhyme scheme** of the poem.

End Rhymes
Sneetches with _____
small with _____
snort with _____
walking with _____
roasts with _____
near with _____
stars with _____
keen with _____
unhappy with _____
need with _____

Rhyme Scheme of Poem

Skills Review

The Sneetches

COMPREHENSION

Reading Comprehension   Circle the correct answer.

1. Which two groups in this poem are competing with each other?
   a. the Sneetches and the McBean family
   b. the Star-Bellies and the Plain-Bellies
   c. McBean and the Fix-It-Up Chappie
   d. the tall Sneetches and the small Sneetches

2. What does Sylvester McMonkey McBean do for the Sneetches?
   f. He lends them money.
   g. He throws them a frankfurter roast.
   h. He removes and reattaches their stars.
   j. He heals their bellies.

3. Which of the following statements is correct?
   a. McBean offers to give the Plain-Bellies stars for ten dollars each.
   b. McBean refuses to remove stars because it is dangerous.
   c. McBean designs new stars for the Sneetches.
   d. McBean's machine can remove and add stars.

4. Which pair of words does *not* rhyme?
   f. *McBean/machine*
   g. *drove/learn*
   h. *speed/guaranteed*
   j. *through/knew*

5. What lesson does this poem teach?
   a. Money equals power.
   b. Popular fashion causes trouble.
   c. People shouldn't be judged by their appearance.
   d. It's impossible to please everyone.

Before You Read

These selections also appear in *Elements of Literature.*

Ode to Mi Gato by Gary Soto
In a Neighborhood in Los Angeles
by Francisco X. Alarcón
Hard on the Gas by Janet S. Wong

LITERARY FOCUS: SPEAKER'S TONE

When you speak, your voice and face show how you feel—sad, happy, angry, and so on. In a poem the **tone** reveals how the speaker feels about a subject or a character. To figure out the tone of a poem, you need to read the words carefully. A poem can express more than one tone.

THE ODE

An **ode** is a poem that is usually written in a formal and dignified style. It is meant to honor an important person or event. Gary Soto's ode, however, uses ordinary language and the rhythms of everyday speech. It celebrates the speaker's love for a cat.

READING SKILLS: FINDING UNITS OF MEANING

The ideas or thoughts in a poem can be arranged in different ways. In Gary Soto's "Ode to Mi Gato," units of meaning are contained within sentences. You have to look carefully for them in the lines of poetry.

Many other poems, including "In a Neighborhood in Los Angeles" and "Hard on the Gas," contain groups of lines called stanzas. A **stanza** is a major section of a poem, like a paragraph in a work of prose. A stanza usually expresses one unit of thought in a poem.

SKILLS FOCUS

Literary Skills
Understand tone; understand elements of an ode.

Reading Skills
Find units of meaning.

Ode to Mi Gato

Gary Soto

He's white
As spilled milk,
My cat who sleeps
With his belly
5 Turned toward
The summer sky.
He loves the sun,
Its warmth like a hand.
He loves tuna cans
10 And milk cartons
With their dribble
Of milk. He loves
Mom when she rattles
The bag of cat food,
15 The brown nuggets
Raining into his bowl.
And my cat loves
Me, because I saved
Him from a dog,
20 Because I dressed him
In a hat and a cape
For Halloween,
Because I dangled
A sock of chicken skin
25 As he stood on his
Hind legs. I love mi gato,
Porque I found
Him on the fender

IDENTIFY

Circle the Spanish words in the title of the poem. *Mi gato* means "my cat."

CLARIFY

A **simile** is an imaginative comparison between things that are seemingly different. Underline the simile in lines 1–2. What two things are being compared?

_____

_____

IDENTIFY

What do you learn about the cat in lines 9–16?

_____

_____

INTERPRET

What is the chicken skin compared to in line 24?

_____

_____

WORD STUDY

Porque (pôr·kā′), in line 27, is Spanish for "because."

IDENTIFY

Pause at line 35. What is the speaker's **tone** as he speaks of his cat?

_____

_____

_____

FLUENCY

Read lines 36–45 silently, and underline words you think are especially important. Note that *huevo* (wā'vð) means "egg." Then, read those lines aloud, and use your voice to convey how the speaker feels about his cat.

CLARIFY

How are lines 56–57 similar to lines 1–2?

_____

_____

_____

_____

CONNECT

An **ode** honors something important to the speaker. What does Soto honor in this poem?

_____

_____

_____

_____

Of an abandoned car.
30   He was a kitten,
     With a meow
     Like the rusty latch
     On a gate. I carried
     Him home in the loop
35   Of my arms.
     I poured milk
     Into him, let him
     Lick chunks of
     Cheese from my palms,
40   And cooked huevo
     After huevo
     Until his purring
     Engine kicked in
     And he cuddled
45   Up to my father's slippers.
     That was last year.
     This spring,
     He's excellent at sleeping
     And no good
50   At hunting. At night
     All the other cats
     In the neighborhood
     Can see him slink
     Around the corner,
55   Or jump from the tree
     Like a splash of
     Milk. We lap up
     His love and
     He laps up his welcome.

In a Neighborhood in Los Angeles

Francisco X. Alarcón

© John Neubauer/Photo Edit, Inc.

I learned
Spanish
from my grandma

mijito[1]
5   don't cry
she'd tell me

on the mornings
my parents
would leave

10   to work
at the fish
canneries

---

1. *mijito* (mē·hē′tð): contraction of *mi hijito,* Spanish for "my little child."

"In a Neighborhood in Los Angeles" from *Body in Flames/Cuerpo en llamas* by Francisco X. Alarcón. Copyright © 1990 by Francisco X. Alarcón. Reproduced by permission of **Chronicle Books, San Francisco.**

IDENTIFY

Circle the words or phrases that are spoken by the grandmother in lines 4–6.

PARAPHRASE

There are no periods in the poem. Lines 1–12 can be read as two sentences. In your own words, restate what lines 1–12 say.

_____

_____

_____

_____

Re-read lines 13–21. What
kind of person is the grandmother?

_____

_____

_____

_____

_____

_____

_____

_____

CLARIFY

Re-read lines 25–30. What
kinds of things does the
grandmother teach the
speaker? What is the speaker's **tone** as he describes her?

_____

_____

_____

_____

_____

_____

_____

_____

_____

_____

my grandma

would chat

15   with chairs

sing them

old

songs

dance

20   waltzes with them

in the kitchen

when she'd say

niño barrigón[2]

she'd laugh

25   with my grandma

I learned

to count clouds

to point out

in flowerpots

30   mint leaves

my grandma

wore moons

on her dress

Mexico's mountains

35   deserts

ocean

---

2. *niño barrigón* (nēn′yô bä′rē·gôn′): Spanish for "potbellied boy."

in her eyes
I'd see them
in her braids

40   I'd touch them
in her voice
smell them

one day
I was told:
45   she went far away

but still
I feel her
with me

whispering
50   in my ear
mijito

—*translated by*
   Francisco Aragon

FLUENCY

Read lines 31–42 aloud several times. Use your voice to express the speaker's feelings.

INFER

What is the meaning of line 45?

_____

_____

_____

_____

_____

_____

_____

INTERPRET

How would you describe the relationship between the speaker and his grandmother?

_____

_____

_____

_____

_____

_____

_____

_____

_____

_____

HARD ON THE GAS

Janet S. Wong

INFER

What do you think the grandfather's life has been like (lines 1–2)?

_____

_____

IDENTIFY

Alliteration is the repetition of consonant sounds in words close together. Circle the examples of alliteration in line 6.

INTERPRET

What does the word *ride* in the last line of the poem refer to?

_____

_____

CONNECT

The poem uses an **extended metaphor** to compare a way of driving to a way of living. What kind of life would be "hard on the gas"?

_____

_____

FLUENCY

Read the entire poem aloud. Use the clues given by the punctuation of the poem.

My grandfather taught himself to drive
rough, the way he learned to live,

push the pedal, hard on the gas,
rush up to 50,
5   coast a bit,

rush, rest, rush, rest—

When you clutch the bar above your right shoulder
he shoots you a look that asks,
Who said the ride would be smooth?

"Hard on the Gas" from *Behind the Wheel: Poems About Driving* by Janet S. Wong. Copyright © 1999 by Janet S. Wong. Reproduced by permission of **Margaret K. McElderry Books, an imprint of Simon & Schuster Children's Publishing Division.**

Ode to Mi Gato / In a Neighborhood in Los Angeles / Hard on the Gas

Tone Chart   **Tone** is the speaker's attitude toward his or her subject. Identify the tone of "Ode to Mi Gato," "In a Neighborhood in Los Angeles," and "Hard on the Gas." Then, give examples from each poem that help to create its tone.

SKILLS FOCUS

Literary Skills
Analyze tone.

"Ode to Mi Gato"	"In a Neighborhood in Los Angeles"	"Hard on the Gas"
Speaker's Tone Joyful	Speaker's Tone Friendly	Speaker's Tone Stubborn
Passages That Create Tone And he cuddled up to my fathers Slippers	Passages That Create Tone my grandma would chat with chairs sing them old songs dance waltzes with them in the kitchen.	Passages That Create Tone My grandfather taught himself to drive rough, the way he learned to live, he sheds you a look that asks, Who said the ride would be smooth?

Skills Review

Ode to Mi Gato / In a Neighborhood in Los Angeles / Hard on the Gas

COMPREHENSION

Reading Comprehension   Circle the letter of the correct answer.

1. The **tone** of "Ode to Mi Gato" might be described by all of the following words *except*

    a. loving   b. humorous   c. playful   d. sad

2. Which of the following is true of "Ode to Mi Gato"?

    f. It has meter.

    g. It has no stanzas.

    h. It rhymes.

    j. It has no speaker.

3. How did the speaker get the cat?

    a. His sister gave the cat to him.

    b. He bought the cat from a pet shop.

    c. He found the cat on a car fender.

    d. A neighbor gave him the cat.

4. The grandmother in Alarcón's poem—

    f. takes care of the speaker

    g. lives in Arizona

    h. takes the child to school each day

    j. dies young

5. What is the speaker's **tone** when he speaks of his grandmother?

    a. sad   b. admiring   c. boastful   d. sarcastic

6. In "Hard on the Gas" the speaker tells about her—

    f. first fast car

    g. grandfather's views on life

    h. fear of living

    j. need to be number one

Before You Read

This selection also appears in *Elements of Literature.*

John Henry Anonymous African American

LITERARY FOCUS: REPETITION

In a poem, a poet may repeat a word, a phrase, a stanza, a sound, or a pattern of words. **Repetition** is a tool that helps the poet create rhythm, a musical sound, a mood, and even suspense. Repetition also helps a poet emphasize an idea.

A **refrain** is a word, phrase, line, or group of lines repeated regularly in a poem or song. A refrain usually appears at the end of a stanza. The wording of a refrain may vary slightly in different parts of a poem.

You are likely to see a refrain in a **ballad,** a song or a poem that tells a story. Like most ballads, "John Henry" contains short stanzas and simple words. Like the characters in many ballads, John Henry is a folk hero. As you read the ballad, note the pattern of repetition in each verse.

READING SKILLS: MAKING PREDICTIONS

Although "John Henry" is a poem, it also tells a story. Get involved in the story of John Henry by making predictions as you read. Here's how:

- Look for clues in the text.
- Connect those clues with things you already know.
- Revise and adjust your predictions as needed.

SKILLS FOCUS

Literary Skills
Understand repetition and refrain.

Reading Skills
Make predictions.

JOHN HENRY

Anonymous African American

> **BACKGROUND: Literature and Folklore**
>
> Nobody knows whether John Henry, the hero of this song, was a real person, but people began singing about him in the early 1870s. He is said to have been an African American laborer in the crew constructing the Big Bend Tunnel of the Chesapeake and Ohio Railroad. According to the legend, someone set up a contest between John Henry and a steam drill. If you can, listen to a recording of the song "John Henry."

IDENTIFY

Underline examples of **repetition** in lines 1–15. What effect does the use of repetition have?

_____

_____

_____

PREDICT

Pause at line 15. John Henry prepares to do battle with the steam drill to see who can drill the holes through rock faster. Who do you think will win? What will happen next?

_____

_____

_____

_____

John Henry was about three days old
Sittin' on his papa's knee.
He picked up a hammer and a little piece of steel
Said, "Hammer's gonna be the death of me, Lord, Lord!
5   Hammer's gonna be the death of me."

The captain said to John Henry,
"Gonna bring that steam drill 'round
Gonna bring that steam drill out on the job
Gonna whop that steel on down, Lord, Lord!
10   Whop that steel on down."

John Henry told his captain,
"A man ain't nothin' but a man
But before I let your steam drill beat me down
I'd die with a hammer in my hand, Lord, Lord!
15   I'd die with a hammer in my hand."

© Getty Images.

John Henry said to his shaker,°
"Shaker, why don't you sing?
I'm throwing thirty pounds from my hips on down
Just listen to that cold steel ring, Lord, Lord!
20   Listen to that cold steel ring."

John Henry said to his shaker,
"Shaker, you'd better pray
'Cause if I miss that little piece of steel
Tomorrow be your buryin' day, Lord, Lord!
25   Tomorrow be your buryin' day."

The shaker said to John Henry,
"I think this mountain's cavin' in!"
John Henry said to his shaker, "Man,
That ain't nothin' but my hammer suckin' wind, Lord, Lord!
30   Nothin' but my hammer suckin' wind."

The man that invented the steam drill
Thought he was mighty fine

° **shaker** *n.:* worker who holds the drill.

INFER

Why will tomorrow be the shaker's "buryin' day" (line 24) if John Henry misses the piece of steel?

_____

_____

_____

_____

_____

_____

_____

_____

_____

_____

_____

_____

_____

_____

_____

_____

IDENTIFY

Circle the words in lines 31–35 that tell you that John Henry won the contest. Then, read the next stanza, and underline the passage that reveals that the machine might have won after all.

DRAW CONCLUSIONS

John Henry's actual story ends at line 40, but the song goes on. Why do you think the last four verses were added to the story?

_____

_____

_____

_____

_____

_____

_____

_____

_____

_____

_____

_____

_____

_____

_____

_____

_____

But John Henry made fifteen feet
The steam drill only made nine, Lord, Lord!
35   The steam drill only made nine.

John Henry hammered in the mountain
His hammer was striking fire
But he worked so hard, he broke his poor heart
He laid down his hammer and he died, Lord, Lord!
40   He laid down his hammer and he died.

John Henry had a little woman
Her name was Polly Ann
John Henry took sick and went to his bed
Polly Ann drove steel like a man, Lord, Lord!
45   Polly Ann drove steel like a man.

John Henry had a little baby
You could hold him in the palm of your hand
The last words I heard that poor boy say,
"My daddy was a steel-driving man, Lord, Lord!
50   My daddy was a steel-driving man."

They took John Henry to the graveyard
And they buried him in the sand
And every locomotive comes a-roaring by
Says, "There lies a steel-driving man, Lord, Lord!
55   There lies a steel-driving man."

Well, every Monday morning
When the bluebirds begin to sing
You can hear John Henry a mile or more
You can hear John Henry's hammer ring, Lord, Lord!
60   You can hear John Henry's hammer ring.

John Henry

Repetition Chart   Like many poems, "John Henry" contains several types of repetition. Re-read the poem, and fill in the chart with examples.

Literary Skills
Analyze repetition.

Types of Repetition	Examples from "John Henry"
words	lord, John Henry
phrases	Whop that steel on down
lines	I'd die with a hammer in my hand.
patterns	dialogue

Skills Review

John Henry

COMPREHENSION

Reading Comprehension   Answer each question.

1. Who is the subject of the ballad?

   The subject is John Henry.

2. What prediction did John Henry make when he was a baby?

   The prediction John Henry made was: He picked up a hammer and a little piece of steel and said "Hammer's gonna be the death of me."

3. What does John Henry mean when he says, "A man ain't nothin' but a man"?

   John Henry can only do what he can, he's a human.

4. In what way does John Henry's prediction come true?

   John Henry died with a hammer in his hand.

5. How does the memory of John Henry live on?

   The memory lives on with songs and stories.

Before You Read

April Rain Song by Langston Hughes
Ankylosaurus by Jack Prelutsky

LITERARY FOCUS: SOUND EFFECTS IN POETRY

What comes to mind when you think about poetry? If you're like many people, you think of sounds. That's because most poems are full of sounds. Poets choose words for how they sound as well as for what they mean. Here are some sound devices you'll find in many poems.

- **Repetition** of a single word, a phrase, a group of lines, a stanza, or a pattern. When a group of lines is repeated in a poem, it is called a refrain.

- **Rhyme** is another form of repetition. For example, *choose* and *lose* rhyme, as do *spaghetti* and *confetti*.

- **Alliteration** is a form of repetition. It is the repetition of a consonant sound in words that are close together. Example: "**M**arigold and **m**imosa **m**urmur in the **m**eadow."

- **Onomatopoeia** (ăn'ō·mat'ō·pē'ə) is the use of a word whose sound imitates or suggests its meaning. *Clank, bark, buzz, roar,* and *hiss* are examples.

READING SKILLS: READING ALOUD

Poetry that contains sound devices comes alive when it is read aloud. Be sure to pause from time to time when you read the poems that follow. Read sections aloud either to a peer or to yourself. Take note of the rhymes, rhythms, and other musical effects created by the poet's word choice.

SKILLS FOCUS

Literary Skills
Understand sound effects in poetry.

Reading Skills
Read poetry aloud.

April Rain Song

Langston Hughes

Let the rain kiss you.

Let the rain beat upon your head with silver liquid drops.

Let the rain sing you a lullaby.

The rain makes still pools on the sidewalk.

5 The rain makes running pools in the gutter.

The rain plays a little sleep-song on our roof at night—

And I love the rain.

© Getty Images.

ANKYLOSAURUS

Jack Prelutsky

Clankity Clankity Clankity Clank!
Ankylosaurus° was built like a tank,
its hide was a fortress as sturdy as steel,
it tended to be an inedible meal.

5   It was armored in front, it was armored behind,
there wasn't a thing on its minuscule mind,
it waddled about on its four stubby legs,
nibbling on plants with a mouthful of pegs.

Ankylosaurus was best left alone,
10   its tail was a cudgel of gristle and bone,
Clankity Clankity Clankity Clank!
Ankylosaurus was built like a tank.

WORD STUDY

A cudgel (kuj'əl), line 10, is a stick or club that has a blunt tip.

IDENTIFY

Read the poem through. Then, mark its **rhyme scheme**.

IDENTIFY

Underline the lines in the poem that are repeated. What effect does the use of **repetition** create?

_____

_____

INTERPRET

What one word would you use to describe ankylosaurus?

_____

FLUENCY

Read the poem aloud, listening to its sounds. Emphasize the "Clankity Clank" lines and the words that rhyme.

° **ankylosaurus** (aŋ'kə·lō·sôr'əs): heavily armored, short-legged dinosaur; also called ankylosaur.

"Ankylosaurus" from *Tyrannosaurus Was a Beast* by Jack Prelutsky. Copyright © 1988 by Jack Prelutsky. Reproduced by permission of **Greenwillow Books**, a division of **HarperCollins Publishers, Inc.**

April Rain Song / Ankylosaurus

SKILLS FOCUS

Literary Skills
Analyze sound effects in poetry.

Sound Effects Chart   Both "April Rain Song" and "Ankylosaurus" are filled with sound effects. Fill in the chart below with some examples from the poems. Not all the sound effects listed are used in each of the poems. Write "None" if you can't find any examples.

Sound Effect	"April Rain Song"	"Ankylosaurus"
repetition		
rhyme		
alliteration		
onomatopoeia		

Skills Review

April Rain Song / Ankylosaurus

COMPREHENSION

Reading Comprehension   Circle the correct answer.

1. The main literary device in "April Rain Song" is—
   a. rhyme
   b. onomatopoeia
   c. repetition
   d. symbolism

2. The creature in "Ankylosaurus" might be described by all of the following words *except*—
   f. clumsy
   g. intelligent
   h. heavy
   j. huge

3. In "Ankylosaurus," "Clankity Clankity Clankity Clank!" is an example of—
   a. rhyme
   b. onomatopoeia
   c. personification
   d. tone

4. "Minuscule mind" contains an example of—
   f. personification
   g. onomatopoeia
   h. alliteration
   j. rhyme

Literary Criticism:
You Be the Judge

© Ryan McVay/Getty Images.

Academic Vocabulary for Collection 8

These are the terms and concepts you should know
as you read and analyze the selections in this collection.

———————

Literary Criticism Analyzing the elements of a literary work (plot, characters, setting, and so on) and evaluating, or judging, its quality.

Character Evaluation Judging how well the characters in a literary work are developed.

The following questions can be used to judge characters:
- Do the characters have weaknesses as well as strengths? Is a character too good to be true?
- Do the characters talk and act like real people?
- Do the characters change and grow as a result of events that take place in the story?

Plot Evaluation Judging whether a plot is believable.

The following questions can be used to judge plot:
- Do the events in the plot grow out of characters' decisions and actions?
- Are there believable causes and effects, or do the events just seem to happen for no clear reason?
- Is the ending satisfying?

The Dog of Pompeii by Louis Untermeyer

LITERARY FOCUS: CREDIBLE CHARACTERS

When we read stories, even fantasy stories, we expect the characters to act the way real people do. We expect them to have strengths and weaknesses. We expect them to grow, change, and make discoveries about themselves. In short, we want the characters to be **credible** (kred′ə·bəl), or believable.

As you read "The Dog of Pompeii," decide whether Tito and Bimbo are credible characters. Does Tito behave like a real boy? Does Bimbo behave like a real dog?

READING SKILLS: MAKING INFERENCES

Making inferences, or educated guesses, about what you read is a way of working with a story's author. You provide details that the author has not included. To make an inference, look for clues that the author *does* provide. Connect these clues to other works you've read or to your own experiences. Then, make your inference. Here's an example.

Details from Story	Experience from Real Life	Sample Inference
Judith is very shy. She gets invited to a huge party. The night of the party Judith gets sick unexpectedly.	Sometimes being nervous or afraid can bring on sickness.	Judith's illness may be caused by her anxiety over going to the party.

SKILLS FOCUS

Literary Skills
Evaluate a character's credibility.

Reading Skills
Make inferences.

Vocabulary Skills
Understand prefixes.

VOCABULARY DEVELOPMENT

PREVIEW SELECTION VOCABULARY

Become familiar with these words before you read "The Dog of Pompeii."

ambitious (am·bish'əs) *adj.:* eager to succeed or to achieve something.

The ambitious citizens of Pompeii hoped to make their city famous.

proverb (präv'ərb) *n.:* short traditional saying that expresses a truth.

"Haste makes waste" is a proverb.

revived (ri·vīvd') *v.:* awakened; brought back to life.

The splashing water revived him, and he sat up.

CLARIFYING WORD MEANINGS: PREFIXES

You can often clarify the meaning of an unfamiliar word by looking at the parts it is made of. A **prefix** is a word part that is added to the beginning of a word or root. Like words, prefixes have meanings. Whenever a prefix is added to a word, the meaning of the original word changes.

Get to know these common prefixes:

Common Prefixes

Prefix	Meaning	Examples
dis–	opposing; away	dishonor, dislike
in–	not	incomplete, incorrect
non–	not	nonhuman, nonprofit
un–	not	unwise, unwell

THE DOG OF POMPEII

Louis Untermeyer

BACKGROUND: Literature and Social Studies

"The Dog of Pompeii" is **historical fiction**. Louis Untermeyer weaved together a fictional story and actual historical events. The story's setting is Pompeii, an ancient Roman city that was buried by a volcanic eruption in A.D. 79.

Tito and his dog Bimbo lived (if you could call it living) under the wall where it joined the inner gate. They really didn't live there; they just slept there. They lived anywhere. Pompeii was one of the gayest of the old Latin towns, but although Tito was never an unhappy boy, he was not exactly a merry one. The streets were always lively with shining chariots and bright red trappings; the open-air theaters rocked with laughing crowds; sham[1] battles and athletic sports were free for the asking in the great stadium. Once a

10 year the Caesar[2] visited the pleasure city and the fireworks lasted for days; the sacrifices[3] in the forum were better than a show.

But Tito saw none of these things. He was blind—had been blind from birth. He was known to everyone in the poorer quarters. But no one could say how old he was, no one remembered his parents, no one could tell where he

---

1. **sham** *adj.:* make-believe.
2. **Caesar** (sē′zər) *n.:* Roman emperor. The word *Caesar* comes from the family name of Julius Caesar, a great general who ruled Rome as dictator from 49 to 44 B.C.
3. **sacrifices** *n.:* offerings (especially of slaughtered animals) to the gods.

Joel Spector/HRW Illustration.

IDENTIFY

Pause at line 21. Who are the two main characters in this story? What is unusual about Tito? What is unusual about Bimbo?

came from. Bimbo was another mystery. As long as people could remember seeing Tito—about twelve or thirteen years—they had seen Bimbo. Bimbo had never left his side.

20 He was not only dog but nurse, pillow, playmate, mother, and father to Tito.

Did I say Bimbo never left his master? (Perhaps I had better say comrade, for if anyone was the master, it was Bimbo.) I was wrong. Bimbo did trust Tito alone exactly three times a day. It was a fixed routine, a custom under-stood between boy and dog since the beginning of their friendship, and the way it worked was this: Early in the morning, shortly after dawn, while Tito was still dreaming, Bimbo would disappear. When Tito awoke, Bimbo would

_____

_____

_____

_____

_____

_____

_____

_____

_____

_____

INFER

Pause at line 50. Why might it be important for Bimbo to stay alert at night?

_____

_____

_____

_____

_____

_____

30 be sitting quietly at his side, his ears cocked, his stump of a tail tapping the ground, and a fresh-baked bread—more like a large round roll—at his feet. Tito would stretch himself; Bimbo would yawn; then they would breakfast. At noon, no matter where they happened to be, Bimbo would put his paw on Tito's knee and the two of them would return to the inner gate. Tito would curl up in the corner (almost like a dog) and go to sleep, while Bimbo, looking quite important (almost like a boy), would disappear again. In half an hour he'd be back with their lunch. Sometimes it

40 would be a piece of fruit or a scrap of meat, often it was nothing but a dry crust. But sometimes there would be one of those flat rich cakes, sprinkled with raisins and sugar, that Tito liked so much. At suppertime the same thing happened, although there was a little less of every-thing, for things were hard to snatch in the evening, with the streets full of people. Besides, Bimbo didn't approve of too much food before going to sleep. A heavy supper made boys too restless and dogs too stodgy[4]—and it was the business of a dog to sleep lightly with one ear open and

50 muscles ready for action.

But, whether there was much or little, hot or cold, fresh or dry, food was always there. Tito never asked where it came from and Bimbo never told him. There was plenty of rainwater in the hollows of soft stones; the old egg woman at the corner sometimes gave him a cupful of strong goat's milk; in the grape season the fat winemaker let him have drippings of the mild juice. So there was no danger of going hungry or thirsty. There was plenty of everything in Pompeii—if you knew where to find it—and if you had a

60 dog like Bimbo.

_____

4. **stodgy** (stä′jē) _adj.:_ heavy and slow in movement.

As I said before, Tito was not the merriest boy in Pompeii. He could not romp with the other youngsters and play "hare and hounds" and "I spy" and "follow your master" and "ball against the building" and "jackstones" and "kings and robbers" with them. But that did not make him sorry for himself. If he could not see the sights that delighted the lads of Pompeii, he could hear and smell things they never noticed. He could really see more with his ears and nose than they could with their eyes. When he and Bimbo went out walking, he knew just where they were going and exactly what was happening.

"Ah," he'd sniff and say, as they passed a handsome villa,[5] "Glaucus Pansa is giving a grand dinner tonight. They're going to have three kinds of bread, and roast pigling, and stuffed goose, and a great stew—I think bear stew—and a fig pie." And Bimbo would note that this would be a good place to visit tomorrow.

Or, "H'm," Tito would murmur, half through his lips, half through his nostrils. "The wife of Marcus Lucretius is expecting her mother. She's shaking out every piece of goods in the house; she's going to use the best clothes—the ones she's been keeping in pine needles and camphor[6]—and there's an extra girl in the kitchen. Come, Bimbo, let's get out of the dust!"

Or, as they passed a small but elegant dwelling opposite the public baths, "Too bad! The tragic poet is ill again. It must be a bad fever this time, for they're trying smoke fumes instead of medicine. Whew! I'm glad I'm not a tragic poet!"

Or, as they neared the forum, "Mm-m! What good things they have in the macellum[7] today!" (It really was a

5. **villa** n.: large house.
6. **camphor** (kam'fər) n.: strong-smelling substance used to keep moths away from clothing. Camphor is still used for this purpose.
7. **macellum** (mə·sel'əm) n.: market, especially a meat market.

INFER

Re-read lines 61–71. Write down three words that describe what you know about Tito's **character** so far.

_____

_____

_____

_____

_____

_____

_____

_____

_____

_____

_____

_____

INTERPRET

What does the author mean when he says in lines 68–69 that Tito could "see more with his ears and nose" than the other boys of Pompeii could see with their eyes? Circle at least three things in lines 72–98 that Tito "sees" with his nose.

IDENTIFY

Re-read lines 89–98. Underline the details that help make Tito a **credible**, or realistic, character.

_____

_____

_____

_____

_____

_____

_____

_____

VISUALIZE

Re-read lines 99–112. List three details that help you picture the forum.

_____

_____

_____

_____

_____

_____

_____

VOCABULARY

ambitious (am·bish'əs) *adj.:* eager to succeed or to achieve something.

sort of butcher-grocer-marketplace, but Tito didn't know any better. He called it the macellum.) "Dates from Africa, and salt oysters from sea caves, and cuttlefish, and new honey, and sweet onions, and—ugh!—water-buffalo steaks. Come, let's see what's what in the forum." And Bimbo, just as curious as his comrade, hurried on. Being a dog, he trusted his ears and nose (like Tito) more than his eyes. And so the two of them entered the center of Pompeii.

100 The forum was the part of the town to which everybody came at least once during the day. It was the central square, and everything happened here. There were no private houses; all was public—the chief temples, the gold and red bazaars, the silk shops, the town hall, the booths belonging to the weavers and jewel merchants, the wealthy woolen market, the shrine of the household gods. Everything glittered here. The buildings looked as if they were new— which, in a sense, they were. The earthquake of twelve years ago had brought down all the old structures and, since the citizens of Pompeii were **ambitious** to rival Naples and

110 even Rome, they had seized the opportunity to rebuild the whole town. And they had done it all within a dozen years. There was scarcely a building that was older than Tito.

Joel Spector/HRW Illustration.

Tito had heard a great deal about the earthquake, though being about a year old at the time, he could scarcely remember it. This particular quake had been a light one—as earthquakes go. The weaker houses had been shaken down, parts of the outworn wall had been wrecked; but there was little loss of life, and the brilliant new Pompeii had taken the place of the old. No one knew what caused these earthquakes. Records showed they had happened in the neighborhood since the beginning of time. Sailors said that it was to teach the lazy city folk a lesson and make them appreciate those who risked the dangers of the sea to bring them luxuries and protect their town from invaders. The priests said that the gods took this way of showing their anger to those who refused to worship properly and who failed to bring enough sacrifices to the altars and (though they didn't say it in so many words) presents to the priests. The tradesmen said that the foreign merchants had corrupted the ground and it was no longer safe to traffic in imported goods that came from strange places and carried a curse with them. Everyone had a different explanation and everyone's explanation was louder and sillier than his neighbor's.

They were talking about it this afternoon as Tito and Bimbo came out of the side street into the public square. The forum was the favorite promenade[8] for rich and poor. What with the priests arguing with the politicians, servants doing the day's shopping, tradesmen crying their wares, women displaying the latest fashions from Greece and Egypt, children playing hide-and-seek among the marble columns, knots of soldiers, sailors, peasants from the provinces[9]—to say nothing of those who merely came to lounge and look on—the square was crowded to its last

INFER

Re-read lines 107–119 carefully. What natural disaster had caused most of Pompeii to be rebuilt? How old was Tito when this disaster happened, and how old is he now? What might have caused Tito to have become orphaned and homeless?

---

8. promenade (präm′ə·nād′) *n*.: public place where people stroll.
9. provinces *n*.: places far from the capital, under Roman control.

VOCABULARY

proverb (präv′ərb) *n.:* short traditional saying that expresses a truth.

inch. His ears even more than his nose guided Tito to the place where the talk was loudest. It was in front of the shrine of the household gods that, naturally enough, the householders were arguing.

"I tell you," rumbled a voice which Tito recognized
150 as bath master Rufus's, "there won't be another earthquake in my lifetime or yours. There may be a tremble or two, but earthquakes, like lightnings, never strike twice in the same place."

"Do they not?" asked a thin voice Tito had never heard. It had a high, sharp ring to it and Tito knew it as the accent of a stranger. "How about the two towns of Sicily that have been ruined three times within fifteen years by the eruptions of Mount Etna? And were they not warned? And does that column of smoke above Vesuvius mean nothing?"

160 "That?" Tito could hear the grunt with which one question answered another. "That's always there. We use it for our weather guide. When the smoke stands up straight, we know we'll have fair weather; when it flattens out, it's sure to be foggy; when it drifts to the east—"

"Yes, yes," cut in the edged voice. "I've heard about your mountain barometer.[10] But the column of smoke seems hundreds of feet higher than usual and it's thickening and spreading like a shadowy tree. They say in Naples—"

"Oh, Naples!" Tito knew this voice by the little squeak
170 that went with it. It was Attilio the cameo cutter.[11] "They talk while we suffer. Little help we got from them last time. Naples commits the crimes and Pompeii pays the price. It's become a **proverb** with us. Let them mind their own business."

"Yes," grumbled Rufus, "and others', too."

---

10. **barometer** (bə·räm′ət·ər) *n.:* instrument for measuring atmospheric pressure. Barometers are used in forecasting changes in the weather.
11. **cameo cutter:** artist who carves small, delicate pictures on gems or shells.

"Very well, my confident friends," responded the thin voice, which now sounded curiously flat. "We also have a proverb—and it is this: *Those who will not listen to men must be taught by the gods.* I say no more. But I leave a last warning. Remember the holy ones. Look to your temples. And when the smoke tree above Vesuvius grows to the shape of an umbrella pine, look to your lives."

Tito could hear the air whistle as the speaker drew his toga about him, and the quick shuffle of feet told him the stranger had gone.

"Now what," said the cameo cutter, "did he mean by that?"

"I wonder," grunted Rufus. "I wonder."

Tito wondered, too. And Bimbo, his head at a thoughtful angle, looked as if he had been doing a heavy piece of pondering. By nightfall the argument had been forgotten. If the smoke had increased, no one saw it in the dark. Besides, it was Caesar's birthday and the town was in a holiday mood. Tito and Bimbo were among the merrymakers, dodging the charioteers who shouted at them. A dozen times they almost upset baskets of sweets and jars of Vesuvian wine, said to be as fiery as the streams inside the volcano, and a dozen times they were cursed and cuffed. But Tito never missed his footing. He was thankful for his keen ears and quick instinct—most thankful of all for Bimbo.

They visited the uncovered theater, and though Tito could not see the faces of the actors, he could follow the play better than most of the audience, for their attention wandered—they were distracted by the scenery, the costumes, the byplay,[12] even by themselves—while Tito's whole attention was centered in what he heard. Then to

---

12. **byplay** *n.*: action taking place outside the main action of a play.

PREDICT

Pause at line 184. Do you think another earthquake will strike Pompeii? Tell what you think will happen next in the story.

INTERPRET

Re-read lines 188–200. Underline the details that help make the town and its people seem realistic.

Joel Spector/HRW Illustration.

the city walls, where the people of Pompeii watched a mock naval battle in which the city was attacked by the sea and saved after thousands of flaming arrows had been
210 exchanged and countless colored torches had been burned. Though the thrill of flaring ships and lighted skies was lost to Tito, the shouts and cheers excited him as much as any, and he cried out with the loudest of them.

The next morning there were two of the beloved raisin-and-sugar cakes for his breakfast. Bimbo was unusually active and thumped his bit of a tail until Tito was afraid he would wear it out. The boy could not imagine whether Bimbo was urging him to some sort of game or was trying to tell him something. After a while, he ceased to notice
220 Bimbo. He felt drowsy. Last night's late hours had tired him. Besides, there was a heavy mist in the air—no, a thick fog rather than a mist—a fog that got into his throat and scraped it and made him cough. He walked as far as the marine gate[13] to get a breath of the sea. But the blanket of haze had spread all over the bay and even the salt air seemed smoky.

He went to bed before dusk and slept. But he did not sleep well. He had too many dreams—dreams of ships

13. **marine gate:** gate in a city wall leading to the sea.

lurching in the forum, of losing his way in a screaming
230 crowd, of armies marching across his chest, of being pulled
over every rough pavement of Pompeii.

He woke early. Or, rather, he was pulled awake. Bimbo
was doing the pulling. The dog had dragged Tito to his feet
and was urging the boy along. Somewhere. Where, Tito did
not know. His feet stumbled uncertainly; he was still half
asleep. For a while he noticed nothing except the fact that it
was hard to breathe. The air was hot. And heavy. So heavy
that he could taste it. The air, it seemed, had turned to
powder—a warm powder that stung his nostrils and burned
240 his sightless eyes.

Then he began to hear sounds. Peculiar sounds. Like
animals under the earth. Hissings and groanings and muf-
fled cries that a dying creature might make dislodging the
stones of his underground cave. There was no doubt of it
now. The noises came from underneath. He not only heard
them—he could feel them. The earth twitched; the twitching changed to an uneven shrugging of the soil. Then, as
Bimbo half pulled, half coaxed him across, the ground
jerked away from his feet and he was thrown against a
250 stone fountain.

The water—hot water—splashing in his face **revived**
him. He got to his feet, Bimbo steadying him, helping him
on again. The noises grew louder; they came closer. The
cries were even more animal-like than before, but now they
came from human throats. A few people, quicker of foot
and more hurried by fear, began to rush by. A family or
two—then a section—then, it seemed, an army broken out
of bounds. Tito, bewildered though he was, could recognize
Rufus as he bellowed past him, like a water buffalo gone
260 mad. Time was lost in a nightmare.

IDENTIFY

Pause at line 240. What
changes in the weather does
Tito notice the next morning?

_____

_____

_____

_____

_____

_____

_____

INFER

Pause at line 250. What do
you think is happening?

_____

_____

_____

_____

_____

_____

_____

VOCABULARY

revived (ri·vīvd′) v.: brought
back to life or to a waking
state.

VISUALIZE

Underline details in lines 241–270 that help you *hear* what Tito hears. Circle details that help you *picture* the terrifying scene.

IDENTIFY

Re-read lines 271–287. What details help make Tito's character seem **credible**?

_____

_____

_____

_____

_____

_____

_____

_____

_____

_____

_____

_____

_____

_____

_____

_____

_____

_____

It was then the crashing began. First a sharp crackling, like a monstrous snapping of twigs; then a roar like the fall of a whole forest of trees; then an explosion that tore earth and sky. The heavens, though Tito could not see them, were shot through with continual flickerings of fire. Lightnings above were answered by thunders beneath. A house fell. Then another. By a miracle the two companions had escaped the dangerous side streets and were in a more open space. It was the forum. They rested here awhile—how long, he

270   did not know.

Tito had no idea of the time of day. He could feel it was black—an unnatural blackness. Something inside— perhaps the lack of breakfast and lunch—told him it was past noon. But it didn't matter. Nothing seemed to matter. He was getting drowsy, too drowsy to walk. But walk he must. He knew it. And Bimbo knew it; the sharp tugs told him so. Nor was it a moment too soon. The sacred ground of the forum was safe no longer. It was beginning to rock, then to pitch, then to split. As they stumbled out of the

280   square, the earth wriggled like a caught snake and all the columns of the temple of Jupiter[14] came down. It was the end of the world—or so it seemed. To walk was not enough now. They must run. Tito was too frightened to know what to do or where to go. He had lost all sense of direction. He started to go back to the inner gate; but Bimbo, straining his back to the last inch, almost pulled his clothes from him. What did the creature want? Had the dog gone mad?

Then suddenly he understood. Bimbo was telling him the way out—urging him there. The sea gate, of course.

290   The sea gate—and then the sea. Far from falling buildings, heaving ground. He turned, Bimbo guiding him across open pits and dangerous pools of bubbling mud, away from buildings that had caught fire and were dropping

---

14. Jupiter: the supreme god in the religion of the Romans.

their burning beams. Tito could no longer tell whether the noises were made by the shrieking sky or the agonized people. He and Bimbo ran on—the only silent beings in a howling world.

New dangers threatened. All Pompeii seemed to be thronging toward the marine gate and, squeezing among the crowds, there was the chance of being trampled to death. But the chance had to be taken. It was growing harder and harder to breathe. What air there was choked him. It was all dust now—dust and pebbles, pebbles as large as beans. They fell on his head, his hands—pumice stones from the black heart of Vesuvius. The mountain was turning itself inside out. Tito remembered a phrase that the stranger had said in the forum two days ago: "Those who will not listen to men must be taught by the gods." The people of Pompeii had refused to heed the warnings; they were being taught now—if it was not too late.

Suddenly it seemed too late for Tito. The red-hot ashes blistered his skin, the stinging vapors tore his throat. He could not go on. He staggered toward a small tree at the side of the road and fell. In a moment Bimbo was beside him. He coaxed. But there was no answer. He licked Tito's hands, his feet, his face. The boy did not stir. Then Bimbo did the last thing he could—the last thing he wanted to do. He bit his comrade, bit him deep in the arm. With a cry of pain, Tito jumped to his feet, Bimbo after him. Tito was in despair, but Bimbo was determined. He drove the boy on, snapping at his heels, worrying his way through the crowd, barking, baring his teeth, heedless of kicks or falling stones. Sick with hunger, half dead with fear and sulfur fumes, Tito pounded on, pursued by Bimbo. How long, he never knew. At last he staggered through the marine gate and felt soft sand under him. Then Tito fainted. . . .

300

310

320

INFER

Underline the details in lines 298–310 that lead you to infer that what is happening here is more than an earthquake. What's your best guess as to what might be happening to Pompeii?

_____

_____

_____

_____

_____

IDENTIFY

Pause at line 326. How does Bimbo help Tito get to the marine gate?

_____

_____

_____

_____

FLUENCY

Re-read this suspenseful passage aloud. This is where you find the story's **climax**, its most exciting moment, when the outcome of the conflict, boy vs. the forces of nature, is decided. Read the short sentences quickly. Use your voice to show increased excitement until the climax, when Tito falls—and Bimbo saves the day.

Pause at line 337. Retell what
has happened to Tito since
Bimbo woke him up that
morning (line 232).

_____

_____

_____

_____

_____

_____

_____

_____

_____

_____

_____

_____

_____

_____

_____

_____

_____

_____

_____

_____

Joel Spector/HRW Illustration.

Someone was dashing seawater over him. Someone
was carrying him toward a boat.

"Bimbo," he called. And then louder, "Bimbo!" But
330 Bimbo had disappeared.

Voices jarred against each other. "Hurry—hurry!"
"To the boats!" "Can't you see the child's frightened and
starving!" "He keeps calling for someone!" "Poor boy, he's
out of his mind." "Here, child—take this!"

They tucked him in among them. The oarlocks
creaked; the oars splashed; the boat rode over toppling
waves. Tito was safe. But he wept continually.

"Bimbo!" he wailed. "Bimbo! Bimbo!"

He could not be comforted.

340   Eighteen hundred years passed. Scientists were restoring the ancient city; excavators[15] were working their way through the stones and trash that had buried the entire town. Much had already been brought to light—statues, bronze instruments, bright mosaics,[16] household articles; even delicate paintings had been preserved by the fall of ashes that had taken over two thousand lives. Columns were dug up, and the forum was beginning to emerge.

It was at a place where the ruins lay deepest that the director paused.

350   "Come here," he called to his assistant. "I think we've discovered the remains of a building in good shape. Here are four huge millstones that were most likely turned by slaves or mules—and here is a whole wall standing with shelves inside it. Why! It must have been a bakery. And here's a curious thing. What do you think I found under this heap where the ashes were thickest? The skeleton of a dog!"

"Amazing!" gasped his assistant. "You'd think a dog would have had sense enough to run away at the time.

360   And what is that flat thing he's holding between his teeth? It can't be a stone."

"No. It must have come from this bakery. You know it looks to me like some sort of cake hardened with the years. And, bless me, if those little black pebbles aren't raisins. A raisin cake almost two thousand years old! I wonder what made him want it at such a moment."

"I wonder," murmured the assistant.

Notes _____

INFER

Re-read lines 350–366. Why did Bimbo return to Pompeii after taking Tito to a safe place? Underline the details that support your ideas.

---

15. **excavators** (eks′kə·vāt′ərz) *n.:* diggers; here, archaeologists.
16. **mosaics** (mō·zā′iks) *n.:* pictures or designs made by inlaying small bits of stone, glass, tile, or other materials in mortar.

The Dog of Pompeii

SKILLS FOCUS

Literary Skills
Evaluate a character's credibility.

Character Evaluation Chart   In the chart below, answer the questions about Tito's character. Give examples from the story as you answer each item. Review your responses. Finally, explain why you think Tito's character is—or is not—credible.

Tito	
Question	**Example from the Story**
Does the character have both strengths and weaknesses? Explain.	
Does the character talk and act as a real person would? Explain.	
Does the character grow and change as a result of story events? Explain.	

☐ **Credible?** Explain. ☐ **Not Credible?** Explain.

_____

_____

_____

_____

Skills Review

The Dog of Pompeii

VOCABULARY AND COMPREHENSION

A. Prefixes   Complete the paragraph by writing the correct words from the Word Bank in the blanks. Then, circle words that contain prefixes meaning "not."

Word Bank

ambitious

proverb

revived

At the game, two fans became unwell and fainted in the summer heat. They were (1) _____ when we brought them into the shade and gave them noncarbonated water to drink. Each team played a(n) (2) _____ game, hoping to remain unbeatable. One fan wore a T-shirt with a(n) (3) _____ printed on it that said "What counts is how you play the game."

B. Reading Comprehension   Answer each question below.

1. Who are the two main characters in the story? Where do they live?

_____

_____

2. What topic do the townspeople argue about?

_____

_____

3. What happens to the town in which Tito and Bimbo lived?

_____

_____

4. At the end of the story, what happens to Tito and Bimbo?

_____

_____

SKILLS FOCUS

Vocabulary Skills
Use prefixes.

This selection also appears in *Elements of Literature.*

Zlateh the Goat by Isaac Bashevis Singer

LITERARY FOCUS: SUSPENSE

Have you ever gripped the armrests of your seat during the final moments of an exciting movie? chewed your fingernails while the final seconds of a big game played out? held your breath when waiting to hear if you had been chosen as a finalist in a contest? That feeling is called **suspense,** a feeling of anxious curiosity about what will happen next.

Feelings of suspense can also build when you read something exciting. Writers sometimes build suspense by dropping hints about what will happen later in a story. "Zlateh the Goat" is not a horror story or a science-fiction cliffhanger. But, as you read, don't be surprised if you find your fingers turning the pages faster and faster to find out what happens to Zlateh the goat.

READING SKILLS: MAKING PREDICTIONS

When you're reading a story and the outcome is uncertain, what do you do? If you're like most people, you fill in the gap. You **predict** what will happen. You try to outsmart the writer by anticipating what's to come. If you read on and your prediction proves to be correct, that's great. In a way, though, you might enjoy being surprised by what actually happens.

Pause at three points as you read "Zlateh the Goat," and predict what you think will happen. Then, compare your predictions with what actually happens later in the story. You may want to use a chart like this one.

PREDICTION	OUTCOME
1.	
2.	
3.	

SKILLS FOCUS

Literary Skills
Understand suspense.

Reading Skills
Make predictions.

Vocabulary Skills
Understand suffixes.

VOCABULARY DEVELOPMENT

PREVIEW SELECTION VOCABULARY

Before you read "Zlateh the Goat," get to know these words.

penetrated (pen'i·trāt'id) *v.:* pierced; made a way through.

> *Sunlight penetrated the clouds.*

cleft (kleft) *adj.:* split; divided.

> *Goats have cleft hooves.*

chaos (kā'äs') *n.:* total confusion or disorder.

> *The storm created chaos outside Aaron's shelter.*

exuded (eg·zyo͞od'id) *v.:* gave off.

> *The hay exuded warmth.*

CLARIFYING WORD MEANINGS: SUFFIXES

Many words are made of more than one part. When you come across an unfamiliar word, look at its parts to see if you recognize any of them. A **suffix** is a word part that is added to the end of a word or root. The more suffixes you know, the more word meanings you'll be able to figure out.

Here are some common suffixes:

Common Suffixes

Suffix	Meaning	Examples
–able	capable of being	likable, laughable
–en	make	deepen, lengthen
–ful	full of	stressful, doubtful
–ion	act or condition of	inspection, reaction
–less	without	penniless, hopeless

Zlateh the Goat

Isaac Bashevis Singer

> **BACKGROUND: Literature and Religion**
>
> "Zlateh the Goat" takes place at Hanukkah (khä′noo·kä′), an eight-day Jewish religious festival usually observed in December. Hanukkah celebrates the rededication of the Temple in Jerusalem, in 165 B.C., following the victory of Jewish fighters over a huge Syrian army. The Temple, which had been taken over by Antiochus, ruler of the Syrians, had been violated and damaged. While the Jews were purifying and repairing the Temple, a miracle occurred. A tiny bit of oil for the holy lamp—barely enough for one day—lasted eight days. Do you see a miracle in Zlateh's story as well?

IDENTIFY

In lines 8–14, underline the details that describe the situation Reuven faces. Why does he decide to sell Zlateh?

_____

_____

_____

_____

_____

_____

_____

"Zlateh the Goat," from *Zlateh the Goat and Other Stories* by Isaac Bashevis Singer, illustrated by Maurice Sendak. Text copyright © 1966 by Isaac Bashevis Singer. Reproduced by permission of **HarperCollins Publishers**.

At Hanukkah time the road from the village to the town is usually covered with snow, but this year the winter had been a mild one. Hanukkah had almost come, yet little snow had fallen. The sun shone most of the time. The peasants complained that because of the dry weather there would be a poor harvest of winter grain. New grass sprouted, and the peasants sent their cattle out to pasture.

For Reuven the furrier[1] it was a bad year, and after long hesitation he decided to sell Zlateh the goat. She was
10 old and gave little milk. Feyvel the town butcher had offered eight gulden[2] for her. Such a sum would buy Hanukkah candles, potatoes and oil for pancakes, gifts for the children, and other holiday necessaries for the house. Reuven told his oldest boy, Aaron, to take the goat to town.

---

1. **furrier** (fur′ē·ər) *n.:* someone who makes and repairs fur garments.
2. **gulden** (gool′dən) *n.:* coins formerly used in several European countries.

Aaron understood what taking the goat to Feyvel meant, but he had to obey his father. Leah, his mother, wiped the tears from her eyes when she heard the news. Aaron's younger sisters, Anna and Miriam, cried loudly. Aaron put on his quilted jacket and a cap with earmuffs,

20 bound a rope around Zlateh's neck, and took along two slices of bread with cheese to eat on the road. Aaron was supposed to deliver the goat by evening, spend the night at the butcher's, and return the next day with the money.

While the family said goodbye to the goat, and Aaron placed the rope around her neck, Zlateh stood as patiently and good-naturedly as ever. She licked Reuven's hand. She shook her small white beard. Zlateh trusted human beings. She knew that they always fed her and never did her any harm.

30 When Aaron brought her out on the road to town, she seemed somewhat astonished. She'd never been led in that

INFER

Pause at line 23. What does "taking the goat to Feyvel" mean? Why is the family unhappy?

_____

_____

_____

_____

_____

_____

_____

_____

INFER

Based on information in lines 24–29, what inference can you make about Zlateh's **character**?

_____

_____

_____

_____

_____

_____

_____

_____

_____

VISUALIZE

Re-read lines 39–46. Underline three details that help you picture the change in the weather.

PREDICT

Pause at line 53. What do you think will happen now that the weather has changed?

_____

_____

_____

_____

_____

_____

VOCABULARY

penetrated (pen'i·trāt'id) v.: pierced; made a way through.

IDENTIFY

How would Aaron have to answer Zlateh's question (lines 58–59)? What do we know that Zlateh doesn't know?

_____

_____

_____

_____

direction before. She looked back at him questioningly, as if to say, "Where are you taking me?" But after a while she seemed to come to the conclusion that a goat shouldn't ask questions. Still, the road was different. They passed new fields, pastures, and huts with thatched roofs. Here and there a dog barked and came running after them, but Aaron chased it away with his stick.

The sun was shining when Aaron left the village.
40 Suddenly the weather changed. A large black cloud with a bluish center appeared in the east and spread itself rapidly over the sky. A cold wind blew in with it. The crows flew low, croaking. At first it looked as if it would rain, but instead it began to hail as in summer. It was early in the day, but it became dark as dusk. After a while the hail turned to snow.

In his twelve years Aaron had seen all kinds of weather, but he had never experienced a snow like this one. It was so dense it shut out the light of the day. In a short time their
50 path was completely covered. The wind became as cold as ice. The road to town was narrow and winding. Aaron no longer knew where he was. He could not see through the snow. The cold soon **penetrated** his quilted jacket.

At first Zlateh didn't seem to mind the change in weather. She too was twelve years old and knew what winter meant. But when her legs sank deeper and deeper into the snow, she began to turn her head and look at Aaron in wonderment. Her mild eyes seemed to ask, "Why are we out in such a storm?" Aaron hoped that a peasant would
60 come along with his cart, but no one passed by.

The snow grew thicker, falling to the ground in large, whirling flakes. Beneath it Aaron's boots touched the softness of a plowed field. He realized that he was no longer on the road. He had gone astray. He could no longer figure out which was east or west, which way was the village, the town. The wind whistled, howled, whirled the snow about in eddies. It looked as if white imps were playing tag on the fields. A white dust rose above the ground. Zlateh stopped. She could walk no longer. Stubbornly she anchored her **cleft** hooves in the earth and bleated as if pleading to be taken home. Icicles hung from her white beard, and her horns were glazed with frost.

Aaron did not want to admit the danger, but he knew just the same that if they did not find shelter, they would freeze to death. This was no ordinary storm. It was a mighty blizzard. The snowfall had reached his knees. His hands were numb, and he could no longer feel his toes. He choked when he breathed. His nose felt like wood, and he rubbed it with snow. Zlateh's bleating began to sound like crying. Those humans in whom she had so much confidence had dragged her into a trap. Aaron began to pray to God for himself and for the innocent animal.

70

80

PREDICT

Pause at line 82—a moment of great **suspense**. Will Aaron and Zlateh freeze to death? How do you think the story will end?

IDENTIFY

Look back at the beginning of the story. Notice in lines 9–10 one of the reasons Aaron's father decides to sell Zlateh. In lines 103–110, underline the "miracle" that happens.

Suddenly he made out the shape of a hill. He wondered what it could be. Who had piled snow into such a huge heap? He moved toward it, dragging Zlateh after him. When he came near it, he realized that it was a large haystack which the snow had blanketed.

Aaron realized immediately that they were saved. With great effort he dug his way through the snow. He was a
90 village boy and knew what to do. When he reached the hay, he hollowed out a nest for himself and the goat. No matter how cold it may be outside, in the hay it is always warm. And hay was food for Zlateh. The moment she smelled it, she became contented and began to eat. Outside, the snow continued to fall. It quickly covered the passageway Aaron had dug. But a boy and an animal need to breathe, and there was hardly any air in their hide-out. Aaron bored a kind of a window through the hay and snow and carefully kept the passage clear.

100 Zlateh, having eaten her fill, sat down on her hind legs and seemed to have regained her confidence in man. Aaron ate his two slices of bread and cheese, but after the difficult journey he was still hungry. He looked at Zlateh and noticed her udders were full. He lay down next to her, placing himself so that when he milked her, he could squirt the milk into his mouth. It was rich and sweet. Zlateh was not accustomed to being milked that way, but she did not resist. On the contrary, she seemed eager to reward Aaron for bringing her to a shelter whose very walls, floor, and ceiling
110 were made of food.

Through the window Aaron could catch a glimpse of the **chaos** outside. The wind carried before it whole drifts of snow. It was completely dark, and he did not know whether night had already come or whether it was the darkness of the storm. Thank God that in the hay it was not cold. The dried hay, grass, and field flowers **exuded** the warmth of the summer sun. Zlateh ate frequently; she nibbled from above, below, from the left and right. Her body gave forth an animal warmth, and Aaron cuddled up to her.

120 He had always loved Zlateh, but now she was like a sister. He was alone, cut off from his family, and wanted to talk.

He began to talk to Zlateh. "Zlateh, what do you think about what has happened to us?" he asked.

"Maaaa," Zlateh answered.

"If we hadn't found this stack of hay, we would both be frozen stiff by now," Aaron said.

"Maaaa," was the goat's reply.

"If the snow keeps on falling like this, we may have to stay here for days," Aaron explained.

130 "Maaaa," Zlateh bleated.

"What does 'Maaaa' mean?" Aaron asked. "You'd better speak up clearly."

"Maaaa. Maaaa," Zlateh tried.

"Well, let it be 'Maaaa' then," Aaron said patiently. "You can't speak, but I know you understand. I need you and you need me. Isn't that right?"

"Maaaa."

Aaron became sleepy. He made a pillow out of some hay, leaned his head on it, and dozed off. Zlateh too fell asleep.

140 When Aaron opened his eyes, he didn't know whether it was morning or night. The snow had blocked up his window. He tried to clear it, but when he had bored through to the length of his arm, he still hadn't reached the outside. Luckily he had his stick with him and was able to break through to the open air. It was still dark outside. The snow continued to fall and the wind wailed, first with one voice and then with many. Sometimes it had the sound of devilish laughter. Zlateh too awoke, and when Aaron greeted

VOCABULARY

exuded (eg·zyo͞od'id) v.: gave off.

IDENTIFY

Re-read lines 88–121. If Aaron or Zlateh had been alone, neither would have survived. List three ways that Zlateh helps Aaron survive. Then, list three ways that Aaron helps Zlateh survive.

_____

_____

_____

FLUENCY

Imagine that each time Zlateh speaks, she is responding to what Aaron says. Write what Zlateh might be saying each time she bleats, "Maaaa." Then, read the boxed passage aloud.

_____

_____

_____

_____

_____

_____

_____

her, she answered, "Maaaa." Yes, Zlateh's language consisted
150 of only one word, but it meant many things. Now she was
saying, "We must accept all that God gives us—heat, cold,
hunger, satisfaction, light, and darkness."

Aaron had awakened hungry. He had eaten up his
food, but Zlateh had plenty of milk.

For three days Aaron and Zlateh stayed in the haystack.
Aaron had always loved Zlateh, but in these three days he
loved her more and more. She fed him with her milk and
helped him keep warm. She comforted him with her
patience. He told her many stories, and she always cocked
160 her ears and listened. When he patted her, she licked his
hand and his face. Then she said, "Maaaa," and he knew it
meant, I love you too.

IDENTIFY

Underline the details in lines
155–162 that describe the
ways in which Zlateh helps
Aaron.

The snow fell for three days, though after the first day it was not as thick and the wind quieted down. Sometimes Aaron felt that there could never have been a summer, that the snow had always fallen, ever since he could remember. He, Aaron, never had a father or mother or sisters. He was a snow child, born of the snow, and so was Zlateh. It was so quiet in the hay that his ears rang in the stillness. Aaron

170 and Zlateh slept all night and a good part of the day. As for Aaron's dreams, they were all about warm weather. He dreamed of green fields, trees covered with blossoms, clear brooks, and singing birds. By the third night the snow had stopped, but Aaron did not dare to find his way home in the darkness. The sky became clear and the moon shone, casting silvery nets on the snow. Aaron dug his way out and looked at the world. It was all white, quiet, dreaming dreams of heavenly splendor. The stars were large and close. The moon swam in the sky as in a sea.

180 On the morning of the fourth day, Aaron heard the ringing of sleigh bells. The haystack was not far from the road. The peasant who drove the sleigh pointed out the way to him—not to the town and Feyvel the butcher, but home to the village. Aaron had decided in the haystack that he would never part with Zlateh.

Aaron's family and their neighbors had searched for the boy and the goat but had found no trace of them during the storm. They feared they were lost. Aaron's mother and sisters cried for him; his father remained silent

190 and gloomy. Suddenly one of the neighbors came running to their house with the news that Aaron and Zlateh were coming up the road.

VISUALIZE

Underline details in lines 163–179 that help you see what Aaron experiences. Circle details that help you imagine sounds (or the complete lack of sound).

INTERPRET

What does the decision in lines 184–185 reveal about Aaron's **character**? How has his experience changed him from the kind of person he was before the storm?

_____
_____
_____
_____
_____
_____
_____
_____
_____
_____
_____
_____
_____
_____
_____
_____
_____
_____

How has Zlateh's relationship to the rest of the family changed? Underline the details in lines 193–208 that support your answer.

_____
_____
_____
_____
_____
_____
_____
_____
_____
_____
_____
_____
_____
_____
_____
_____
_____
_____
_____
_____
_____

There was great joy in the family. Aaron told them how he had found the stack of hay and how Zlateh had fed him with her milk. Aaron's sisters kissed and hugged Zlateh and gave her a special treat of chopped carrots and potato peels, which Zlateh gobbled up hungrily.

Nobody ever again thought of selling Zlateh, and now that the cold weather had finally set in, the villagers needed

200 the services of Reuven the furrier once more. When Hanukkah came, Aaron's mother was able to fry pancakes every evening, and Zlateh got her portion too. Even though Zlateh had her own pen, she often came to the kitchen, knocking on the door with her horns to indicate that she was ready to visit, and she was always admitted. In the evening, Aaron, Miriam, and Anna played dreidel.[3] Zlateh sat near the stove, watching the children and the flickering of the Hanukkah candles.

Once in a while Aaron would ask her, "Zlateh, do you

210 remember the three days we spent together?"

And Zlateh would scratch her neck with a horn, shake her white bearded head, and come out with the single sound which expressed all her thoughts, and all her love.

---

3. **dreidel** (drā′dəl): spinning top played with at Hanukkah. Its four sides display Hebrew letters that stand for "A great miracle happened there."

Zlateh the Goat

Plot Map   The plot events in "Zlateh the Goat" work together to build suspense. Re-create the plot events by filling in the plot map below. Then, use a star to mark the point at which your interest in the story began to increase. Use a question mark to indicate any plot event you thought was contrived, or not believable.

Literary Skills
Analyze plot;
evaluate a plot's
credibility.

Event 6

Event 5

Event 4

Event 3

Event 2

Event 1

Was the story ☐ credible? ☐ not credible?

Explain.

_____

_____

_____

_____

Zlateh the Goat

VOCABULARY AND COMPREHENSION

Word Bank

penetrated

cleft

chaos

exuded

A. Suffixes   Write in the blanks the correct words from the Word Bank to complete the paragraph. Then, circle words in the passage that contain suffixes meaning "full of" and "act or condition of."

Jan smeared ink on the small (1) _____ block and then pressed the block onto a sheet of paper to make a print. Each print showed the division of the block. Jan was careful to use just enough ink so that it (2) _____ the paper but not the table. She knew there would be (3) _____, or total confusion, if her mother found a stain on the dining-room table. Finishing her print, Jan (4) _____ pride in her work of art.

B. Reading Comprehension   Answer each question below.

1. Where is Aaron taking Zlateh? Why? _____

_____

2. What happens on their journey? _____

_____

3. What do Aaron and Zlateh do to survive? _____

_____

4. At the end of the story, what does the family decide to do about

Zlateh? _____

_____

SKILLS FOCUS

Vocabulary Skills
Use suffixes.

Ola and the Grim *retold by* Eric A. Kimmel

LITERARY FOCUS: EVALUATING CHARACTERS AND PLOT

Do you remember the last time you were disappointed in a movie you saw? Was it because the characters were too good to be true? Did the characters' actions make no sense? How about a movie you loved? Were the characters lovable and true to life? Was the plot exciting and believable?

As with viewing a film, when you read a story, you **evaluate,** or judge, its characters and plot. You decide whether the characters are **credible,** or believable. (Even if the character is a three-headed monster, you want to believe it's real.) You also decide whether the plot develops logically from the conflict. Use the tips below to help you evaluate the characters and plot of "Ola and the Grim."

READING SKILLS: EVALUATING THE TEXT

Use these tips to evaluate the characters and plot of "Ola and the Grim."

Tips for Evaluating Characters	Tips for Evaluating Plot
• Do the characters have strengths as well as weaknesses as real people do? • Do the characters talk and act as real people do? • Do the characters grow and change as a result of the events in the story?	• Do the plot events grow naturally out of the decisions and actions of the characters? • Do many events result from luck, or are there believable causes and effects? • Do events unfold the way they would in real life?

SKILLS FOCUS

Literary Skills
Evaluate characters and plot.

Reading Skills
Evaluate the text.

Vocabulary Skills
Understand synonyms.

VOCABULARY DEVELOPMENT

PREVIEW SELECTION VOCABULARY

Before you read "Ola and the Grim," become familiar with these words.

persisted (pər·sist′id) *v.:* kept on.

> *Although no one encouraged him, he persisted in his practice.*

adequate (ad′i·kwət) *adj.:* good enough.

> *He was an adequate fiddler but not a great one.*

mottled (mät′′ld) *adj.:* streaked or spotted in different colors or shades.

> *He recognized the mottled green skin of the troll.*

CLARIFYING WORD MEANINGS: SYNONYMS

Synonyms are words that share meaning. When you learn a new word, you should also learn its synonyms. Doing so will not only help you remember the meaning of the unfamiliar word but also will help you increase your vocabulary. In the examples that follow, the synonym for each boldface word appears in parentheses.

- The pony's **mottled** (spotted) coat was black and white.
- Although we were tired, we **persisted** (continued) on our journey.
- The pitcher's curveball was **adequate** (sufficient) enough to strike out several hitters.

Ola and the Grim

A Norwegian folk tale *retold by* Eric A. Kimmel

Once there was—or perhaps there was not—a boy named
Ola. He lived on a farm not far from the sea, on the road
that leads to the great city of Bergen. Ola loved the fiddle.
He would walk for miles to hear a talented fiddler play.

He saved all his money, and one proud day Ola
brought home his very own fiddle. His grandfather showed
him how to hold the bow and draw it across the strings.

SKREEK! A terrible noise came out. It sounded like
two cats fighting. Ola dropped the bow in surprise. His
10 mother picked it up.

"Don't be discouraged, Ola," she said. "Fiddles sound
like that when one is learning to play. There will be many
sour notes. Keep practicing. The music will come."

Ola practiced and practiced. Whenever he found a
spare moment, he took his fiddle and played. He practiced
in the barn and in the shade of haystacks until his father
asked him to stop. His fiddling frightened the animals. The
cows stopped giving milk. The hens stopped laying eggs.
The sheep scattered, and the sheepdogs that herded them
20 ran off and were nowhere to be found.

From then on, Ola practiced away from the farm.
He sat under trees in the forest and on lonely rocks at the
seashore. Crabs scurried into the surf. Seals dived deep.
Sea gulls screamed overhead. But Ola **persisted,** even when
the seabirds spattered him with their droppings. He kept
sawing away at his fiddle. Ola practiced hour after hour,
day after day. None of it did any good. He still played as
badly as ever. His fiddle sounded like roosters crowing,

IDENTIFY

Pause after the first sentence.
Circle the words that tell you
that this story may be out of
the ordinary.

EVALUATE

Pause at line 20. Ola's
audience extends beyond
his family. Do you think the
reactions of the animals are
believable?

_____

_____

_____

_____

_____

_____

_____

_____

_____

_____

VOCABULARY

persisted (pər·sist'id) *v.:*
kept on.

WORD STUDY

Pause at line 32. Underline the similes the writer uses to let us know what Ola's fiddling sounded like. (A **simile** is a comparison of two or more seemingly unlike things.)

WORD STUDY

A tankard (line 43) is a large drinking cup with a handle and often a hinged lid.

A troll (line 51) is a figure in Scandinavian folklore. Trolls are from a race of imaginary beings, often with special powers or skills.

PREDICT

Re-read lines 51–59. Will the fosse-grim help Ola? Explain.

_____

_____

_____

_____

_____

_____

_____

_____

_____

_____

_____

30 donkeys braying, oxen bellowing, wagons with axles that needed greasing—everything but what a fiddle should sound like. His family covered their ears. No one wanted to tell Ola to give up. But everyone hoped he would.

One day there was a wedding at a neighboring farm. A fiddler came all the way from Bergen. All the guests agreed he was the finest fiddler they had ever heard. While the man rested between dances, Ola came up and spoke to him.

"Sir, can you give me some advice? I want to be a fiddler like you and make everybody merry. I practice 40 and practice, but I never get any better, no matter how hard I try. Everything sounds like noise. I can't even keep my fiddle in tune. Can you tell me what to do?"

The fiddler put down his tankard. He leaned over to Ola and whispered in his ear, "How badly do you want to play?"

"Oh, very badly, sir!"

"I was once like you," the fiddler said. "I, too, wanted to play badly. And I did. Very badly! So I went to see the *fosse-grim*."

50 "Who's that?" Ola asked.

"The fosse-grim is a troll. He lives below a waterfall. Sometimes, if you listen closely, you'll hear him playing his harp. The grim is a master musician. He can play any instrument. He can teach you how to play your fiddle. But he won't do it for nothing. You must bring him a gift. The greater the gift, the greater the learning."

"What sort of gift should I bring?" Ola asked.

"The fosse-grim likes meat," the fiddler said. "Bring him something to eat."

60　The next day Ola finished his chores early. He took his
fiddle and set out for the mountains. "I'm going to practice
awhile," he told his family.

"Come back before dark," his father said. "I don't want
the trolls to get you."

"Take something to eat in case you get hungry," his
mother added.

No one told Ola not to go. As much as they cared
about him, they were grateful not to have to hear him
practicing.

70　Ola stopped at the smokehouse. He stuffed a large
sausage into his knapsack. Then he set out, following the
path that wound along the stream.

The path took Ola high into the mountains. It led to
the foot of a rushing waterfall.

Ola stood by the falls, listening. He heard music in
the tumbling water that sounded like notes played on a

EVALUATE

Pause at line 69, and think over Ola's relationship with his family. Do their words and actions seem **credible,** or believable? Explain.

_____
_____
_____
_____
_____
_____
_____
_____
_____
_____
_____
_____
_____
_____
_____
_____
_____
_____

IDENTIFY

Underline the words in the paragraph beginning at line 75 that **personify** the music— that is, that describe the music doing things that only humans do.

harp. The sweet, mysterious music sang to the waterfall. It danced in the silver spray. Ola had never heard anything so beautiful in his life. There is magic in this place, he

80 thought.

"Grim!" he called. "Fosse-Grim, are you here?"

A curious creature emerged from the pool beneath the falls. Its skin was **mottled** green, and it cradled a harp in its arms. Strands of green, silky hair, like long threads of algae, hung to its shoulders. It drew its fingers across the harp and spoke in a voice like splashing water.

"What do you want, boy?"

"I need your help, Grim," Ola said. "I want to play the fiddle so badly."

90 "Let me hear you."

Ola took his fiddle from his knapsack. Tuning the strings as best he could, he took up his bow and began to play.

"Stop! Stop!" cried the grim. "You're hurting my ears! There is nothing I can teach you, boy. You want to play badly. And you do!"

"Don't mock me, Grim," Ola said. "You know what I mean. I want to become a good fiddler. Can you help me?"

"I can," the grim said. "But I won't do it for nothing.

100 What did you bring me?"

Ola held out the sausage. The grim snatched it right away. He bit off the end, "Ugh! Tough and stringy! Can't you afford decent sausage, boy? Never mind. I'll give you what it's worth. I can at least teach you how to tune that fiddle. Listen closely. I'll pluck a string on my harp. You match it. Let's begin."

The grim plucked a note. Ola tried to tune his fiddle string to it, but the note slipped away. It was like trying to catch fish barehanded.

Illustration by Denny Bond.

IDENTIFY

What **simile** is used on this page to help you imagine what happens inside Ola's head? Underline it.

IDENTIFY

Pause at line 123. What part of Ola's problem has been resolved?

_____

_____

_____

_____

_____

_____

_____

_____

_____

_____

_____

_____

_____

_____

_____

_____

_____

_____

IDENTIFY

Pause at line 130. What further problems does Ola have in his quest to learn to play the fiddle? Underline them.

110   "No, no, no!" the grim yelled. "That's too high! Now you're too low! What's the matter with you? Are your ears blocked? Can you hear anything?"

    The grim stretched out his long, green arm. He pressed the palm of his hand against Ola's ear. Ola felt something inside his head SNAP! It popped and crackled like ice breaking on a pond. Suddenly he heard the sounds around him clearly. It was as if he were listening for the first time.

    "Try again," the grim said.

    This time Ola tuned his strings effortlessly. And they

120 stayed in tune, no matter how long he played.

    "Thank you, Grim," Ola said.

    "Keep practicing," the grim snorted as he dived beneath the ripples.

Ola raced home. He tuned his fiddle and sawed away. "Listen to me now!" he cried to everyone. "I can play in tune." And he did, for the first time!

    However, there is more to fiddling than playing in tune. Ola still squeaked and scraped. His timing was off; his fingering incorrect. Every song he attempted became

130 a hopeless muddle.

Pause at line 154. What do Ola and the grim have in common? In what ways are the two characters very different?

_____
_____
_____
_____
_____
_____
_____
_____
_____
_____
_____
_____
_____
_____
_____
_____
_____

"Keep practicing, Ola. You're getting better," his mother said.

But Ola knew that wasn't true. He could not hope to get anywhere on his own, no matter how hard he practiced. It was time to visit the grim.

Ola packed his knapsack and fiddle. He followed the stream up into the mountains. When he reached the waterfall, he called out, "Grim, come up from the pool! I need you!"

140 The waters rippled. The fosse-grim appeared, cradling his harp. "What do you want, boy?"

"I want to play the fiddle in the worst way. Help me, please!"

The grim laughed. "You don't need me. You already play in the worst way. You're the worst fiddler I ever heard. You couldn't get any worse if you tried."

"Don't mock me, Grim!" Ola pleaded. "You know what I mean. Playing in tune is not enough. I need to know so much more."

150 "Nothing buys nothing," the grim replied. "What did you bring me?"

"A whole leg of mutton!" Ola took the meat from his knapsack. He tossed it to the grim, who gnawed it down to the bone.

"That's worth something," the grim finally said, smacking his lips. "Take out your fiddle. We'll play together."

The grim came out of the pool. He sat beside Ola, pressing the boy's fingers down with his left hand and 160 pulling his wrist back and forth with his right.

"Ow! You're pinching me!" Ola cried.

"Stop complaining! Open yourself to the music. Feel its wonder. Let it take you."

Ola played and played. The grim guided his fingers from note to note. Ola felt as if he had walked through a hidden door into a secret realm. He lost himself in the music that poured from his fiddle like a mountain brook streaming down a waterfall.

170 At last the grim said, "Enough! I've given you a leg of mutton's worth of music. Those tunes are in your fingers now. Practice every day so you don't forget them. Otherwise, you'll have to bring me another leg of mutton to have me teach you again."

"Will I be a good fiddler?" Ola asked.

"**Adequate.** Nothing more. What do you expect for a leg of mutton? You'll earn your living playing at weddings and festivals. At least people won't run away when you take out your fiddle. Isn't that what you wanted?"

"I guess so," said Ola.

180 But it wasn't. Everyone loved Ola's playing now. His family begged him to take out his fiddle in the evening, after the day's work was done. Neighbors invited him to their farms to play for them. Whenever a joyous occasion arose, people sent for Ola to play. "You're a great fiddler, Ola!" everyone said.

It wasn't so, and Ola knew it. A vast gulf lay between what Ola wanted to play and what he could play. He heard music everywhere: in the wind, in trees, rippling fields of wheat and rushing streams, in surging ocean waves and 190 quiet mountain meadows. He tried to capture it with his fiddle, but the notes slipped away. Ola felt like a fisherman carried out to sea by a running tide. He sees the land clearly, but he cannot reach it, no matter how hard he rows.

"I must visit the fosse-grim," Ola said to himself.

INFER

Pause at line 179. Is this what Ola wants? Explain.

_____

_____

_____

_____

_____

WORD STUDY

Pause at line 193. Underline the extended **simile** that the writer uses to help us imagine how Ola feels about his music.

PREDICT

Pause at line 194. What is it that Ola wants now? What will he do to get it?

_____

_____

_____

_____

_____

_____

IDENTIFY

Pause at line 208. Have you noticed that the amount of food Ola brings the grim gets larger and larger? What has he brought the grim now?

_____

_____

_____

_____

INTERPRET

What does the grim mean when he says, "Did you expect to buy greatness for a side of beef" (lines 222–223)? Do you agree that "Pain is the price of genius"?

_____

_____

_____

_____

_____

_____

_____

_____

_____

_____

_____

_____

Once more Ola followed the stream. He struggled up the path, bent double with the weight of a whole side of beef on his shoulders.

"Grim, come out! I need you!" Ola called to the waterfall.

200 The fosse-grim emerged from the pool. "What do you want, boy?"

"Grim, it is not enough to be a good fiddler. I want to be a great fiddler. I want to be able to play the music I hear, the music I love. I will practice night and day. I will do anything you ask. Look! I have brought you half of a whole steer. If it is not enough, I will go back down the mountain for more. Tell me what I must do, Grim, to become the fiddler I want to be."

"Put down the beef and take out your fiddle," the grim
210 said. He climbed out of the pool to sit beside Ola. "You and I will play together. Keep playing, no matter what happens. Play until I tell you to stop."

The grim took hold of Ola's wrist and fingers. Together they began to play: songs, scales, exercises. Hour after hour. Ola's wrists began to cramp.

"Let me rest, Grim! My hands ache!"

"Keep playing!" The grim pulled Ola's arm back and forth. He pressed the boy's fingers onto the strings until blisters rose from his fingertips.

220 "Let me go, Grim! You're torturing me! This is more than I can endure!"

"What a fool you are! Did you expect to buy greatness for a side of beef? Pain is the price of genius. The great ones of the world are always disappointed, neglected, misunderstood. And still they keep on. But look at you! A few little blisters and you're ready to quit. Go ahead! What do I care? I have your beef. Dolts like you keep me well fed."

Ola set his jaw. He clamped the fiddle beneath his chin. "No. I will go on."

230   "Then play!"

Ola and the grim played through the night until the sun came up. By then, Ola's hands had tightened into claws, the fiddle's strings had snapped, and the bow hung in pieces.

"But you're a real fiddler now," said the grim. "Go! Make your way in the world. I have nothing more to teach you."

Ola left without a word of thanks. He felt too weary to speak. He stumbled down the mountain, and it was many weeks before he had the strength to take up his

240   fiddle again.

But when he did . . .

Years later, a special performance took place in Bergen's concert hall. People came from all over Scandinavia to hear Ole Bull, Norway's most famous violinist. All the critics agreed, "Ole Bull has no peer. He is the finest musician in Scandinavia. The best in Europe. The greatest in the world."

At the reception afterward a small, odd-looking man with a mottled green complexion was seen heaping his plate at the smorgasbord in back of the hall. A Swedish

250   countess asked him, "Did you enjoy the concert? It astonishes me that a human being can possess such natural talent."

To which the odd little man replied, "Talent? Bah! It's courage, dedication, and hard work. Ola couldn't play a note when we began. You've no idea what I went through just to teach him to tune his fiddle!"

IDENTIFY

Pause at line 236. How has Ola's problem been resolved?

_____

_____

_____

EVALUATE

The fosse-grim is a creature of fantasy, but how is the relationship between the fosse-grim and Ola realistic?

_____

_____

_____

_____

_____

EVALUATE

The concluding section of the story in Bergen's concert hall contains a mix of fact and fantasy. What do you think is actually true here?

_____

_____

_____

_____

_____

_____

Ola and the Grim

Evaluation Chart   In a sentence, tell how credible you find the character of Ola to be. Give three examples of his actions or feelings to support your evaluation. Then, answer questions about the story's plot. In the bottom box, tell whether or not you think the plot is credible.

Character Evaluation	
Is Ola credible? Explain.	
Story detail 1:	
Story detail 2:	
Story detail 3:	

Plot Evaluation	
What does Ola want?	
What complications arise?	
How is Ola's problem resolved?	
Is the plot credible? Explain.	

Skills Review

Ola and the Grim

VOCABULARY AND COMPREHENSION

A. Synonyms Write words from the Word Bank to replace the synonyms in italic type.

The fiddler *continued* (1) _____ with his advice to Ola. He said, "If you want to be a fiddler, you have to visit the grim who lives below a waterfall. He'll teach you." The grim turned out to be an odd-looking creature with *spotted* (2) _____ green skin. Ola played badly for the grim. With practice, however, his playing became *sufficient* (3) _____ to entertain at weddings. Later, his playing became great.

B. Reading Comprehension Answer each question below.

1. What does Ola want? _____

_____

_____

2. Who helps Ola get what he wants? _____

_____

_____

3. What price does Ola pay for the help he gets? _____

_____

_____

4. In what ways is Ola like a real person? _____

_____

_____

Part Two

Reading Informational Texts

Academic Vocabulary for Part Two

These are the terms you should know
as you read and analyze the informational selections in this section.

_____

Main Idea The most important point in a text or section of text.

Summary A brief restatement of the main events or ideas in a text.

Comparison Description of how two or more things are alike.

Contrast Description of how two or more things are different.

Argument A position supported by evidence.

Evidence Details a writer uses to support his or her position. Evidence
may include facts, statistics, quotations, and case studies.

Assertion A statement or a claim.

Citation Text evidence that supports an assertion.

Logic Correct reasoning, based on facts.

Fallacious Reasoning False reasoning. Types of false reasoning
include hasty generalizations, circular reasoning, and only-cause
fallacy.

● ● ●

Text Features Special type, such as boldface, italics, and capitals, and
bullets that call attention to important information.

Headings Titles at the tops of pages or sections.

Illustrations Drawings, photos, art, graphs, maps, or other visuals.

Captions Descriptions of art, illustrations, charts, or maps. A caption
usually appears beneath or next to the visual it describes.

Tricky Science by Steve Miller

READING SKILLS: ANALYZING STRUCTURAL FEATURES OF POPULAR MEDIA

You use different kinds of popular media to obtain information: newspapers, magazines, radio, and television. You also can find information on a wealth of topics online. The best way to get what you need from such an array of media is to become familiar with structural features they use. Here are some features and how they are used:

- **The title**   Most articles have titles that reveal the main topic of the piece. Most titles also try to grab your interest.
- **Headings**   Headings are words or phrases used to break up the text of an article into sections. If you scan an article's headings, you'll get an overview of what the article will be about.
- **Illustrations**   Many articles are illustrated with drawings, photographs, maps, graphs, and tables. Information about these visuals is often explained in **captions,** or brief text passages.

VOCABULARY DEVELOPMENT: PREVIEW SELECTION VOCABULARY

Before you read "Tricky Science," get to know these words:

abductions (ab·duk′shənz) *n.:* kidnappings.

Some people have claimed that they were victims of alien abductions.

hoax (hōks) *n.:* trick or fraud.

Edgar Allan Poe's story about crossing the Atlantic Ocean in three days by balloon was a hoax.

herds (hʉrdz) *n.:* groups of cattle, sheep, or other animals.

One imaginative story described herds of bison grazing on the moon.

sapphire (saf′īr) *n.:* deep-blue variety of corundum, a precious stone.

According to the tale, creatures with batlike wings lived in temples of sapphire, a precious blue gemstone.

traces (trā′səz) *n.:* marks left by a past person, thing, or event.

A stuffed hippopotamus foot supposedly found in Scotland had traces of mud on it.

SKILLS FOCUS

Reading Skills
Analyze structural features of media.

from *Muse* magazine, September 2000

Tricky Science

Steve Miller

Do you believe in alien **abductions** or that a spaceship crashed in the desert near Roswell, New Mexico, in 1947? Do you believe a meteor the size of Manhattan smashed into the earth, killing the dinosaurs, or that people have walked on the moon? Which is more believable: that there is a monster swimming around in Loch Ness or that there's a black hole at the center of our galaxy sucking up everything passing nearby?

10   How do you decide what to believe? Do you believe something because it sounds right, or because there's nothing obviously wrong with it, or because it was published in the newspaper? Perhaps you believe science stories if scientists believe them. That's a good answer. But is this method foolproof?

    It's actually pretty easy to pull off a scientific **hoax.** Most people are used to believing what they hear, especially if it has to do with science. Scientists like to think that even if they are fooled at first, someone usually comes along and figures out the truth. Obviously that's happened with all

20 the hoaxes we know about. But what about the *really* great hoaxes? They still haven't been uncovered! Deciding what's true and what's false isn't easy.

At Home on the Moon

On 25 August 1835, the *New York Sun* ran a story about some extraordinary discoveries made by the famous astronomer Sir John Herschel. The paper claimed Herschel had just assembled the world's largest telescope in South Africa, with a lens 24 feet in diameter. (The largest lens ever made is only 40 inches.) When he aimed it at the moon, he

30 spied some truly amazing things. Over the next week, the newspaper told the story of his observations. (Herschel really *was* in South Africa at the time, so no one could check with him.)

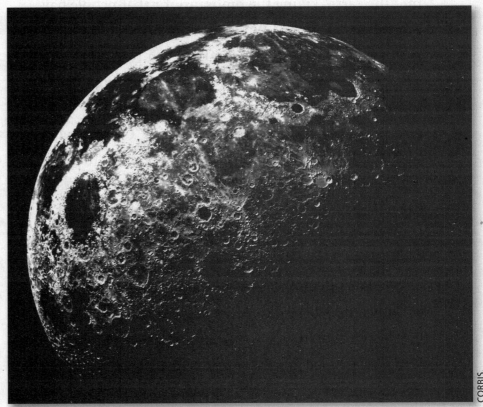

CORBIS.

The moon.

What did he see? A landscape of forests and plains, broad rivers, and beautiful white beaches. Masses of gold were draped over rock ledges. There was a crystal river of quartz five miles wide and 340 miles long. Oh, the planet was inhabited, too. Grazing on the plains were **herds** of bison with flaps over their eyes to protect them from the

40 sun. (Sort of like the bill of a baseball cap, even though baseball hadn't been invented yet.) There were blue antelopes with a single horn (can't forget the unicorn), and a kind of huge beaver that had no tail and walked on its hind legs. But these were no ordinary beavers. They carried their babies in their arms like people, built huts to live in, and used fire to heat their homes. Most amazing of all, there were creatures that looked human, but had large bat-like wings. The expressions on their faces were human (that's some telescope) and they built beautiful temples of

50 **sapphire.**

You're probably thinking this is an obvious fraud. But 165 years ago, people didn't know that much about the moon and they had a lot of respect for authority. And since Herschel was the most famous astronomer in the world with the world's best telescope, of course he saw things no one else had ever seen. After all, what would you think if it was a report from NASA about life on Mars? (OK, maybe you wouldn't believe the part about the bison with a baseball cap—but how about a football helmet?)

60 It turned out that a reporter named Richard Locke spun the whole thing as a joke. He claimed to have been surprised that anyone believed it. But since he was selling so many papers, he kept going for awhile. When Sir John Herschel heard about it, he had a good laugh, but said he

FLUENCY

Read the boxed paragraph to a small group of classmates. Can they identify the author's remarks by the tone of your voice? Re-read the paragraph, and try to improve your speed and the smoothness of your delivery.

VOCABULARY

herds (hʉrdz) *n.:* groups of cattle, sheep, or other animals.

sapphire (saf'īr) *n.:* deep-blue variety of corundum, a precious stone.

IDENTIFY

Locate and underline the reasons people believed what Herschel told them (lines 51–59).

IDENTIFY CAUSE & EFFECT

Pause at line 63. Why did Richard Locke keep publishing the false reports?

_____

_____

_____

_____

_____

_____

_____

_____

Why do you think this
section of the article
appears in a tinted box?

_____

_____

_____

_____

_____

_____

Circle the word *hotheaded*
(line 71). This passage says
that the hotheaded borer's
head was so hot it could
drill through ice. *Hotheaded,*
however, has another meaning. What do we mean
when we say a person is
hotheaded?

_____

_____

_____

What does "Nessie" in the
heading refer to?

_____

_____

_____

_____

_____

was afraid his real report was going to be much less interesting. But many of the people who fell for the joke didn't
think it was so funny.

WHEN IN DOUBT, CHECK THE DATE

Occasionally—most often in April—a hoax is just for fun. In
70   *1995,* Discover *magazine reported the discovery of a truly
unusual creature in Antarctica. The hotheaded naked ice
borer looks like a naked mole-rat with a big bulb on its head.
Since it burns calories fast, it's very warm, and it uses its hot
head to bore tunnels through the ice.*

   *The most amazing thing about the hothead is its hunting
technique. Whole families of the warm, ugly creatures gather
beneath a penguin, melting the ice with their heads until the
snow collapses and the bird is trapped below. Then the hot-
heads devour it. The creatures were discovered by Aprille*
80   *Pazzo (pazzo is "fool" in Italian).*

   Other April Fool's jokes in Discover *have included a
Neanderthal tuba made from a hollowed-out mastodon tusk,
a huge bellows to blow pollution away from Los Angeles (hey,
it might work), and the discovery of the bigon, an elementary
particle as big as a bowling ball. .*

Nessie, Is That You?

Hundreds of people claim to have seen Nessie, the Loch
Ness monster. Some have even claimed to have taken pictures of it. The most famous photograph of all was shot in
90   1934 by R. Kenneth Wilson, a respected surgeon from
London. The photo shows a head and long neck sticking
out of the water. Ripples at the base of the neck suggest the
creature is swimming.

For decades, people argued about this picture. Did it show a dinosaur, a log that looked like a neck and head, or a duck in the distance? (Try drawing something that looks like a dinosaur, a log, *and* a duck. It's pretty hard to do!) Then in 1993, a man named Christian Spurling confessed that the photograph was a hoax. He had helped his stepfa-

100 ther, Marmaduke Weatherell, build a model neck and head on top of a toy windup submarine. The photograph was taken as the sub puttered around underwater. Eventually the model sank. (It probably became a toy for a baby monster.)

TEXT STRUCTURE

How does the photo of the Loch Ness monster help you understand the hoax?

_____

_____

_____

_____

_____

_____

Associated Press.

Is this the Loch Ness monster?

VOCABULARY

traces (trā'sәz) *n.:* marks left by a past person, thing, or event.

IDENTIFY
CAUSE & EFFECT

Underline the reasons Weatherell faked the photograph of the Loch Ness monster (lines 105–121).

INTERPRET

What do you think is meant by "Stone Age people" (line 129)? Read the rest of the paragraph to see if you find a clue.

Weatherell took the photo to get revenge. He was upset because he had been fired from his job as monster hunter—and it probably wasn't easy to find a new job of the same sort. Someone had actually paid him money the year before to look for evidence of a creature in the lake. And guess what? He found it! There were footprints of a large animal, proof of Nessie's existence. He made casts of the footprints, and then someone noticed that the monster prints were remarkably similar to hippopotamus prints. That, in itself, was strange, since hippos are somewhat rare in Scotland. Someone else uncovered a stuffed hippopotamus foot with **traces** of mud—also not too common. (It isn't clear, though, whether Weatherell made the prints himself or whether he fell for someone else's trick.) The blunder cost him his job. Out of disgust and anger he came up with the idea of the faked photo and got Dr. Wilson to help him.

Does this prove that the Loch Ness monster doesn't exist? No, but it does remove one of the strongest pieces of evidence. Still, there are a few people who believe the photograph is genuine and the *real* hoax is the story of the toy submarine. This shows that some people will continue to believe in some hoaxes no matter what.

At Home in the Forest

The last Stone Age people were discovered in 1971 by a Philippine government official named Manuel Elizalde— maybe. Called the Tasaday, these people lived in a cave deep in the rain forest. They didn't farm or herd animals. Instead they lived on wild yams, grubs, berries, and frogs. They had no contact with other people, even those living just a few miles away, for thousands of years. The 26 Tasaday had no

Johnny Villena/Associated Press.

Manuel Elizalde.

IDENTIFY

Pause at line 154. What allowed the Tasaday hoax to continue for fifteen years?

tools except stone axes and no clothing other than forest leaves. No one expected to find people this isolated in the second half of the 20th century.

Their story caught the world's imagination. Because
140 of his position in the Philippine government, Elizalde was able to control contact with the Tasaday, and all information about them came from him. Very few scientists were allowed to study the tribe—Elizalde said he wanted to protect them from the outside world. A lot of people agreed with him and figured that scientists would rob the Tasaday of their innocence.

This situation continued for 15 years until the Philippine government fell. As soon as they could, journalists went to the jungle to visit the Tasaday. They found
150 them living in regular houses, wearing Western clothes, and tending gardens just like those of other rural people in the southern Philippines. They told reporters and scientists that the whole thing was a hoax, and that they had gone along with it because Elizalde had paid them to.

Photograph of the Tasaday, distributed by Elizalde.

Associated Press.

INTERPRET

According to the article, why were so many people fooled by these scientific hoaxes?

So why did Elizalde make it all up? Probably just to get attention. And why did people believe it? In part because Elizalde, like Herschel, was supposed to be an authority, and in part because they couldn't check the story them-selves. Also, probably just because it's fun to believe that

160 there are still undiscovered places in the world.

Tricky Science

Magazine Features Chart   You can use the features of a magazine article to find different kinds of information. Fill out this magazine features chart after you read "Tricky Science."

SKILLS FOCUS

Reading Skills
Analyze structural features of media.

Article Title:

_____

_____

_____

Illustrations & Captions (What Are They About?):

_____

_____

_____

_____

_____

Headings (What Are They?):

_____

_____

_____

_____

_____

_____

_____

_____

_____

_____

Main Idea of Article:

_____

_____

_____

_____

_____

_____

_____

Tricky Science

VOCABULARY AND COMPREHENSION

Word Bank

abductions
hoax
herds
sapphire
traces

A. Selection Vocabulary: Words in Context   Write words from the Word Bank to complete the paragraph. Use each word only once.

   Could it all have been just a cruel (1) _____?
People and things started disappearing from Fenton Forks. When the
(2) _____ were first discovered, nobody panicked too
much. But when (3) _____ of cattle from MacDuffie's
farm and the precious (4) _____ from Mrs. Thane's
home vanished, people started to worry and wonder more and more.
With no clues or (5) _____ of the missing people,
animals, and jewel, the strange events remain a mystery.

B. Reading Comprehension   Answer each question below.

1. According to the author of "Tricky Science," why is it easy for people
   to pull off a scientific hoax? _____

   _____

2. Why did the *New York Sun*'s reporter pretend to be Sir John Herschel
   when he wrote the reports about life on the moon? _____

   _____

3. How did Christian Spurling and his stepfather create a photograph
   of Nessie? _____

   _____

4. Why was the hoax about the Tasaday undiscovered for so long?

   _____

   _____

Before You Read

The Samurai by Paul Varley

READING SKILLS: TAKING NOTES

Taking notes is particularly useful when you read informational texts. Notes should be written in your own words. Whenever you need to copy a writer's exact words, enclose them in quotation marks and write down the source and page number where you found the quotation.

Here are some tips for taking notes:

- Use index cards or small sheets of notebook paper.
- Read through the selection once to find the main ideas.
- Make a card or note for each main idea.

VOCABULARY DEVELOPMENT: PREVIEW SELECTION VOCABULARY

Get to know these words before you read "The Samurai."

samurai (sam′ə·rī′) *n.:* Japanese warriors.

The samurai were a military class in ancient Japan.

provinces (präv′ins·əz) *n.:* administrative divisions of a country.

The samurai first appeared in the eastern provinces of the country.

frontier (frun·tir′) *n.:* developing, often still uncivilized or lawless region of a country.

The Kantō plain at that time was a frontier that needed governing.

shogun (shō′gun′) *n.:* any of the military governors of Japan who, until 1868, had absolute rule.

The shogun was a military leader who became governor of Japan.

tumultuous (too·mul′choo·əs) *adj.:* full of disturbance or upheaval; unsettled.

Because many vassals rebelled against their lords, the fifteenth and sixteenth centuries in Japan were tumultuous.

SKILLS FOCUS

Reading Skills
Understand a text by taking logical notes.

from Faces: The Magazine About People

The Samurai

Paul Varley

TEXT STRUCTURE

Locate the author's name and the captions in this article. Circle them.

VOCABULARY

samurai (sam'ə·rī') *n.:* Japanese warriors. Note the meaning of the word given in the text.

provinces (präv'ins·əz) *n.:* administrative divisions of a country.

DECODING TIP

You can often find a clue to the meaning of an unfamiliar new word by breaking it up into smaller words that you know. Look at the word *oversight* (line 19). What smaller words do you see? Circle the words. Use the meanings of the smaller words to help you define *oversight.*

_____

_____

VOCABULARY

frontier (frun·tir') *n.:* developing, often still uncivilized or lawless region of a country.

A **samurai** is "one who serves." In ancient times, the term described lowly servants supplied to the households of elderly people by the Japanese government. Later it became one of several terms used for members of the warrior class that developed in the **provinces** of Japan during the tenth century. Although the word *bushi* ("military gentry") appears most often in old official records, the term *samurai* has become widely known among people outside Japan. Today the Japanese themselves also use this word when 10 they refer to the fighting men of their country before modern times.

The samurai first appeared in the eastern provinces of Japan—that is, in the Kantō plain that contains the modern city of Tokyo. In the tenth century, the central government consisted of court officials in the service of the emperor in Kyoto, then the capital city. The samurai arose because these officials paid little attention to affairs in the provinces except for making sure that they received the income from their agricultural estates. Without effective oversight from 20 the Kyoto court, men in the provinces took up arms to become a professional military class.

In that period, the Kantō was a **frontier** area, rich in farmland and especially in need of men to maintain order as the territory developed. The samurai in the Kantō and elsewhere organized themselves into bands whose members were joined together as lords and vassals (followers under a lord's protection), much like the knights of medieval Europe.

30 Although Japan is far from Europe and had no contact with Europeans until the mid-sixteenth century, the Japanese developed a system of organizing society remarkably similar to that of medieval Europe. This system, known as feudalism, took root in Japan with the founding of its first military government, or shogunate (government headed by a *shogun,* or "great general"), in 1185. As in Europe, feudalism in Japan was based almost entirely on agriculture. Land divided into estates, or manors, was worked by peasants called serfs who had to remain on the land and could not move about freely. Feudalism also

40 featured a ruling warrior or military class made up of lords and their vassals.

In samurai society, a vassal was supposed to give absolute, unquestioning loyalty to his lord and even be prepared to die for him in battle. In fact, the relationship between a lord and vassal went both ways: In return for performing military service, a vassal expected rewards and protection from his lord. The idea of the loyal, self-sacrificing vassal was often ignored. Many vassals, especially in the **tumultuous** fifteenth and sixteenth

50 centuries, betrayed or rebelled against their lords.

The samurai continued to rule Japan until the beginning of the modern period in 1868. During the time of the last military government, the shogunate of the Tokugawa family (1600–1867), Japan remained almost entirely at peace. Deprived of their profession of warfare, many samurai lived idly on payments provided by their lords.

VOCABULARY

shogun (shō′gun′) *n.:* any of the military governors of Japan who, until 1868, had absolute rule.

WORD STUDY

Underline the definitions of these words, which are given right in context on this page: *shogunate; serfs; vassals.*

FLUENCY

Read the boxed passage aloud as if you were reading to a group of classmates who are taking notes as you read. Make sure you emphasize the words and phrases that are given special treatment in the paragraph—those in italics, in parentheses, and within quote marks.

VOCABULARY

tumultuous (tōō·mul′chōō·əs) *adj.:* full of disturbance or upheaval; unsettled.

Frightening the enemy was part of the strategy of the samurai. In battle, these warriors wore fierce-looking masks and fought fiercely, too.

IDENTIFY

Re-read lines 51–60. According to the article, what happened to the samurai during the shogunate of the Tokugawa family? Underline this information. How did this historical happening contribute to the development of the martial art that is still practiced today?

Others entered government service or professions such as teaching. As a substitute for actual fighting, the samurai of the Tokugawa period developed the martial arts still

60 practiced by many people in Japan and elsewhere.

Members of the samurai class overthrew the Tokugawa shogunate and brought Japan into the Western-dominated modern world in the late nineteenth century. Although samurai status was officially dissolved in the 1870s, many people of samurai background continued to provide leadership in modernizing Japan. Moreover, samurai values remained deeply ingrained in the behavior of many Japanese at least through World War II.

This samurai was photographed in 1860.

Notes

The Samurai

Notes Organizer   Effective notes include only the main idea and key supporting details in a passage. As you take notes, put the information in your own words. You can use the author's words, too—but be sure to put quotation marks around them to show that you have copied them directly from the text.

As you read "The Samurai," fill out the following note cards.

Main Idea:	Main Idea:
Details:	Details:

Main Idea:	Main Idea:
Details:	Details:

Main Idea:

Details:

Skills Review

The Samurai

VOCABULARY AND COMPREHENSION

A. Selection Vocabulary: Words in Context Write words from the Word Bank to complete the paragraph below. Use each word only once.

The situation in the various (1) _____ of sixteenth-century Japan could be described only as dangerous and (2) _____. All month long various (3) _____ had ridden through the land to announce that the (4) _____ was going to visit to check on each area's defenses. There were rumors that hostile forces were gathering on the (5) _____, and the leaders were taking no chances.

B. Reading Comprehension Answer each question below.

1. Who were the samurai?

_____

_____

2. When did the samurai live?

_____

_____

3. What was the purpose of the samurai?

_____

_____

4. Why did the samurai cease to exist?

_____

_____

Myths in Our Lives

by Joseph Bruchac

READING SKILLS: EVALUATING EVIDENCE

When you evaluate something, you judge its value or worth. In reading informational texts, you need to evaluate the evidence that is used to support the writer's ideas. There are many types of **evidence,** including facts, quotations, statistics, and case studies (specific examples that illustrate the point). Opinions may be valid evidence if they are supported by facts.

Ask yourself the following questions as you read "Myths in Our Lives":

- Does the evidence support the writer's conclusion?
- Would other kinds of evidence or support have worked better?
- Should the writer have presented *more* evidence?

VOCABULARY DEVELOPMENT: PREVIEW SELECTION VOCABULARY

Take time to learn these words before you begin the selection.

chaos (kā′äs′) *n.:* disordered, formless matter, supposed to have existed before the universe took its present, orderly shape.

> *In many different mythologies, chaos precedes the creation of the world.*

ritual (rich′oo·əl) *n.:* form or system of rites, religious or otherwise.

> *In some Native American cultures, the vision quest is an important ritual.*

ancient (ān′chənt) *adj.:* belonging to long ago.

> *Classical mythology is the mythology of ancient Greece and Rome.*

essential (ə·sen′shəl) *adj.:* basic; fundamental.

> *An essential difference between classical mythology and earlier mythologies is that the Greeks depicted their gods in human form.*

foundations (foun·dā′shənz) *n.:* fundamentals or beginnings of something.

> *In large part, ancient Greece provided the foundations of Western civilization.*

SKILLS FOCUS

Reading Skills
Evaluate evidence.

Myths in Our Lives

Joseph Bruchac

Myths Make Us Human

Probably the first stories people ever told were myths—stories that explain people's relationships with the gods and with the powers of creation. Myths are central to human experience. All over the world—in Europe and Asia, in Australia and Africa, in North America and South America, on the many Pacific Islands—we find great bodies of myths.

Although the myths may differ greatly in their details, all of them explain how, long ago, things came to be.
10 Polynesian people tell how the god Maui goes fishing and catches the Hawaiian Islands on his magical hook, pulling them up out of the deep. Lakota Indian people tell how life on earth began with Tunka-shila, "Grandfather Rock," rising up out of fire to create dry land and clouds. The Greeks tell how, out of **Chaos,** Earth and Sky were born.

Myths may also explain such big questions as why we suffer, why seasons change, why a religious **ritual** is practiced, or what happens after death. These are serious matters, so it is wise to treat all myths with respect.

20 ### Myths of Greece and Rome

In the Western world the best-known myths are from **ancient** Greece and Rome. There are a number of reasons for that. First, these myths are great stories that contain **essential** truths about life. Second, Western civilization is based largely on the social and cultural **foundations** of ancient Greece. Most European languages, including English, contain words from Greek and Latin. (*Myth*, for example, comes from the Greek *mythos*, "story.") Third, tales of the Greek and Roman gods and goddesses have 30 been written down for more than two thousand years. We have had a long time to become familiar with them.

It's important to remember that the myths of ancient Greece and Rome are only one small part of the body of myths. There are thousands of different cultures, and myths are part of every one.

The Myths of Our Lives

Medusa.

Bettmann/CORBIS.

In many ways our own lives echo the great mythic tales about journeys of heroes. Like those heroes, we are 40 born, we must grow and learn how to overcome problems, we are given advice by those who are older and wiser, and we must all, finally, face the challenge of death. Whether it is the story of Perseus guided by a wise goddess as he seeks to defeat the monster Medusa or it is the Native American Ojibway tale of Manabozho taking the advice of his wise grandmother as he fights the Fever Monster, a great myth helps us to understand the joys and challenges of our own lives.

Myths in Our Lives

Evidence Organizer   In "Myths in Our Lives" Joseph Bruchac draws several conclusions about mythology. Determine whether or not Bruchac's conclusions are sound by filling in the chart below with supporting evidence you find in the article.

Conclusion
"Myths are central to human experience."
Evidence (Find Examples):
_____
_____
_____
_____

Conclusion
"In the Western world the best-known myths are from ancient Greece and Rome."
Evidence (Find Reasons or Explanations):
_____
_____
_____
_____

Conclusion
"Our own lives echo the great mythic tales about journeys of heroes."
Evidence (Find Examples):
_____
_____
_____
_____

Skills Review

Myths in Our Lives

VOCABULARY AND COMPREHENSION

Word Bank

chaos
ritual
ancient
essential
foundations

A. Selection Vocabulary: Words in Context   Write words from the Word Bank to complete the paragraph. Use each word only once.

Long, long ago, to (1) _____ people, the world was a mystery. In order to understand (2) _____ truths about the world, people asked questions. The answers to these questions became the (3) _____ for myths. Some myths, for example, explained how our universe came into existence out of (4) _____. Others explained the beginnings of a specific religious (5) _____. Myths not only entertain but also teach important lessons.

B. Reading Comprehension   Answer each question below.

1. What three examples does Bruchac give to support his conclusion that all mythologies tell how things came to be?

   _____

   _____

2. What three reasons does Bruchac give to support his conclusion that the best-known myths of the Western world are from ancient Greece and Rome?

   _____

   _____

3. According to Bruchac, how are our own lives like the lives of the mythic heroes?

   _____

   _____

Before You Read

Puppy Love or Hamster Heaven?

READING SKILLS: ANALYZING COMPARISON AND CONTRAST

It's natural to compare and contrast people, situations, and things in order to understand them better. When you **compare,** you show how two or more things are alike. When you **contrast,** you show how two or more things are different. When writers compare and contrast, they generally arrange their ideas in one of two organizational patterns: the **point-by-point pattern** and the **block pattern.** A point-by-point pattern discusses one feature at a time of the subjects that are being compared. A block pattern covers all the points of comparison for the first subject, and then all the points of comparison for the others. Look at the examples below.

Point-by-Point Pattern

Points of Comparison	Subjects
Human contact	• Dogs like to be petted. • Hamsters don't like to be petted.
Playfulness	• Dogs like to play with owners. • Hamsters prefer to explore on their own.
Need for care	• Dogs require lots of daily care. • Hamsters can be left alone for days.

Block Pattern

Subjects	Points of Comparison
Dogs	• Like to be petted • Like to play with owners • Require lots of daily care
Hamsters	• Do not like to be petted • Prefer exploring to playing • Can be left on their own a lot

SKILLS FOCUS

Reading Skills
Analyze a comparison-contrast article.

Puppy Love or Hamster Heaven?

© EyeWire, Inc.

IDENTIFY

Read the title of this article. What two things do you think will be compared in it?

_____

_____

IDENTIFY

Re-read lines 7–16. State three ways dogs relate to people.

_____

_____

_____

_____

_____

Your friends have one, maybe even two or three. The neighbors have one. Does it seem that everyone has one but you? No, it is not the latest video game, but something much more fun—a family pet. Dogs and hamsters both make good family pets, but they are different in the way they relate to people and in their needs.

Dogs and hamsters are both fun to hold and pet, but they relate to people in different ways. For instance, dogs enjoy human contact. They love to play fetch, chase, and
10 tug-of-war with their owners. Dogs like to be petted, and most dogs will roll over to have their bellies rubbed. Dogs are also affectionate and love licking their owners' faces. However, dogs need lots of care, too. They need fresh food and water every day, and they need regular exercise. They also need someone to take care of them when their owners go out of town.

Hamsters are very different from dogs. Having contact with people is not important to them. They like to sleep when people want to play. Unlike dogs, hamsters do not like being petted. Many will hide when their owners want to pick them up. Hamsters are also very independent. They like to spend their time exploring. Hamsters may be low on affection, but they need less daily care than dogs do. They need food and water just as dogs do, but an owner usually fills up the food and water dishes only once a week. Hamsters need exercise too, but they get their exercise by running on wheels in their cages. If their owners go out of town, hamsters can be left alone.

Dogs and hamsters both make good pets. Dogs provide plenty of affection, but they are also high maintenance. Hamsters are definitely low maintenance, but they are also less cuddly. The choice is yours.

© G. K. and Vikki Hart/Getty Images.

COMPARE & CONTRAST

Re-read lines 17–28. Underline four details that show how hamsters are different from dogs.

ANALYZE

Review the structure of this article. Are the details organized point by point, or are they organized in a block pattern? Explain.

_____

_____

_____

_____

_____

_____

_____

CONNECT

Think about what you've just read. Which kind of pet, a dog or a hamster, appeals to you more? Explain.

_____

_____

_____

_____

_____

_____

_____

_____

Puppy Love or Hamster Heaven?

SKILLS FOCUS

Reading Skills
Analyze text structures: analyze a comparison-and-contrast article.

Venn Diagram   A **Venn diagram** is a chart in which you can record and show similarities and differences between two things. Compare and contrast the qualities of the pets described in the text by filling in the Venn diagram below.

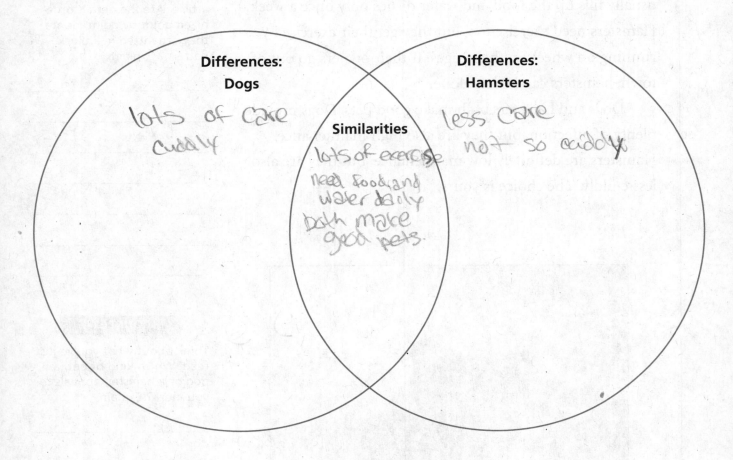

Differences:
Dogs

lots of care
cuddly

Similarities

lots of exercise
need food and
water daily
both make
good pets.

Differences:
Hamsters

less care
not so cuddly

Skills Review

Puppy Love or Hamster Heaven?

COMPREHENSION

Reading Comprehension   Write **T** or **F** next to each statement to tell if it is true or false.

T **1.** Dogs are higher maintenance pets than hamsters are.

F **2.** People who like dogs don't like hamsters.

T **3.** Hamsters prefer sleeping to playing.

F **4.** Hamsters are affectionate with humans.

T **5.** Dogs provide more affection than hamsters do.

T **6.** Hamsters can be left alone for long periods.

F **7.** Hamsters do not need exercise.

F **8.** Hamsters make cuddly pets.

F **9.** Both dogs and hamsters need their food and water replaced daily.

F **10.** Hamsters like to have their bellies rubbed.

Before You Read

What Is Stress?

by Jerrold Greenberg, Ed.D., and Robert Gold, Ph.D.

READING SKILLS: FINDING AND ANALYZING MAIN IDEAS

When you read an informational text, you need to take note of two things: its topic and its main idea. The **topic** is the subject of a piece of writing. The **main idea** is the most important thing said about that topic. The topic of an essay might be, for example, "Myths." The main idea might be "Myths are central to human experience."

Sometimes a writer states a main idea directly. At other times the idea is **implied,** or suggested; you must then infer or guess what it is. When you read "What Is Stress?" try using the **TLC strategy.** Find the **T**opic. **L**ook for the least important sentences, and set them aside. **C**onnect the other ideas with the topic to come up with the main idea.

VOCABULARY DEVELOPMENT: PREVIEW SELECTION VOCABULARY

Get to know these words before you read "What Is Stress?"

potentially (pō·ten′shə·lē) *adv.:* possibly.

Racquel knew that her appearance before the class was potentially embarrassing.

motivate (mōt′ə·vāt′) *v.:* move to take action.

Stress can motivate us to excel.

mobilized (mō′bə·līzd′) *v.:* organized for action; readied.

In times of stress the body's resources are mobilized to confront a threat.

eliminate (ē·lim′ə·nāt′) *v.:* get rid of; remove.

It is impossible to eliminate all situations that cause stress.

SKILLS FOCUS

Reading Skills
Find main ideas.

What Is Stress?

by Jerrold Greenberg, Ed.D., and Robert Gold, Ph.D.

*Racquel had no idea how she was going to do it—the idea
of getting up in front of her English class terrified her.
What if she went totally blank and forgot
everything she was going to say?*

*She could pretend to be sick and stay home the day she was
supposed to give her speech, but she knew she would
have to give it anyway when she went back to
school. There wasn't any way out of it, and it
was making Racquel a nervous wreck.*

If you, like Racquel, have had physical reactions to a change
in your life situation, you have experienced stress. All of us
do. The key is learning how to manage stress so that it
doesn't make you miserable or sick.

Before you can cope with stress, you have to know
how it develops. First, a situation arises that is new or
potentially unpleasant. This situation is called a stressor.
In Racquel's case, the stressor was the speech that she had
to give in her English class. Racquel felt anxious, her heart
raced, and her hands started sweating when she thought
about the speech. What she was experiencing was a stress
response, the body's reaction to a stressor.

It is important to remember that stressors only have
the *potential* to cause a stress response. For some people,
giving a speech would not cause a stress response. It's only

10

TEXT STRUCTURE

Skim this article. Circle its
subheadings. What other
feature do you find?

_____

_____

_____

_____

_____

VOCABULARY

potentially (pō·ten′shə·lē)
adv.: possibly.

TEXT STRUCTURE

The **topic** of this section is stressors. What examples of stressors do the writers provide? Number them. You should find eight.

_____
_____
_____
_____
_____
_____
_____
_____
_____
_____
_____
_____

when a stressor does cause a stress response that stress results. Therefore, stress is the combination of the presence of a stressor and the occurrence of a stress response.

Stressors

20 Stressors can occur in almost every area of life. At school, you may experience stress when you try out for a sport or the school play or if you have trouble becoming part of a certain social group. You may feel stress if you don't have the money to buy the clothes you want for a school dance or if other students pick on you.

A stressor can be something as simple as trying to get paper clips untangled, getting stuck at a red light when you're in a hurry, or getting a busy signal when you really need to talk with someone. If you let them, these kinds of 30 "daily hassles" can add up and cause a tremendous amount of stress.

Even positive situations can be stressors. Making the all-star basketball team is an example of a positive life-changing event that can cause stress.

Having some stressors is perfectly normal and healthy. They **motivate** us to confront challenges and accomplish things. The ideal balance is to be able to deal with stressors effectively so we don't become ill from too much stress.

The Stress Response

40 The stress response occurs because of the relationship between your brain and the rest of your body. Your brain recognizes a stressor and evaluates it. If your brain decides that the stressor isn't anything to worry about, nothing happens to your body. But if the stressor is seen as a threat, your brain tells your body to produce certain chemicals that contribute to the stress response.

VOCABULARY

motivate (mōt′ə·vāt′) v.: move to take action.

Why does the brain tell the rest of the body to respond this way? It doesn't seem as though the stress response would help us at all. It certainly didn't help Racquel prepare for her speech. When could the stress response possibly be helpful to us?

Well, imagine that you are walking down the street and a huge dog suddenly leaps at you from behind a garbage truck, snarling, teeth bared, and ready to bite you. What do you do? Do you try to defend yourself against the dog, or do you run away as fast as you can? Whichever you do—fight the dog or run away—will require you to act immediately and with great physical effort.

The stress response makes it possible for you to protect yourself. Your body produces the hormone called adrenaline, which gives you the rush of extra energy you need. Your breathing speeds up, which helps get more oxygen throughout your body. Your heart beats faster, which increases the flow of blood to your muscles. And your muscles tense up, which prepares you to move quickly.

At the same time these changes are occurring, other changes are also taking place throughout your body. Because all your physical resources are **mobilized** to help you respond to danger, other body functions take a back seat. The digestive system may begin to function strangely. Less saliva is produced, because it is a low priority to your body during times of physical danger. As a result, your mouth becomes dry.

The stress response is sometimes called the "fight-or-flight" response because it prepares you to either "fight" or "take flight." It prepares you to do something *physical.* So when you are physically threatened and need to respond physically, the stress response is helpful.

TEXT STRUCTURE

The writer poses two questions in lines 47–51. Underline the questions. Then, read on and answer the questions.

_____

_____

_____

_____

_____

_____

_____

_____

VOCABULARY

mobilized (mō′bə·līzd′) *v.:* organized for action; readied.

IDENTIFY CAUSE & EFFECT

Pause at line 73. What cause and effect explain why your mouth goes dry when you are stressed?

_____

_____

_____

_____

_____

_____

However, your body also responds the same way to 80 a *nonphysical* threat. Giving a speech can cause the same stress response as being attacked by an animal. But giving a speech, unlike defending yourself against an animal attack, does not require you to release stress in any physical way. The stress that is not released can make you physically ill.

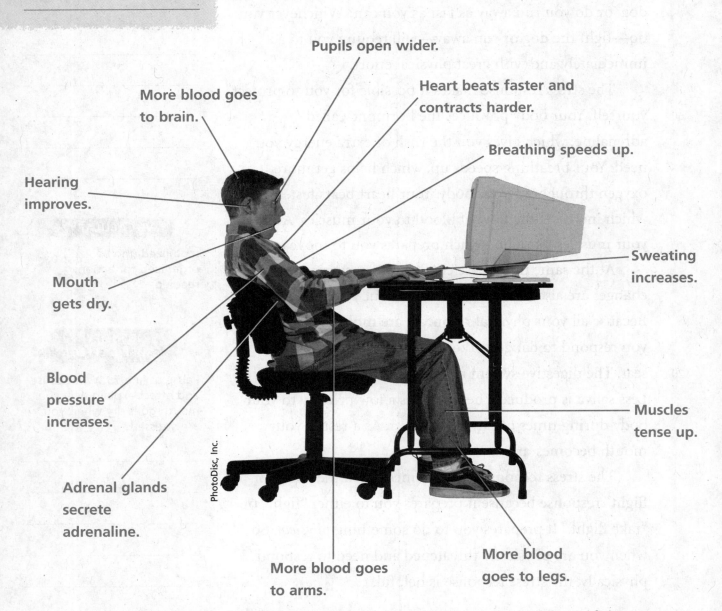

Pupils open wider.

More blood goes to brain.

Heart beats faster and contracts harder.

Breathing speeds up.

Hearing improves.

Sweating increases.

Mouth gets dry.

Blood pressure increases.

Muscles tense up.

PhotoDisc, Inc.

Adrenal glands secrete adrenaline.

More blood goes to arms.

More blood goes to legs.

The physical changes of the stress response prepare the body to run away or to stay and fight.

Selective Awareness

Though you can **eliminate** some stressors from your life, you cannot get rid of all of them. You can, however, use selective awareness to make your stressors less disturbing. Selective awareness is choosing to focus on the aspects of a situation that make you feel better. For example, if your stressor is having to make a speech in one of your classes, you could choose to focus on the positive aspect of the situation—having a chance to present your ideas to others.

Make a list of five stressors in your life, and then write the positive aspects of each one. It may also be helpful to take time just before you go to sleep each night to recall all the *good* things about the day. Pat yourself on the back for what you accomplished and the problems you handled successfully.

90

VOCABULARY

eliminate (ē·lim′ə·nāt′) *v.*: get rid of; remove.

TEXT STRUCTURE

Skim the text under this heading. What is the **topic**? How do you know?

_____

_____

_____

_____

_____

_____

_____

_____

_____

_____

_____

_____

_____

_____

_____

_____

_____

What Is Stress?

Main Idea Chart   In the chart below, list the topics discussed in "What Is Stress?" Then, list details that tell about each topic. Review your work, and then identify the main idea of the article.

Topic	Details
Main Idea	

Skills Review

What Is Stress?

VOCABULARY AND COMPREHENSION

A. Selection Vocabulary: Words in Context   Write words from the Word Bank to complete the paragraph. Use each word only once.

I wasn't looking forward to the afternoon. The fact was that in the last few days nothing was able to (1) _____ me to study for my test. The stress was beginning to build up! Then, I gave myself a pep talk. I (2) _____ my studying instincts. From now on, I would (3) _____ napping during my free period and study. If I failed to complete my studying, life could (4) _____ become very unpleasant for me.

B. Reading Comprehension   Circle the letter of the correct response to each item.

1. The **topic** of "What Is Stress?" is—

   a. giving speeches   **c.** anger

   b. headaches   **d.** stress

2. Which statement expresses a **main idea** in "What Is Stress?"

   f. The stress response can be a helpful phenomenon.

   g. Stress is entirely mental, with no physical component.

   h. Experts agree about stress.

   j. Managing stress is an impossible task.

3. What is "selective awareness," as defined in the article?

   a. The ability to learn while napping.

   b. Focusing only on certain aspects of a situation.

   c. Identifying one out of three causes of stress.

   d. Choosing to avoid all stressful situations.

The Ancient Library of Alexandria by Anne Nolting

READING SKILLS: MAKING ASSERTIONS ABOUT A TEXT

If you're like most people, you make assertions all the time. An **assertion** is a statement or a claim. Keep in mind that not all assertions are valid. In order to be reasonable, your assertion must be supported with evidence. When evidence comes from a text source, it is called a **citation.**

SAMPLE ASSERTION: Sandy should get the lead in the school play.

SAMPLE EVIDENCE: Sandy sings and acts really well. Her audition was terrific. Last year, she showed up at all rehearsals on time, and she came prepared.

You will be reading "The Ancient Library of Alexandria" and making assertions about the text when you are done. Use these tips to help you:

- Identify the facts in the text and think them over.
- Use evidence from the text to make an assertion.
- Evaluate your assertion. Look to see how well the evidence in the text supports it.

VOCABULARY DEVELOPMENT: PREVIEW SELECTION VOCABULARY

You may find it helpful to learn these words before reading.

universal (yōō′nə·vʉr′səl) *adj.:* regarded as complete; whole.

Ptolemy established the first universal library at Alexandria.

deposited (dē·päz′it·id) *v.:* entrusted for safekeeping; put.

Books written on papyrus scrolls were deposited in a library at Alexandria.

stationary (stā′shə·ner′ē) *adj.:* unmoving; fixed or still.

Aristarchus asserted that Earth was not stationary because it revolved around a sun.

edicts (ē′dikts′) *n.:* orders; decrees.

Theodosius, the Roman emperor, published edicts that led to the destruction of many documents.

SKILLS FOCUS

Reading Skills
Make assertions
about a text.

from Cricket, May 2000

The Ancient Library of Alexandria

Anne Nolting .

BACKGROUND: Informational Text and Social Studies

Here's what you need to know before you begin reading:

- Ancient books were written on papyrus and rolled into scrolls.
- The Library of Alexandria, in Egypt, was the first universal library. This means that it was the first library where scrolls from different countries were collected.
- The library was not only a place to read. It was also a great center where people came to do research, debate, discuss, study, teach, and share ideas. In many ways the library was like an educational resort, because people who came from distant lands lived and ate at the library.

About 2,300 years ago, a great king ruled the country of Egypt. His name was Ptolemy I Soter, and he was a wise and inquisitive monarch with a deep longing for knowledge. His wish was for Egypt to become the most powerful nation in the world.

"You must read, great Ptolemy," his friend Demetrius urged. "This is the way to understand how to use power wisely."

10 Demetrius supplied Ptolemy with every document in Egypt. The books were written on thin, dried papyrus sheets and rolled into large scrolls.

WORD STUDY

Underline *inquisitive* (in·kwiz′ə·tiv) in line 3. What words in this first paragraph help you guess what it means? Circle the clues.

Inquisitive means "eager to learn."

_____

_____

_____

_____

_____

TEXT STRUCTURE

This article combines information with illustrations and photographs. Preview the visuals provided. What do you learn from them?

_____

_____

_____

_____

_____

_____

_____

_____

_____

_____

_____

_____

_____

IDENTIFY

The author makes a statement that Alexandria became the greatest center of trade in the world (lines 18–19). Circle this **assertion**. Then, read on, and underline facts and examples that support this assertion.

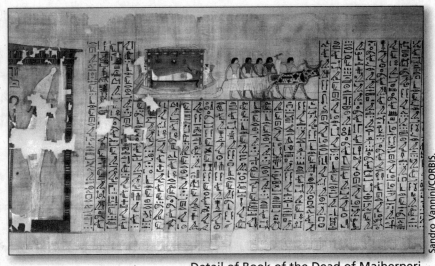

Detail of Book of the Dead of Maiherperi.

As Ptolemy studied the Egyptian scrolls, he became more and more curious about the world outside his country. He realized that wealthy empires would trade their goods with Egypt if his country welcomed them with a safe port. In 300 B.C., the ruler ordered the building of a mighty fleet of ships to patrol in the Mediterranean Sea. Within a few years, the beautiful capital city of Alexandria became the greatest center of trade in the world. From his magnifi-
20 cent white-marble palace, Ptolemy watched the ships from distant countries sail into port. The docks at Alexandria were covered with fabulous products from far-off lands. Tin came from the British Isles, silk from China, cotton from India. But it was in the captain's quarters of these great boats that Ptolemy discovered the most precious cargo of all. The ships carried scrolls describing life in remote lands.

Ptolemy addressed a letter to be carried from Alexandria on every departing ship. "To all the
30 Sovereignties and Governors on Earth," he wrote. "Send me every kind of written work your country has to offer.

I would like to read the words of your poets and historians, your doctors and inventors. I would like to study the works of your astrologers, mathematicians, and geniuses. Do not hesitate to send all of these!"

Ptolemy appointed Demetrius the first librarian for his collection of books. Demetrius organized the translations of the "ships' collection," and the number of scrolls grew rapidly. Ptolemy erected a colossal building next to his palace in Alexandria. He called it *Mouseion,* or Shrine of the Muses, and dreamed it would become a treasury that would store every document in the world. A branch was established at the temple of Serapis. Thus the first **universal** library was born.

After Ptolemy I died, his successors continued to collect scrolls, and the great library of Alexandria flourished. The priest Manetho wrote a three-scroll work on Egypt's history and religion under Ptolemy II, who also authorized seventy Jewish scholars to translate the Old Testament from Hebrew into Greek. All these works were **deposited** in the great library. Scholars from distant lands traveled to Egypt. They came to study, to teach, and to share their inventions. Poets, astronomers, physicists, mathematicians, zoologists, and doctors of many different races lived together at the library. They ate their meals in one gigantic dining hall, and the high ceiling reverberated with echoes from the lively debates.

The chambers of the great library were spacious and bright. Visitors sat on luxurious couches to enjoy the lilting voices of the poets and to listen to the melodies played by musicians. Across the hall, doctors carried out research in vast laboratories and dissecting rooms. In still another chamber, inventors gathered to assemble their new contraptions. Day and night the library pulsed with activity.

WORD STUDY

Circle the word *colossal* (line 39). The dictionary meaning is "stupendous; so great in size or force or extent as to inspire awe." The dictionary gives this example of its use: "the colossal crumbling ruins of an ancient temple." Why do you think it's a good word choice here?

_____

_____

_____

WORD STUDY

A few words in this selection are in italicized type. Circle *Mouseion* (line 40). Then, skip three paragraphs in the text to find and circle the italicized word *bibliothekai* (line 72). These are Greek words. Right after each word, you'll find its definition.

VOCABULARY

universal (yo͞o'nə·vur'səl) *adj.:* regarded as complete; whole.

deposited (dē·päz'it·id) *v.:* entrusted for safekeeping; put.

IDENTIFY

Circle the author's **assertion** that scholars came to study, teach, and share their inventions (line 52). Then continue reading, and underline facts and examples that support this statement.

At dusk, astronomers met on the rooftop observatory to map the constellations. At dawn, botanists could be seen ambling through terraced gardens where they observed new varieties of fruit trees and crops. Behind the library walls, animal keepers tended the world's first-known zoo.

70 Open walkways, bordered by lovely fountains and lotus flowers, divided the courtyards from the library chambers. Along these walks stood the *bibliothekai,* the name given to the niches, or cubbyholes, filled with scrolls. The library stored 500,000 scrolls, and none of them ever left the library. Scholars sat on small stools near the niches to read, unrolling the papyrus sheets on their laps to view the columns of writing. Some of the scrolls were twenty feet long!

The most knowledgeable people in the world traveled 80 to Egypt to study and lecture at the great Library of Alexandria. The names of many geniuses have been lost, but the few men and women who have been remembered offer us a glimpse into the exciting life of research at this great library.

The geographer Eratosthenes served as the director of the Library of Alexandria for forty years, beginning in 245 B.C. He was a brilliant mathematician and astronomer whose geometric calculations proved that the earth was a sphere. Eratosthenes calculated the size of the earth by 90 measuring the lengths of shadows cast by sticks placed in the Egyptian cities of Alexandria and Elephantine. From measurements taken at noon on the summer solstice, he estimated earth's diameter to be 7,850 miles (12,630 kilometers). This is very close to the measurement of 7,900 miles (12,700 kilometers) we use today. Building upon Eratosthenes' research, geographers began to map possible trade routes to India eastward across the Indian Ocean.

Another brilliant scholar who worked at the library was Aristarchus, a Greek astronomer. The earth, he claimed, is not **stationary.** He concluded that the world is one of many planets that revolve around a sun. He wrote treatises, or theories, proving his ideas. Democritus, a philosopher, added his thoughts. "The Milky Way is not the spilled milk of the goddess," Democritus explained. "It is composed of stars, millions of stars."

The great inventors used the library courtyards to test their designs. Archimedes constructed many machines, including the lever. "Give me a place to stand on," Archimedes declared, "and I will move the earth." Heron, another inventor of Alexandria, added his works to the library. He wrote *Automata,* the first book on robots. Callimachus produced a 120-scroll catalog of authors and their works in the library.

Not all scholars who worked in the library were men. Hypatia was a gifted mathematician and astronomer whose fame spread to many countries. She taught at the library, wrote manuscripts, and worked on many of her own inventions, including an astrolabe, an instrument to measure the angle of a star from the horizon.

For seven centuries, the most brilliant minds in the world contributed their ideas to the storehouse of knowledge in Alexandria. Then, during one brief, chaotic time in history, the scrolls that told the stories of the world disappeared. What tragedies occurred to destroy this first great universal library?

First, in 47 B.C., a fire broke out in the great library's warehouses during Julius Caesar's Alexandrine War. Then, around A.D. 270, the Palace Quarter was destroyed and the library seriously damaged. Later, in A.D. 391, the branch

---

stationary (stā′shə·ner′ē) *adj.:* unmoving; fixed or still.

If you wanted to describe how the leaves of a tree look when the air is calm, would you choose the word *stationary* or *unmoving* to describe the leaves? Explain.

_____

_____

_____

_____

_____

IDENTIFY

The author asserts that an exciting life of research took place at this great library in Alexandria. Circle the names of four great scholars mentioned in lines 107–115.

WORD STUDY

Hypatia (hī·pā′shə) invented the astrolabe, which measures the angle of a star on the horizon (line 118). What other words come from the root *astro–,* meaning "star"?

_____

_____

_____

_____

_____

Profile of Greek mathematician Hypatia.

IDENTIFY

In lines 124–125, the writer poses a question. What facts does she go on to cite to answer the question?

_____

_____

_____

_____

_____

_____

_____

_____

INFER

In these times a pagan (line 137) was any person who worshipped the gods of ancient Greece or Rome or the gods of the so-called barbarians. The prefix *anti–* means "against." What would *antipagan* feelings be?

_____

_____

_____

_____

VOCABULARY

edicts (ē′dikts′) *n.:* orders; decrees.

130 library and the temple of Serapis were destroyed. The main library survived but in a much diminished state.

At that time Emperor Theodosius ruled the Roman Empire. His beliefs differed from those of the scholars who taught at the Library of Alexandria. Most of the scholars based their studies on the Greek tradition of mathematics and philosophy. The Christian emperor believed that ancient Greek scholars were pagans. He published **edicts** that closed the temples and destroyed written documents that did not agree with his doctrines.

140 Theodosius died in A.D. 395, and antipagan feelings grew stronger. In A.D. 415, Hypatia was set upon by a mob of religious fanatics in the streets and brutally murdered. Many scrolls, so faithfully collected for centuries, were burned as fuel for the public baths.

A painting on papyrus of a tomb painting from ancient Egypt. Lotus flowers are shown at the right.

About A.D. 640, the Arabs invaded the city of Alexandria. The library was in ruins when the Arabs arrived, but they salvaged some of the remaining documents. As the Roman Empire fell to barbaric tribes and Europe entered the Dark Ages, the Arabs preserved the world's rich culture of mathematics, astronomy, and science.

150

Today there are libraries in every town, and books of every kind are available to everyone. The words of ancient and present-day writers are standing on open shelves, waiting for any reader to encounter them.

Notes _____

_____

_____

_____

_____

_____

_____

_____

_____

_____

The Ancient Library of Alexandria

Reading Skills
Make assertions
about a text.

Assertion Web   After you finish reading "The Ancient Library of Alexandria," you can make assertions about it. To make an assertion, think about what you learned from the text. Ask yourself, *What statement or claim can I make about the information I read? Is there evidence to support this assertion?* Then, complete the graphic organizer below. Make an assertion, and support it with citations or evidence from the article.

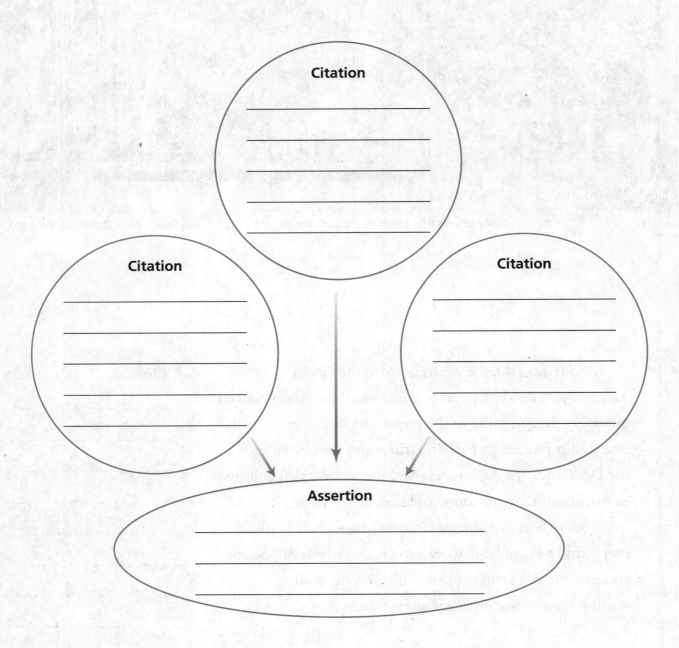

Skills Review

The Ancient Library of Alexandria

VOCABULARY AND COMPREHENSION

A. Selection Vocabulary: Words in Context Write words from the Word Bank to complete the paragraph below. Use each word only once.

The library in Alexandria was the first (1) _____ library ever. The great works of scholars were (2) _____ there. One such scholar was Aristarchus; he claimed that Earth was not (3) _____ but revolved around the sun. The orders, or (4) _____, of Theodosius may have prompted his followers to seize and burn scrolls considered pagan.

B. Reading Comprehension Circle the letter of the best response.

1. How does the author support her **assertion** that Ptolemy was wise?

   a. By saying that Ptolemy read widely and had a longing for knowledge

   b. By saying that Ptolemy had good advisers

   c. By saying that Ptolemy wanted power

   d. By saying that Ptolemy created great buildings

2. The author asserts that the most knowledgeable people in the world came to the library. This is a reasonable **assertion** because—

   f. the scholars included men and women

   g. the author quotes famous people who testify to this

   h. there were many scrolls found in the library

   j. the author names the people who traveled there

3. What **evidence** did Eratosthenes provide to support his assertion that Earth was a sphere?

   a. He showed that many planets revolve around a sun.

   b. He mapped the constellations.

   c. He estimated Earth's diameter.

   d. He said that the Milky Way was composed of millions of stars.

Before You Read

Save Our Earth

from The World Almanac for Kids 2001

READING SKILLS: ANALYZING PERSUASIVE TECHNIQUES

Persuasion is the use of language or visual images intended to get people to think or act in a certain way. Writers may use several persuasive techniques. Not all of these techniques are valid, or acceptable, forms of reasoning. **Logic** is correct reasoning. When you put together facts and draw conclusions based on those facts, you are using logical reasoning. **Emotional appeals** get readers' feelings involved. Writers use vivid language, reasons, examples, and personal-experience stories that appeal to basic feelings such as fear, love, and anger.

Fallacious reasoning is false reasoning. It at first seems reasonable but contains flaws. Here are some examples of fallacious reasoning:

- **Hasty generalizations** are broad statements based on incomplete evidence. *All poems rhyme* is a hasty generalization based on only partial evidence.
- **Circular reasoning** repeats an argument instead of supporting it with reasons and evidence: *We have the best school newspaper because no other school paper is as good as ours.*
- **Only-cause fallacy** claims that a situation is the result of only one cause: *I could have passed the test if I had been given more time.*

As you read informational texts, be aware of persuasive techniques that are logical and of those that can mislead you.

SKILLS FOCUS

Reading Skills
Analyze persuasive techniques.

from The World Almanac for Kids 2001

Save Our Earth

Protecting Our Water

Every living thing needs water to live. Many animals also
depend on water as a home. People not only drink water,
but also use it to cook, clean, cool machinery in factories,
produce power, and irrigate farmland.

Where Does Water Come From?

Although about two thirds of the Earth's surface is water,
we are able to use only a tiny fraction of it. Seawater makes
up 97% of Earth's water, and 2% is frozen in glaciers and
10   ice around the north and south poles. Freshwater makes up
only 1% of our water, and only part of that is close enough
to Earth's surface for us to use.

     The water we can use comes from lakes, rivers,
reservoirs, and groundwater. Groundwater is melted snow
or rain that seeps deep below the surface of the Earth and
collects in pools called aquifers.

     Overall, the world has enough freshwater, but some-
times it is not available exactly where it is needed. Extreme
water shortages, or droughts, can occur when an area gets
20   too little rain or has very hot weather over a long period of
time, causing water supplies to dry up.

TEXT STRUCTURE

Skim this article. What two
parts is it divided into? What
do its headings tell you
about its coverage?

_____

_____

_____

_____

_____

IDENTIFY

Circle the statistics in the
second paragraph. How does
the writer answer the question in the heading?

_____

_____

_____

WORD STUDY

Underline the context clue
that defines *droughts*
(drouts), in line 19.

The writer poses a question in line 22. How is it answered? Are these answers examples of facts or opinions?

_____

_____

_____

_____

_____

_____

_____

_____

_____

_____

Like many scientific articles, this one includes charts. Where is most water used at home?

_____

_____

_____

_____

The writer poses another question in line 31. Underline the answers to the question.

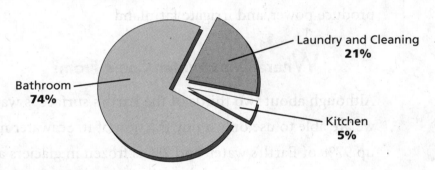

HOW MUCH WATER DO WE USE?

◆ Average American's daily cooking, washing, flushing, and lawn care: 183 gallons

◆ An average load of wash in a washing machine: 50 gallons

◆ 10-minute shower or a bath: 25–50 gallons

◆ One load of dishes in a dishwasher: 12–20 gallons

◆ One person's daily drinking and eating: 2 quarts

EyeWire, Inc.

30

How Water Is Used at Home

Laundry and Cleaning
21%

Bathroom
74%

Kitchen
5%

What Is Threatening Our Water?

Water is polluted when it is not fit for its intended uses, such as drinking, swimming, watering crops, or serving as a habitat. Polluted water can cause disease and kill fish and other animals. Some major water pollutants include sewage, chemicals from factories, fertilizers and weed killers, and leakage from landfills. Water pollution is being reduced in some areas, such as Lake Erie, the Willamette River in Oregon, Boston Harbor, and the

40 Hudson River in New York State. Companies continue to look for better ways to get rid of wastes, and many farmers are trying new ways to grow crops without using polluting fertilizers or chemicals.

The Importance of Forests

Trees and forests are very important to the environment. In addition to holding water, trees hold the soil in place. Trees use carbon dioxide and give off oxygen, which animals and plants need for survival. And they provide homes and food for millions of types of animals.

50   Cutting down trees—usually to use the land for something besides a forest—is called deforestation. Although people often have good reasons for cutting down trees, deforestation can have serious effects. In the Amazon rain forest in South America, for example, thousands of plant and animal species are being lost before scientists can even learn about them. In the Pacific Northwest, there is a conflict between logging companies that want to cut down trees for lumber and people who want to preserve the ancient forests.

60 **Why Do We Cut Down Trees?** People cut down trees for many reasons. When the population grows, people cut down trees to clear space to build houses, schools, factories, and other buildings. People may clear land to plant crops and graze livestock. Sometimes all the trees in an area are cut and sold for lumber and paper.

TEXT STRUCTURE

What topic will be discussed on this page?

_____

_____

_____

TEXT STRUCTURE

How does the writer support the **assertion** in line 45?

_____

_____

_____

_____

_____

_____

_____

_____

_____

_____

_____

WORD STUDY

The word *deforestation* (line 51) is defined in context. Underline the definition.

TEXT STRUCTURE

To answer the question in line 66, the writer cites a series of causes and effects. What happens when trees are cut down?

_____

_____

_____

_____

_____

_____

_____

_____

_____

_____

_____

_____

_____

_____

_____

_____

TEXT STRUCTURE

How does the writer answer the question in line 77? Put a number in front of each answer.

What Happens When Trees Are Cut Down? Cutting down trees can affect the climate. After rain falls on a forest, mist rises and new rain clouds form. When forests are cut down, this cycle is disrupted, and the area eventu-

70 ally grows drier, causing a change in the local climate.

If huge areas of trees are cut down, the carbon dioxide they would have used builds up in the atmosphere and contributes to the greenhouse effect. And without trees to hold the soil and absorb water, rain washes topsoil away, a process called soil erosion. Farming on the poorer soil that is left can be very hard.

What Are We Doing to Save Forests? In many countries trees are being planted faster than they are being cut down. Foresting companies are working on

80 more efficient methods of replacing and growing forests. In addition, communities and individuals are helping to save forests by recycling paper.

Save Our Earth

Chart of Appeals   Examine the persuasive details from "Save Our Earth" listed in the chart below. Then, in the right-hand column, explain whether each detail is a logical appeal or an emotional appeal.

SKILLS FOCUS

Reading Skills
Analyze persuasive techniques.

Detail from "Save Our Earth"	Type of Persuasive Appeal
"Save Our Earth"	
"Extreme water shortages . . . can occur when an area gets too little rain or has very hot weather over a long period of time . . ."	
"Polluted water can cause disease and kill fish and other animals."	
"In the Amazon rain forest in South America, for example, thousands of plant and animal species are being lost before scientists can even learn about them."	

Save Our Earth

COMPREHENSION

Reading Comprehension   Write **T** or **F** next to each statement to tell whether it is true or false.

_____ **1.** Groundwater is freshwater that collects below the surface of Earth.

_____ **2.** The main reason for drought is the lack of rivers and reservoirs.

_____ **3.** Most water used in American homes is used for laundry and cleaning.

_____ **4.** A major cause of water pollution is the use of fertilizers and chemicals.

_____ **5.** The cutting down of trees is a major cause of soil erosion.

_____ **6.** In the Amazon rain forest, the cutting down of trees has wiped out species of animals and plants.

_____ **7.** The people who want to cut down trees are mostly environmentalists.

_____ **8.** The cutting down of trees can cause changes in local climate.

_____ **9.** When trees are cut down, carbon dioxide can build up in the atmosphere.

_____ **10.** The cutting down of trees preserves topsoil.

Vocabulary Development

Pronunciation guides, in parentheses, are provided for the vocabulary words in this book. The following key will help you use those pronunciation guides.

As a practice in using a pronunciation guide, sound out the words used as examples in the list that follows. See if you can hear the way the same vowel might be sounded in different words. For example, say "at" and "ate" aloud. Can you hear the difference in the way "a" sounds?

The symbol ə is called a **schwa**. A schwa is used by many dictionaries to indicate a sort of weak sound like the "a" in "ago." Some people say the schwa sounds like "eh." A vowel sounded like a schwa is never accented.

The vocabulary words in this book are also provided with a part-of-speech label. The parts of speech are *n.* (noun), *v.* (verb), *pro.* (pronoun), *adj.* (adjective), *adv.* (adverb), *prep.* (preposition), *conj.* (conjunction), and *interj.* (interjection). To learn about the parts of speech, consult the *Holt Handbook*.

To learn more about the vocabulary words, consult your dictionary. You will find that many of the words defined here have several other meanings.

---

at, āte, cär; ten, ēve; is, īce; gō, hôrn, look, tool; oil, out; up, fur; ə *for unstressed vowels, as* a *in* ago, u *in* focus; ' *as in* Latin (lat'ʼn); chin; she; zh *as in* azure (azh'ər); thin, *the;* ŋ *as in* ring (riŋ)

Notes

Notes

Notes

Notes

Notes

Notes

Notes

Notes

Notes

Notes

Notes

Notes

Notes

Notes